Y0-BQP-000

Wordless/Almost Wordless
Picture Books

Wordless/Almost Wordless Picture Books
A Guide

Virginia H. Richey
Katharyn E. Puckett

1992
LIBRARIES UNLIMITED, INC.
Englewood, Colorado

LIBRARIES UNLIMITED, INC.
P.O. Box 6633
Englewood, CO 80155-6633

Library of Congress Cataloging-in-Publication Data

Richey, Virginia H.
   Wordless/almost wordless picture books : a guide / Virginia H. Richey and Katharyn E. Puckett.
   xvi, 223 p. 17x25 cm.
   Includes bibliographical references and indexes.
   ISBN 0-87287-878-3
   1. Picture books for children--Bibliography.   2. Illustrated books, Children's--Bibliography.   3. Children's literature--Bibliography.   I. Puckett, Katharyn E.   II. Title.
Z1037.R47   1991
011'.62--dc20   91-29364
                                                                       CIP

Contents

Foreword

The wordless picture book is a unique, challenging, and rewarding experience for both the creator and the reader. It requires the fullest use of an artist's visual storytelling skills and personal interpretation on the part of the viewer.

The narrative aspects of picture making have always interested me. Early on, I realized that creating a sequence of images was more interesting than just a single picture. Once I had created a character or a fantasy world, I wanted to stay and explore it. While a student at the Rhode Island School of Design, I began to clarify and develop some of the main visual concepts I am still exploring today. During this time, my roommate told me about a book he had seen in the rare book collection of his hometown library. The book had no words, he said, and the story was told entirely through woodcut illustrations.

It was more than a year before I was finally able to see a copy of *Madman's Drum* by Lynd Ward. Published in 1930, it is a remarkable book. Complex emotions and themes are explored in more than 250 black-and-white images (Ward did three novels for adults: *Gods' Man*, *Madman's Drum*, and *Wild Pilgrimage*). The book had a tremendous impact on me. It showed me many things about conveying information visually and about the pacing and rhythm of a story. It connected with ideas of my own that I was exploring.

For my degree project during my senior year at RISD, I created my first wordless picture book. It was my first major attempt at making one, and it had me hooked. My first book as an author/illustrator was wordless, as was my third book.

Creating a wordless picture book requires great care and clarity in every aspect of the picture making. Because the images are the "text," everything in them must contribute not only to the advancement of the plot but to revealing the emotions and feelings of the characters. There are no words to tell us how characters are feeling or what they are thinking. Gestures, posture, and facial expressions alone must describe a personality. The same care is necessary to "read" the pictures. Readers who glance quickly through the pages may miss significant details that enrich a story and characterizations.

It is in the reading of the pictures that the major difference between books with text and those books without text lies. In a book with words, the reader hears the voice of the author—the text—which sets the tone and tells the story. With the wordless book, it is the reader's own voice that interprets and recounts the narrative. Readers bring their own personal responses to the book, and they guide themselves through it. Readers are made more active participants in the story.

This partnership with the reader is what excites me about this genre. I enjoy the fact that different people see many different things in my books. What I had not foreseen when I began making wordless picture books were the uses they have in various teaching situations. I have heard from teachers around the country who have used wordless books as stimuli in all types of creative writing classes.

Language and ESL teachers have sent me student interpretations of my books. Recently, a drama teacher told me how she used my book *Tuesday* as a springboard for class improvisations. These responses have been a gratifying and eye-opening revelation.

I am thrilled that this guide has been compiled. It is a wonderful resource for discovering a truly creative, and unfortunately too often neglected, field of books.

David Wiesner
Winner, Caldecott Medal Award,
1992, for *Tuesday*

Preface

This guide will help you identify wordless and almost wordless books. In these books, the illustration carries the meaning; it might tell a story, demonstrate a concept, or provide information. A reader who cannot decipher any print can still derive the intended meaning from these works. The illustration can be read in the way that print is read. If some print is present, it does not change the message of the illustration but enhances it. The usual roles of text and art are reversed in this genre of picture books.

The selection of titles included in based on the presence or absence of print and the independence of the work from print. Some titles identified by others as wordless books are not included in this bibliography. Upon examination, these books were found to contain significant amounts of print and are more accurately assessed as picture storybooks, in which text and print together contribute to meaning. Other books are not included because they were not available for personal review.

Within the confines of our "wordless/almost wordless" designation we attempted to be inclusive. Some titles are included which, due to their unusual format, are unlikely to be in a circulating library, although they do appear on a number of lists. Older and out-of-print titles are included because they may still be in school or public library collections and, hopefully, may be reprinted as use of the genre expands. In identifying titles, many published lists, textbooks, and unpublished dissertations were examined. A selected bibliography of these is included. This guide was closed in May 1991 and represents publication through that date.

How to Use This Book

Alphabetical Author Listing. The body of the guide consists of an alphabetical listing by author, with each entry numbered. Each citation was determined by the information printed in the copy of the book which was examined. Thus, International Standard Book Numbers (ISBNs) and dates of publication may vary from other citations. Many titles were originally published in other countries, and the date of publication used is generally the U.S. copyright date.

Information is listed in this order: Author, reteller, translator. Title. Illustrator. Publisher, date. International Standard Book Number (ISBN), Library of Congress number (LC). Series title. Description of print use. Format.

There is a brief annotation for each title. This annotation includes plot or nonfiction content and an indication of the type of illustration used, to help the reader decide whether the book would be useful or to distinguish between similarly titled books. There are no age-level recommendations because we believe that wordless books transcend age levels.

Title Index. This section contains an alphabetical listing of all titles in the bibliography, with their entry number.

Format Index. This section identifies titles with unusual formats, using the following terms:

Accordion fold—books with pages that are folded into pleats and that are not bound to a center spine.

Back to back—books with two separate contents, one accessible from one cover, and one from the opposite cover.

Board pages—books printed on sturdy cardboard pages, thicker and heavier than ordinary paper.

Die-cut pages—irregularly shaped pages that produce a three-dimensional effect when overlaying each other.

Die-cut windows—an opening in one page allowing part of the following page to be viewed.

Flaps—a cutout portion of the page is lifted to reveal a part of the illustration.

Flip book—the pages are rapidly fanned, and the illustration appears to move.

Half pages—a half page is set between two larger pages so that the overall illustration is changed when only the half page is turned.

Mix-and-match—cut pages can be combined with each other to produce varied illustrations.

Pop-up—portions of the illustration are engineered to rise from the surface of the page to create a three-dimensional picture.

Portfolio—a folder contains unbound, sequenced illustrations.

Pull tab—pages are engineered so that the illustration changes when a tab is pulled.

Sideways—the book is bound so that the illustration is read from the end farthest from the binding, rather than in the normal way.

Index to Use of Print. This section identifies the degree to which the book contains print. The following designations have been used and defined as follows:

Almost wordless-dialog: print that appears is the direct speech of the characters.

Almost wordless-labels: print reinforces the identification of pictures by placing the word for the picture on the page.

Almost wordless-sentences: complete sentences reinforce the meaning of the illustration.

Almost wordless-sounds: the print representation of a sound such as an animal noise appears on the page.

Wordless-frame: the wordless body of the book is set off with a beginning, and sometimes an ending, phrase.

Wordless-signs: signs appear in the illustration as part of the illustration.

Wordless-symbols: symbols such as numerals or letters appear on the page.

Wordless-no print: no print appears in the illustration or the body of the book.

Wordless-titles: the wordless illustration has a print title, often used to separate short sequences.

Wordless-exclamations: single words such as "help" or "oops" are printed in illustration.

Wordless-hidden print: text appears only when tab is pulled or flap is lifted.

Wordless sequence in book: although the story is somewhat print dependent, a major wordless sequence appears.

Series Index. This section lists the titles covered in this book that are in publishers' series. This is not a complete list of all titles in a series. Books that were not included in this guide were not included in the listing.

Illustrator (When Not Author) Index. This section lists only those illustrators who are not also the author of the book.

Subject Index. This section enables the reader to locate books by subject or theme. It goes beyond assigning subjects based on the central theme or characters of the title. In pulling together text sets, or thematic units, the teacher or librarian often needs to find only a part of a book that can be compared to other works. We have tried to identify some of the ideas and individual illustrations and themes in books that could be used together in this way. The subject lists might also be used as idea sparkers for text sets.

The subject heading "Translation" has been used to identify titles originally published in a language other than English. The subject heading "Guide page" indicates either a print page providing guidance to the contents of the book or a print page inviting further use of the book.

The subject headings relative to the use of photography as illustration are included because of specific uses for this medium.

The *See* and *See also* references are interfiled in the subject list.

ABBREVIATIONS USED

(board)	cardboard pages
Illus.	illustrator
ISBN	International Standard Book Number
(lib.)	library edition
LC	Library of Congress
(pbk.)	paperback edition
ret.	reteller
tr.	translator

Acknowledgments

The authors have many people to thank for their assistance in completing this project: Elizabeth Richey for her knowledge of punctuation, and the rest of our families—Thayr and Will Richey, Marllece and James Puckett for their encouragement. Thanks to our editors, Dr. David Loertscher and Louis Ruybal. We would also like to acknowledge Robert Trinkle, director of the Monroe County (Indiana) Public Library, and the staff of the Children's Department: John Anderson, Mary D'Eliso, Patty Callison, Stephanie Gaston, and Mary Frasier.

We appreciate the support of our many friends in the library field, including Marian Armstrong and Judy Dye, Indiana University School of Library and Information Science; Sara Laughlin, Stone Hills Library Network; Yvonne Oliger, Bedford Public Library; Karen Boswell and Susan Jacobson, Monroe County Community School Corporation; Margaret Lieberman and Lois Johnson, West Vigo Elementary School; Marvis Cannon, Indiana State University Lab School; Audrey Britch, Nappanee Public Library; and Ann Spenner, West Lafayette Public Library.

Our thanks also to friends in the book trade: Sara Holmes, Book Corner; Shirley Mullin and Michael Mullin, Kids INK; Danna and Arthur Jackson, Between the Lines.

This book would not have been possible without the national interlibrary loan network and the more than fifty libraries that generously shared their resources with us through interlibrary loan. We are most grateful to them and for the persistence of the interlibrary loan team at Monroe County Public Library: D'Arcy Danielson, Karen Nissen, and Mary Paladino.

Resource List for Wordless
Picture Book Bibliographies

Abrahamson, Richard F. "An Update on Wordless Picture Books with an Annotated Bibliography." *The Reading Teacher* (January 1981): 417-21.

Carty, Elaine T. "A Study of the Observed Book Usage Patterns of Early Primary Grade Children Using Wordless Picture Books with Suggested Utilization Guidelines." Ph.D. dissertation, Temple University, 1983, 248-56.

Clapp, Kay. "Wordless Book Bibliography." In *Ideas and Insights: Language Arts in the Elementary School*, edited by Dorothy J. Watson. Urbana, Illinois: National Council of Teachers of English, 1987, 226-28.

Ellis, DiAnn Waskul, and Fannie Wiley Preston. "Enhancing Beginning Reading Using Wordless Picture Books in a Cross-age Tutoring Program." *The Reading Teacher* (April 1984): 392-98.

Fisher, Carol J., and C. Ann Terry. *Children's Language and the Language Arts*. 2d ed. New York: McGraw-Hill, 1982, 330-31.

Gillespie, John T., ed. "Stories without Words." In *Best Books for Children: Preschool through the Middle Grades*. New York: Bowker, 1985, 15-17.

Grasty, Patricia Elaine. "The Status of Wordless Picture Books, 1960-1976." Ph.D. dissertation, Temple University, 1978.

Jett-Simpson, Mary. "Wordless Picture Books—Pictures and Thousands of Words." In *Reading Resource Book*. Atlanta, Georgia: Humanics Limited, 1986, 77-82.

Kauffman, Dorothy. "An Identification and Description of Wordless Picture Story Books for Children Published in the United States from 1930 to 1980." Ph.D. dissertation, University of Maryland, 1981, 179-85.

Let's Read Together: Books for Family Enjoyment. 4th ed., Chicago: ALA, 1981, 6-7.

Lima, Carolyn W. *A to Zoo: Subject Access to Children's Picture Books*. 3d ed. New York: Bowker, 1989, 345-47.

Lipson, Eden Ross. *The New York Times Parents' Guide to the Best Books for Children*. New York: Random House, Times Books, 1988, 4-8.

Oklahoma State Department of Education. "Wordless Picture Books Bibliography." *Library Resources No. 47*, January 1986.

Stewig, John Warren. "Wordless Picture Books." In *Children and Literature*. Chicago: Rand McNally College Publishing, 1980, 157-58.

Sutherland, Zena. *Children and Books*, 7th ed. Glenview, Illinois: Scott, Foresman, 1986, 101-3.

Tiedt, Iria McClellan, et al. *Reading/Thinking/Writing: A Holistic Language and Literacy Program for the K-8 Classroom*. Needham Heights, Massachusetts: Allyn & Bacon, 1989, 354-55.

Williams, Helen E. "Books without Words." In *Independent Reading K-3*. Williamsport, Pennsylvania: Brodart, 1980, 21-32.

Wilson, George, and Joyce Moss. *Books for Children to Read Alone: A Guide for Parents and Librarians*. New York: Bowker, 1988, 1-14.

Alphabetical Listing of Authors

1. Adams, Pam. **Angels.** Illus.: Adams, Pam. Child's Play, 1974.
    ISBN: 0-85953-034-5 (board). Series: Child's Play Pre-Reading Books. Wordless - no print, Format - board pages.

    Five angelic children, seen from the front, are shown from the back as they really are—mischievous, active, and sometimes naughty. Blocky, bright-colored pictures show them cooking, painting, playing indoors and out, having pillow fights, fussing, squabbling, and getting into things.

2. Adams, Pam. **Zoo, The.** Illus.: Adams, Pam. Child's Play, 1974.
    ISBN: 0-85953-032-9 (board). Series: Child's Play Pre-Reading Books. Wordless - no print, Format - board pages.

    A father takes his two children to the zoo. The children's activity parallels the various animals they see: i.e. they swing on the bars as they watch monkeys. Brightly colored, simply formed pictures show animal differences, habitats and compare animals with people.

3. Adoff, Arnold. **Ma nda La.** Illus.: McCully, Emily Arnold. Harper and Row, 1971.
    ISBN: 06-020085-5; 06-020086-3 (lib); LC: 76-146-000. Almost wordless - sounds.

    A young African boy and his family prepare their fields, plant and harvest their corn, and then feast on it. Bold energetic illustrations convey family warmth and joy. Sounds represented by the two-letter syllables can be recited as a chant or poem to accompany the illustrations.

4. Alexander, Martha. **Bobo's Dream.** Illus.: Alexander, Martha. Dial, 1970.
    LC: 73-102825. Wordless - signs.

    As a young black football player reads under a tree, his dachshund's bone is taken by a large dog. After the boy rescues the bone, the little dog dreams of being big and bold and rescuing the boy from bullies. The delicate lines and muted colors convey the dog's growing self-esteem.

5. Alexander, Martha. **Magic Box, The.** Illus.: Alexander, Martha. Dial, 1984.
    ISBN: 0-8037-0051-2 (set, pbk.); LC: 83-45365. Wordless - no print, Format - flip book.

    Two children, chased by a witch, take refuge in a large green box. The box becomes a crocodile-like monster and frightens the witch away. The sequence appears to move as the pages of this small book are flipped.

6.   Alexander, Martha. **Magic Hat, The.** Illus.: Alexander, Martha. Dial, 1984.
ISBN: 0-8037-0051-2 (set, pbk.); LC: 83-45364. Wordless - no print, Format -
flip book.

A boy magician produces a rabbit from a top hat, but as the proud bunny takes a
bow, a dove appears from the hat and flies around. The rabbit uses the magic wand to
make the dove disappear, then dances happily. The simply drawn pictures appear to
move as the pages of the book are flipped.

7.   Alexander, Martha. **Magic Picture, The.** Illus.: Alexander, Martha. Dial, 1984.
ISBN: 0-8037-0051-2 (set, pbk.); LC: 83-45366. Wordless - no print, Format -
flip book.

A boy in a baseball cap places a plate with three brownies on it in front of a picture of twin girls. While he is out of the room, the twins step out of the picture and take
the brownies, feeding one to the dog under the table. Flipping the pages makes the
drawings move.

8.   Alexander, Martha. **Out! Out! Out!** Illus.: Alexander, Martha. Dial, 1968.
ISBN: 68-15251. Wordless - no print.

When a bird flies in the open window, a toddler watches as his mother, the
delivery man, and the custodian try various ways to catch the bird or drive it out. After
the adults have given up, the toddler creates a trail of cereal, which the bird follows out
the window. Pale green and gray pastel illustrations.

9.   Aliki. **Go Tell Aunt Rhody.** Illus.: Aliki. Macmillan, 1974.
ISBN: 0-02-700410-4; LC: 74-681. Wordless sequence in book.

The first sixteen pages bear the words to the old folksong "Go Tell Aunt
Rhody," while the illustration develops a story line involving a group of children and
the elderly aunt who is working on a quilt. Eight wordless pages complete the story
after the song ends. Music for the song appears in the back.

10.   Amery, Heather. **Farm Picture Book, The.** Illus.: Cartwright, Stephen. EDC
Publishing, 1986.
ISBN: 0-7460-0128-2 (board). Series: Usborne Picture Book. Wordless - no
print, Format - board pages.

Amusing cartoon-like, double-page spreads show farm animals and activities.
Each picture features out-of-context objects (such as the cake in the chicken's feed)
and a hidden yellow duck to find.

11.   Amery, Heather. **Seaside Picture Book, The.** Illus.: Cartwright, Stephen. EDC
Publishing, 1988.
ISBN: 0-7460-0137-1 (board). Series: Usborne Picture Book. Wordless - no print,
Format - board pages.

The cartoon-like children filling each busy page are involved in a great variety
of beach activities, from playing in the sand to buying ice cream from a stand. Each
drawing contains a yellow duck to find among the colorful details.

12.   Amery, Heather. **Zoo Picture Book, The.** Illus.: Cartwright, Stephen. EDC Publishing, 1986.
ISBN: 0-7460-0127-4 (board). Series: Usborne Picture Book. Wordless - no print, Format - board pages.

Colorful, busy cartoons show the activity and animals at the zoo. In each spread, there is some object out of place, such as the umbrella hanging in the lion's enclosure and the tennis shoe on a goat in the petting zoo. A small yellow duck is among the details of each picture.

13.   Amoss, Berthe. **By the Sea.** Illus.: Amoss, Berthe. Parents Magazine Press, 1969.
LC: 74-77783. Wordless - no print.

A little boy is carried off by his red kite, and his dog follows with a red balloon. Their airborne adventures end in a sandpile, which they turn into a sand castle before heading off down the beach. The black and white line drawings are enhanced with bright red accents.

14.   Amoss, Berthe. **What Did You Lose, Santa?** Illus.: Amoss, Berthe. Harper and Row, 1987.
ISBN: 0-6694-00197-X; LC: 86-33633. Wordless - signs.

Simple black and white line drawings with bright red and green highlights show Santa and Mrs. Claus on a slapstick search preceding his annual journey. When found, a banner reading "Peace on Earth" is attached to the back of the sleigh.

15.   Andersen, Hans Christian; retold by M. Eulalia Valeri; tr. by Leland Northam. **Ugly Duckling, The.** Illus.: Rius, Maria. Silver-Burdett, 1985.
ISBN: 0-382-09071-3; LC: 84-52782. Series: Tell Me a Story. Wordless - no print.

The major scenes of the story of the ugly duckling who becomes the most beautiful of swans are illustrated with paintings that capture the tale's European background. The pictures serve as memory aids as the story is recounted, rather than depicting each detail of the plot.

16.   Anderson, Lena. **Bunny Bath.** Illus.: Anderson, Lena. R&S, dist. by Farrar, Straus, & Giroux, 1990.
ISBN: 91-29-59652-1; LC: 89-063049. Wordless - no print.

Bunny awakes as the boy comes in from playing outside in winter. Boy undresses, handing each item, from wet red mittens to polka-dotted underpants, to Bunny as he takes them off. Left-hand scenes show boy and Bunny, while right side shows the item of clothing in detail. Finally boy pulls out a rubber duck and they take a bath.

17.   Anderson, Lena. **Bunny Box.** Illus.: Anderson, Lena. R&S Books, 1991.
ISBN: 91-29-59858-3; LC: 90-9053. Wordless - no print.

A child sits sobbing on the side of a bed, with a worried little bunny watching. The big bunny wheels in a box full of toys, and as each toy is taken out (and rejected), the toy is shown on one side in an isolated picture. The little bunny finally climbs into the box and pulls out the missing bedtime cuddly blanket.

18.   Anderson, Lena. **Bunny Fun.** Illus.: Anderson, Lena. R&S Books, 1991.
        ISBN: 91-29-59860-5; LC: 90-9052. Wordless - no print.
        A small child and a small bunny are out fishing when the big bunny joins them.
As the story unfolds on the left-hand page, the objects that further the story are isolated
and shown on the right-hand page—for example, as the big bunny gets out bait, a
worm is pictured on the opposite page. Sketches in dull colors.

19.   Anderson, Lena. **Bunny Party.** Illus.: Anderson, Lena. R&S, dist. by Farrar,
        Straus, & Giroux, 1987.
        ISBN: 91-29-59134-1; LC: 88-61822. Wordless - no print.
        A shaggy-headed toddler is delighted when Bunny begins setting the plain
wooden table, bringing in first a cloth, then utensils, flowers, a chair, and finally a red
pot of something good to eat. Soft watercolors show a full scene on the left page and
an object close-up on the right.

20.   Anderson, Lena. **Bunny Story.** Illus.: Anderson, Lena. R&S, dist. by Farrar,
        Straus, & Giroux, 1988.
        ISBN: 91-29-59132-5; LC: 88-82129. Wordless - signs.
        Bunny is ready to read a bedtime story, but the bed is empty. Child brings vari-
ous animals in, but none are the right kind. Finally, the child brings a baby bunny—and
listens to Bunny reading the bedtime story. A white background surrounds the softly
colored, shaggy-headed child and round-eyed bunny.

21.   Anderson, Lena. **Bunny Surprise.** Illus.: Anderson, Lena. R&S, dist. by Far-
        rar, Straus, & Giroux, 1986.
        ISBN: 91-29-59654-8; LC: 89-063050. Wordless - no print.
        A tousle-headed, white-haired child wakes, hearing Bunny coming. Bunny
brings one package after another, each package shaped like the vegetable or fruit inside
(which is shown in close-up on the right side page). When Bunny indicates that's all,
boy looks sad, but Bunny is only teasing and comes with a pacifier at last.

22.   Anno, Mitsumasa. **Anno's Alphabet: An Adventure in Imagination.** Illus.:
        Anno, Mitsumasa. Thomas Y. Crowell, 1974.
        ISBN: 0-690-00540-7; 0-690-00541-5 (lib.). Wordless - symbols.
        Each letter of the alphabet appears as if crafted from wood, but with a curious
paradoxical twist. The objects representing each letter contain imaginative visual
tricks. Detailed borders hide line drawings of more objects beginning with the initial
letter for the alert reader to find.

23.   Anno, Mitsumasa. **Anno's Animals.** Illus.: Anno, Mitsumasa. William Collins,
        Inc., 1979.
        ISBN: 0-529-05545-7; 0-529-05546-5 (lib); LC: 79-11721. Wordless - no print.
        Hidden pictures within pictures, each page presents a visual challenge to find
the animals, birds, and people camouflaged in the forest. The use of broken line,
densely drawn but vaguely detailed tree and leaf background with the only color green,
make this a very challenging visual game.

24. Anno, Mitsumasa. **Anno's Britain.** Illus.: Anno, Mitsumasa. Philomel Books, 1982. ISBN: 0-399-20861-5. Wordless - no print.

Anno's familiar figure on horseback travels through England, Wales, and Scotland in elaborate and detailed watercolor scenes. Characters from history and literature, typical British activities such as fox-hunting and cricket, and famous landmarks blend into a montage of all that reminds one of Britain.

25. Anno, Mitsumasa. **Anno's Counting Book.** Illus.: Anno, Mitsumasa. Thomas Y. Crowell, 1975.
ISBN: 0-690-01287-X; 0-690-01288-8 (lib.); LC: 76-28977. Wordless - symbols.

From a snowy, empty scene representing zero to a Christmas-time village showing twelve, each picture shows a countryside changing through the seasons. A column of blocks to the left of each page guides the reader in counting as details are added. Mathematical concepts such as sets add dimension to the simply drawn pages.

26. Anno, Mitsumasa. **Anno's Counting House.** Illus.: Anno, Mitsumasa. Philomel Books, 1982.
ISBN: 0-399-20896-8; LC: 82-617. Wordless - no print, Format - die-cut windows.

As ten little people move themselves and their furnishings from one house to another, basic numerical relationships and properties are demonstrated. Die-cut windows in the facade of each house enable a reader to peek into the page to come. Anno combines colorful figures with black line drawings.

27. Anno, Mitsumasa. **Anno's Faces.** Illus.: Anno, Mitsumasa. Philomel Books, 1989. ISBN: 0-399-21711-8; LC: 88-25030. Almost wordless - labels.

Framed by a light line, various vegetables and fruits are drawn on each page. Some of the forty-seven are familiar, such as peas or oranges, and some are less common, including the persimmon, mangosteen and Japanese pear. All become comical figures when a see-through plastic card embellished with a face is slipped over.

28. Anno, Mitsumasa. **Anno's Flea Market.** Illus.: Anno, Mitsumasa. Philomel Books, 1984.
ISBN: 0-399-21031-8. Wordless - no print.

A European-looking square becomes filled with more and more people coming with goods to sell. The objects displayed reflect mankind's history and progress. The interactions of shoppers and visual jokes in the detailed watercolor pictures call for careful viewing. At the end of the day, the square empties.

29. Anno, Mitsumasa. **Anno's Italy.** Illus.: Anno, Mitsumasa. Collins, 1978.
ISBN: 0-529-05559-7; 0-529-05560-0 (lib.); LC: 79-17649. Wordless - signs.

Anno's journey across Italy is shown in detailed ink and watercolor. The rural and city scenes contain hidden images from fine arts, religion, history, and folklore, with the Biblical theme of the life of Christ interwoven with people's daily activities.

30.   Anno, Mitsumasa. **Anno's Journey.** Illus.: Anno, Mitsumasa. Philomel Books, 1977.
ISBN: 0-399-20762-7; 0-399-20952-2 (pbk.); LC: 77-16336. Wordless - no print.

In richly detailed watercolors, a lone traveler journeys across old-world Europe on horseback. He observes people at work and play in cities, villages, and the country-side. Literary characters, historical figures, works of art, and folklore are part of the changing landscape.

31.   Anno, Mitsumasa. **Anno's Peekaboo.** Illus.: Anno, Mitsumasa. Philomel
Books, 1987.
ISBN: 0-399-21520-4; LC: 87-7255. Wordless - no print, Format - half pages.

Die-cut pages in the shape of hands alternate with simple watercolor shapes of animals and people that invite the reader to play the game "peekaboo."

32.   Anno, Mitsumasa. **Anno's U.S.A.** Illus.: Anno, Mitsumasa. Philomel Books, 1983.
ISBN: 0-399-20974-3; 0-399-21060-1 (lib.). Wordless - signs.

Anno's traveler begins in the West and travels east across the United States, passing landmarks, literary and historical characters, historical events, and typical activities of people at work and play. The tiny figure on horseback makes his way in each double-page spread of detailed outline and watercolor scenes.

33.   Anno, Mitsumasa. **Dr. Anno's Magical Midnight Circus.** Illus.: Anno, Mitsumasa.
Weatherhill, 1972.
ISBN: 0-8348-2011-0; LC: 72-78598. Wordless - frame.

At midnight the artist's table becomes filled with tiny people putting on a dream-like circus as "Peppe the Clown" turns the pages of a book left lying there. The full-color, double-page paintings blend real objects with the antics of the little charac-ters to create whimsical and inventive scenes.

34.   Anno, Mitsumasa. **Topsy-Turvies: Pictures to Stretch the Imagination.**
Illus.: Anno, Mitsumasa. Walker/Weatherhill, 1970.
ISBN: 0-8348-2004-8; LC: 71-96054. Wordless - signs.

In this book, Anno explores the tricks perspective can play. The impossible becomes visible in each double-page spread as little men demonstrate that up can be down and inside can be outside. The busy activity of the characters adds to the narra-tive quality of the illustrations.

35.   Ardizzone, Edward. **Wrong Side of the Bed, The.** Illus.: Ardizzone, Edward.
Doubleday, 1970.
LC: 79-89132. Wordless - no print.

The day starts badly for a child in rumpled pajamas standing on the wrong side of his bed and goes to worse as his activity takes him from problem to problem. Cross-hatched pen and ink drawings enable the reader to follow the child's emotions through bad day irritations until he finds a way to apologize to his mother.

36. Arnosky, Jim. **Mouse Numbers and Letters.** Illus.: Arnosky, Jim. Harcourt, Brace, Jovanovich, 1982.
    ISBN: 0-15-256022-X; LC: 81-13305. Wordless - symbols.

    On a trip to the beach, a jaunty mouse encounters ten groups of objects to be counted from one to ten, then backwards as he returns from his trip. Mouse uses twigs to construct the letters of the alphabet before tiring and falling asleep. Black line drawings with numerals, objects to count, and letters in red.

37. Arnosky, Jim. **Mouse Writing.** Illus.: Arnosky, Jim. Harcourt, Brace, Jovanovich, 1983.
    ISBN: 0-15-256028-9; LC: 83-4298. Wordless - symbols.

    Within blue borders, two sketchily drawn mice skate across an ice-covered pond, creating the letters of the cursive alphabet in blue. The larger mouse is identified as "Cap" and skates out the capital letters while the small one, "LC," does the lowercase ones, all within the context of a simple winter story.

38. Arnosky, Jim. **Mud Time and More: Nathaniel Stories.** Illus.: Arnosky, Jim. Addison Wesley, 1979.
    ISBN: 0-201-00173-X; LC: 78-10864. Wordless - titles.

    Four short stories show Nathaniel's Yankee ingenuity as he faces country situations: an exceptionally muddy road, an angry ram, putting up a weathervane, and picking apples. Small black-and-white line drawings convey a New Englander's dry humor as each tale becomes exaggerated.

39. Arnosky, Jim. **Nathaniel.** Illus.: Arnosky, Jim. Addison-Wesley, 1978.
    ISBN: 0-201-00171-3; LC: 77-13505. Wordless sequence in book.

    Three wordless stories, a letter ordering a new hat, and a diary entry develop the character of Nathaniel, a New Englander with a dry sense of humor and prone to mishap. The wordless sequences depict wood gathering complicated by a bear, Nathaniel's struggle to control a wayward diary, and raising a swan.

40. Aruego, Jose. **Look What I Can Do.** Illus.: Aruego, Jose. Scribner, 1971.
    ISBN: 684-12493-9; LC: 73-158880. Wordless - frame.

    When one water buffalo challenges another to "look what I can do," an animated romp through the jungle begins, with each one trying to outdo the other. The exploits of the two are shown in large, exaggerated, double-page spreads in muted colors. As the show-offs stop in exhaustion, a third buffalo arrives to taunt them.

41. Aruego, Jose and Ariane Dewey. **We Hide, You Seek.** Illus.: Aruego, Jose. Greenwillow, 1979.
    ISBN: 0-688-80201-X; 0-688-84201-1 (lib.). Almost wordless - dialog.

    Humorous paintings show in colorful detail a game of hide-and-seek played by a red rhinoceros and a variety of animals from plain, desert, swamp, and river. The rhino seeks the other animals in each habitat until demanding a turn to hide—and finds the perfect spot in the middle of a herd of red rhinoceroses.

42.   Asch, Frank. **Blue Balloon, The.** Illus.: Asch, Frank. McGraw-Hill, 1971.
      LC: 76-160704. Almost wordless - labels.

      This is the story of an unhappy green balloon and the person who tries to control
it. Many interpretations are possible for the strange sequences of events that unfold.
The simple outline illustrations contrast with the complex changes that occur in the
story.

43.   Asch, Frank. **In the Eye of the Teddy.** Illus.: Asch, Frank. Harper and Row, 1973.
      ISBN: 06-020151-7; 06-020152-5 (lib.); LC: 73-5156. Wordless - no print.

      Black-and-white illustrations move into the eye of the teddy and back out in
the eye of a little boy holding the teddy. The black eye is full of bizarre and surreal
images floating past, which include the boy nude and the bear dressed.

44.   Azarian, Mary. **Farmer's Alphabet, A.** Illus.: Azarian, Mary. David R.
      Godine, 1981.
      ISBN: 0-87923-394-X; 0-87923-397-4 (pbk.); LC: 80-84938. Almost wordless
      - labels.

      In sturdy New England images, each letter is represented by a rural image, from
Apple to Zinnia. Woodblock prints of snow-covered barns, maple sugar gathering, and
cast-iron wood-burning stoves reflect the author's Vermont experiences. Upper-and
lowercase letters and one word per page are printed in red.

45.   Baker, Jeannie. **Window.** Illus.: Baker, Jeannie. Greenwillow, 1991.
      ISBN: 0-688-08917-8; 0-688-08918-6 (lib.); LC: 90-3922. Wordless - signs.

      A changing countryside is shown in collage constructions. The view from a sin-
gle window alters from year to year as people move in, and slowly the wilderness is
replaced with a city. A baby held in his mother's arms to look out on the woods grows
into a man who moves to a new forest to begin the process again.

46.   Baker, Madeleine. **I Got Lost.** Illus.: Baker, Madeleine. The Wright Group, 1987.
      ISBN: 1-55624-460-6 (pbk.); 1-55624-251-4 (set). Series: This Weekend.
      Wordless - signs.

      On a shopping expedition, a girl who stops to look at a bookrack becomes lost.
She searches, follows the wrong woman, and is finally reunited with her family. Flat
drawings.

47.   Baker, Madeleine. **We Went to the Pond.** Illus.: Baker, Madeleine. The Wright
      Group, 1987.
      ISBN: 1-55624-461-4 (pbk.); 1-55624-251-4(set). Series: This Weekend.
      Wordless - signs.

      A family is seen eating breakfast, putting on boots, and taking a remote-control
boat to the park. While the older children float the boat, the youngest boy feeds the
ducks. Later they travel by car to a large pond for a toy boat race, which their boat
wins. The flatly colored outline drawings are stiffly realistic.

48. Bakken, Harald. **Special String, The.** Illus.: Richter, Mischa. Prentice-Hall, 1981. ISBN: 0-13-826370-1; LC: 81-7333. Wordless - no print.

A boy finds a piece of red string and as he follows it, rolling it into a ball, he finds many people who need the help of a bit of string. It becomes a clothesline, a lasso, a tightrope, and many other useful things, until he meets a girl collecting string and they go fishing. Black sketches with the string in red.

49. Ball, Sara. **Animals in Africa.** Illus.: Ball, Sara. ARS edition, 1987. ISBN: 1-5602-1112-1 (board). Wordless - no print, Format - mix-and-match; board pages.

Wild animals of Africa appear in family scenes in this spiral-bound flip book. Each page is divided into thirds, so that the scenes can be combined in many different ways. A natural habitat serves as background for the many species shown. Reprinted as *Somewhere in Africa.*

50. Ball, Sara. **Farmyard Families.** Illus.: Ball, Sara. WJ Fantasy, Inc., 1990. ISBN: 1-56021-024-9 (board). Wordless - no print, Format - mix-and-match; board pages.

The farmyard in front of a barn serves as background for a variety of farm animals and their young. Each cardboard page is split in thirds so that three sections can be separately changed, creating hundreds of scenes. The lively animals are simply drawn and short sequences are carried from one page to another.

51. Ball, Sara. **Somewhere in Canada.** Illus.: Ball, Sara. Vanwell Publishing, Ltd, 1987. ISBN: 0-86724-138-1 (board). Wordless - no print, Format - mix-and-match; board pages.

In the North woods near a pond, a variety of wildlife play and feed. Raccoons, squirrels, mountain goats, deer, otters, opossums, beavers, mountain lions, bears, ducks, and wolves are included. Reprinted as *Somewhere in America* by W.J. Fantasy, Inc.

52. Ball, Sara. **Teddy.** Illus.: Ball, Sara. ARS edition, 1990. ISBN: 3-7607-7038-X (board). Wordless - no print, Format - board pages.

This tiny (2.5" x 2.5") book has thick board pages that lift to reveal the various stages of a bear dressing. The appealing brown teddy bear adds one piece of colorful clothing at a time. A tiny bear in the same color as the piece of clothing is added to a row at the top of each page, accumulating to eleven.

53. Bancheck, Linda. **Snake In, Snake Out.** Illus.: Arnold, Elaine. Thomas Y. Crowell, 1978. ISBN: 0-690-03852-6; 0-690-03853-4 (lib.). Almost wordless - labels.

While demonstrating prepositions such as *in* and *on,* a lively story unfolds. A box is delivered to an old woman, who releases a snake and parrot from it. The two animals proceed to explore the house as she chases them from spot to spot. The humorous black-and-white drawings show the events in detail.

54.   Bang, Molly. **Grey Lady and the Strawberry Snatcher, The.** Illus.: Bang, Molly. Four Winds Press, 1980.
ISBN: 0-590-07547-0; LC: 79-21243. Wordless - no print.
Remarkable paintings show the grey lady purchasing ripe red strawberries and being trailed and chased by the blue-skinned, purple-hatted strawberry snatcher. In sophisticated, imaginative sequences, foreshadowing and visual puns enrich the tale as the grey lady escapes and the thief finds a taste for blackberries.

55.   Barner, Bob. **Elephant's Visit, The.** Illus.: Barner, Bob. Atlantic-Little, Brown, 1975.
ISBN: 0-316-56315-3 (lib.); LC: 75-12605. Wordless - no print.
The large gray elephant is a welcome weekend guest, but he is too big for his host's chair, tub, and bed. When the little man takes his friend on a picnic, they wreck both car and rowboat. The clumsy elephant makes a mess wherever he is, and the host is glad when mother comes to take the guest home. Sunny colors.

56.   Barton, Byron. **Applebet Story.** Illus.: Barton, Byron. Viking, 1973.
ISBN: 670-12964-X; LC: 72-91395. Almost wordless - labels.
One word for each letter of the alphabet appears on each page, while the illustrations trace the wild journey of a ripe apple blown into a city. In each gray and white picture, the bright red apple is in the center of action, from landing on a tray of chocolate sundaes to falling from a balloon into a zoo.

57.   Barton, Byron. **Elephant.** Illus.: Barton, Byron. Seabury Press, 1971.
LC: 74-154301. Wordless - signs.
A little girl's obsession with elephants is shown in simple outline drawings as she sees elephants in books, on TV, on posters and in the toy shop. Even her dreams are full of elephants. A visit to a real elephant in a zoo contrasts the giant gray animal with the simple forms she's been seeing.

58.   Barton, Byron. **Where's Al?** Illus.: Barton, Byron. Houghton Mifflin, 1972.
ISBN: 0-395-28765-0; LC: 78-171866. Almost wordless - dialog.
Al is a white and black spotted puppy who chases a stick on a crowded street and becomes lost. His boy calls, but cannot find Al. In outline drawings with solid colors, the boy is seen on one page as he misses Al and posts notices. On the opposite page, Al's experiences alone are shown, until the two find each other again.

59.   Baum, Willi. **Birds of a Feather.** Illus.: Baum, Willi. Addison-Wesley, 1969.
ISBN: 0-201-00421-6; LC: 76-88685. Wordless - no print.
In this retelling of a fable, one vain bird leaves the flock to decorate himself with borrowed feathers from a lady's hat. The others stare at his finery until he is taken by a bird-catcher and caged with exotic birds. When he flings off his fancy feather disguise, he's set free to return to his flock.

60.   Benjamin, Alan. **Rat-a-Tat, Pitter Pat.** Illus.: Miller, Margaret. Thomas Y.
      Crowell, 1987.
      ISBN: 0-690-04609-X; 0-690-04611-1 (lib.); LC: 87-568. Almost wordless -
      sounds.
      Words describing sounds are matched in rhyming pairs and shown in black-and-
white photographs. The pictures show children or scenes familiar to childhood in
demonstrating the sounds; for example, a child with a toy steam engine appears above
"choo choo" and the opposite page shows a cow for "moo."

61.   Bester, Roger. **Guess What?** Illus.: Bester, Roger. Crown, 1980.
      ISBN: 0-517-54104-1; LC: 79-24945. Almost wordless - sentences.
      Although there are many words in this book, they echo the photographs so well
that one could respond to the puzzle format without using them. Close-up photographs
of animal parts and habitats are the clues to a riddle; a clear picture of each animal
provides the answer on the next page.

62.   Blades, Ann. **Fall.** Illus.: Blades, Ann. Lothrop Lee and Shepard, 1989.
      ISBN: 0-688-09232-2 (board). Series: Seasons. Wordless - no print, Format -
      board pages.
      A northern woods in the autumn is the background for various activities such as
swinging on a tire, waving to the engineer of a train, helping get firewood ready for
winter, and looking at wildlife. Two children are shown in the softly colored pictures.

63.   Blades, Ann. **Spring.** Illus.: Blades, Ann. Lothrop Lee and Shepard, 1989.
      ISBN: 0-688-09230-6 (board). Series: Seasons. Wordless - no print, Format -
      board pages.
      Two children on a springtime visit to a zoo see many baby animals in the
exhibits. Soft colors hint at flowering trees and plants.

64.   Blades, Ann. **Summer.** Illus.: Blades, Ann. Lothrop Lee and Shepard, 1989.
      ISBN: 0-688-09231-4 (board). Series: Seasons. Wordless - no print, Format -
      board pages.
      Two children are seen in a variety of outdoor activities on a farm. They play
hide-and-seek in the yard, ride a horse, swim in a pond, watch the plowing, and play
with the piglets. Soft color illustrations with various small animals to identify in each
picture.

65.   Blades, Ann. **Winter.** Illus.: Blades, Ann. Lothrop Lee and Shepard, 1989.
      ISBN: 0-688-09233-0 (board). Series: Seasons. Wordless - no print, Format -
      board pages.
      Two children spend a winter's day playing in the snow: hiking in the woods,
building a snowman, sledding, and after the moon comes out, ice skating. Winter tones
and frosty colors convey the coldness of the season, but the warmly dressed children
enjoy being outside.

66. Blanco, Josette. **On the Farm.** Illus.: d'Ham, Claude. Child's Play, 1975.
     ISBN: 0-859530-036-1 (pbk.); 0-85953-040-X. Series: Moments, Book 2.
     Wordless - no print, Format - half pages.

     Three short vignettes of farm life are shown in bold color and simple form using a European folk art style. In each segment, the event is shown by flipping two half pages. The girl in wooden shoes gathering eggs in a basket, the boy herding sheep, and the busy farmyard show old-fashioned farm practices.

67. Blanco, Josette. **Playtime.** Illus.: d'Ham, Claude. Child's Play, 1975.
     ISBN: 0-85953-038-8 (pbk.); 0-85953-042-6. Series: Moments, Book 4. Wordless - no print, Format - half pages.

     Three short sequences show children playing in a swimming pool, in the woods, and in the mountains. A mishap tumbles a fully dressed lady into the pool. The hide-and-seek game in the woods shows an autumn setting. The game of cowboys and Indians includes falling into a stream and catching pants on fire.

68. Blanco, Josette. **Sport.** Illus.: d'Ham, Claude. Child's Play, 1975.
     ISBN: 0-85953-035-3 (pbk.); 0-85953-039-6. Series: Moments, Book 1. Wordless - no print, Format - half pages.

     Three short glimpses of boys playing hockey, skiing, and running a race feature one child falling each time, which changes the anticipated outcome. Within each simple, colorful picture, the passage of time is shown in background positions as the half pages are turned.

69. Blanco, Josette. **Weather, The.** Illus.: d'Ham, Claude. Child's Play, 1975.
     ISBN: 0-85953-037-X (pbk.); 0-85953-041-8. Series: Moments, Book 3.
     Wordless - no print, Format - half pages.

     Rain in the late spring, a nighttime storm at sea, and children playing in snow in an alpine setting form the three colorful short stories in this book. Against a double-page frame, two half pages turn to show the advancement of events illustrated in a stylized manner.

70. Bonners, Susan. **Just in Passing.** Illus.: Bonners, Susan. Lothrop Lee and Shepard, 1989.
     ISBN: 0-688-07712-9; 0-688-07711-0 (lib.); LC: 88-22021. Wordless - no print.

     A tiny baby on his mother's shoulder yawns as a grey-haired woman passes, starting a sequence in which the yawn is passed from person to person throughout the city and countryside until it returns again to the same baby. Delicately colored pictures show the infectious nature of yawning.

71. Bradman, Tony. **Sandal, The.** Illus.: Dupasquier, Philippe. Viking Kestrel, 1990.
     ISBN: 0-670-82992-7. Wordless sequence in book.

     A wordless sequence shows "Yesterday, 77 BC" when a Roman child loses her sandal while dangling her foot from a bridge. "Today" combines narrative and strip pictures to show a modern family seeing the Roman sandal in a museum and losing a similar sandal. "Tomorrow" shows a futuristic family carrying out the same story.

72. Briggs, Raymond. **Snowman: Building the Snowman, The.** Illus.: Briggs, Raymond. Little Brown, 1985.
ISBN: 0-316-10813-8 (board); LC: 85-80328. Series: The Snowman. Wordless - no print, Format - board pages.

In scenes from the opening of the film of Raymond Briggs's *The Snowman,* the boy wakes, sees the snow, and builds the snowman. This short sequence ends with the boy going inside after the snowman is finished.

73. Briggs, Raymond. **Snowman: Dressing Up, The.** Illus.: Briggs, Raymond. Little Brown, 1985.
ISBN: 0-316-10814-6 (board); LC: 85-80327. Series: The Snowman. Wordless - no print, Format - board pages.

Scenes taken from the film made of Raymond Briggs's book *The Snowman* show the boy and snowman exploring the house. The snowman discovers a snowman ornament on the tree, tries on various fruit noses, dresses in clothes, and dances with the boy in his room.

74. Briggs, Raymond. **Snowman, The.** Illus.: Briggs, Raymond. Random House, 1978.
ISBN: 0-394-88466-3; 0-394-93973-5 (lib.); LC: 78-55904. Wordless - no print.

Delighted by the snow, a boy eagerly creates a snowman. In the night, the snowman magically comes to life, and together they explore the boy's house and fly away on a journey above the frozen countryside. Softly colored illustrations in variously sized panels show the story in detail.

75. Briggs, Raymond. **Snowman: The Party, The.** Illus.: Briggs, Raymond. Little, Brown, 1985.
ISBN: 0-316-10816-2 (board); LC: 85-80325. Series: The Snowman. Wordless - no print, Format - board pages.

Snowman and Santa enjoy a boisterous party in the northern woods in various scenes from the film *The Snowman,* based on the book of the same name. The boy who originally made the snowman dances and pets the reindeer. Final scenes show the boy and snowman flying off.

76. Briggs, Raymond. **Snowman: Walking in the Air, The.** Illus.: Briggs, Raymond. Little Brown, 1985.
ISBN: 0-316-10815-4 (board); LC: 85-80326. Series: The Snowman. Wordless - no print, Format - board pages.

Sections taken from Raymond Briggs's *The Snowman,* a film made from the book of the same title, show the boy and snowman flying from the boy's yard to the far north. As they fly, other snow people join them, and the sequence ends as they arrive in the northern woods.

77. Brinckloe, Julie. **Spider Web, The.** Illus.: Brinckloe, Julie. Doubleday, 1974. ISBN: 0-385-04829-7; 0-385-02821-0 (lib.); LC: 73-20695. Wordless - no print.

A falling leaf settles among high grass in a yard. A spider carefully weaves a web, strand by strand, incorporating the leaf. Just as the spider completes her delicate work of art, a lawn mower cuts down everything in its way. Effective textures and use of white space in the detailed black-and-white illustrations.

78. Brown, Craig. **Patchwork Farmer, The.** Illus.: Brown, Craig. Greenwillow, 1989. ISBN: 0-688-07735-8; 0-688-07736-6 (lib.); LC: 88-29229. Wordless - no print.

Each time this cheerful farmer goes out to work, he rips his old overalls. As he uses more and more fabric scraps to mend each hole, the overalls come to look like the patchwork pattern of his land. Pointillist outlines show the shaggy-haired farmer always in profile and give texture to his increasingly dilapidated pants.

79. Brown, Marcia. **All Butterflies: An ABC.** Illus.: Brown, Marcia. Scribners, 1974. ISBN: 0-684-13771-2; LC: 73-19364. Almost wordless - labels.

The alphabet connection is only apparent through the word pairs on each double-page spread: "ice-cold jumpers," for example, goes with a scene of polar bears playing on an ice floe. The butterfly motif is carried throughout the book in each colorful woodcut.

80. Bruna, Dick. **Another Story to Tell.** Illus.: Bruna, Dick. Methuen, 1974. ISBN: 0-458-92680-9. Wordless - no print.

On a winter day, a little person dresses and goes outside to play in the snow and try skiing. Big outline shapes filled with strong color will attract younger children to this title.

81. Bruna, Dick. **Miffy's Dream.** Illus.: Bruna, Dick. Price Stern Sloan, 1984. ISBN: 0-8431-1545-9. Wordless - no print.

Miffy, a small white rabbit, floats along on a cloud and meets a small brown rabbit. Together they explore the night sky, stars, and the moon before falling asleep. Very simple forms with few visual clues leave the story vague but appealing in its strong design with heavy black outline and clear color.

82. Bruna, Dick. **Story to Tell, A.** Illus.: Bruna, Dick. Price Stern Sloan, 1984. ISBN: 0-416-38231-9. Wordless - no print.

Heavy black outlines and simple forms in primary colors are used in a story that can be interpreted various ways. A person wakes, goes through a morning routine, and takes a walk, finding a small crying doll or baby. The person comforts and takes home the small one and they play and go through an evening routine.

83.   Brychta, Alex. **Arrow, The.** Illus.: Brychta, Alex. Oxford, 1987.
        ISBN: 0-19-272166-6 (pbk.). Series: Cat on the Mat Books. Almost wordless - sounds.

    A cartoon style cat sets up a target and fires an arrow at it. The arrow misses initially, but goes around the world before finally returning to the center of the target. Words representing the sounds made as the arrow strikes famous landmarks appear on each page.

84.   Burgin, Norma. **Just Out for a Walk.** Illus.: Burgin, Norma. The Wright Group,
        1987. ISBN: 1-55624-491-6 (pbk.). Series: More and More. Wordless - no print.

    Sunshine tempts a dark-haired boy outside. He gets ready for his walk by thinking about things he might need if he is cold, hungry, or lost. By the time he leaves, he has collected armfuls of things he might need if it rains, gets dark, or for any other possibility.

85.   Burningham, John. **ABC.** Illus.: Burningham, John. Crown, 1985.
        ISBN: 0-517-55960-9; LC: 85-13219. Series: It's Great to Learn! Almost
        wordless - labels.

    Lightly colored sketches show a boy in straw hat interacting with an object or animal for each letter of the alphabet. In each scene, the word beginning with the letter appears with the upper- and lowercase letter. Pushing the queen in a wheelbarrow or carrying carrots to rabbit, the boy is cheerfully active.

86.   Burningham, John. **Cluck Baa.** Illus.: Burningham, John. Viking, 1984.
        ISBN: 0-670-22580-0; LC: 83-25979. Almost wordless - labels.

    Simple black line drawings with light touches of color portray a toddler making animal sounds along with the animal. The child is posed in the same posture as the animal and the word for the sound appears on the top of the page. For example, the child spreads arms near the spread-winged goose under the word *Hiss.*

87.   Burningham, John. **Come Away from the Water, Shirley.** Illus.: Burningham,
        John. Thomas Y. Crowell, 1977.
        ISBN: 0-690-01360-4; 0-690-01361-2 (lib.); LC: 77-483. Wordless sequence in book.

    On the left-hand page Shirley's parents set up chairs and relax on a beach, while on the right-hand page Shirley and a stray dog enact a fantasy pirate adventure. Typical parental comments are made as the adults pass a mundane time, oblivious to Shirley's spirited adventure told in a colorful wordless sequence.

88.   Burningham, John. **Count Up: Learning Sets.** Illus.: Burningham, John.
        Viking, 1983.
        ISBN: 0-670-24410-4 (board); LC: 82-051282. Series: Viking Number Play.
        Wordless - symbols, Format - accordion fold.

    Each page folds out to elaborate on the initial picture, giving action to the children or animals representing each set. The one monkey on one bike has one accident, the two dogs have two parachutes, three frogs leap from three lily pads, four elephants lose four hats, and five children hold five balloons.

89. Burningham, John. **Five Down: Numbers as Signs.** Illus.: Burningham, John. Viking, 1983.
ISBN: 0-670-31698-9 (board); LC: 82-051279. Series: Viking Number Play. Wordless - symbols, Format - accordion fold.

As each page from one to five unfolds, a large numeral appears as if it were a physical object being held by the appropriate number of people or animals. As the page is lifted up, the numeral suffers a disaster. Two children quarreling over the 2, for example, pull it into two pieces.

90. Burningham, John. **John Burningham's 1 2 3.** Illus.: Burningham, John. Crown, 1985.
ISBN: 0-517-55962-5; LC: 85-13212. Series: It's Great to Learn! Almost wordless - labels.

One by one, ten children of assorted ages climb into a tree to play until a tiger decides to join them and frightens them away. Softly colored pencil and line illustrations span two pages with the numeral and word for each number of children on the lower right.

91. Burningham, John. **John Burningham's Colors.** Illus.: Burningham, John. Crown, 1986.
ISBN: 0-517-55961-7; LC: 85-12582. Series: It's Great to Learn! Almost wordless - labels.

Eleven colors are introduced with the word for the color and a hat in the color. A following illustration shows the activity of a boy wearing the hat. Shade and tones of the color are presented in various outdoor scenes as the boy drives a red car, holds yellow balloons, walks a gray dog in the rain, and so on.

92. Burningham, John. **John Burningham's Opposites.** Illus.: Burningham, John. Crown, 1985.
ISBN: 0-517-55963-3; LC: 85-13218. Series: It's Great to Learn! Almost wordless - labels.

Lightly colored drawings feature a cheerful boy demonstrating various concepts. In straw hat and striped shirt he lifts an elephant for *heavy* and balances a giant balloon for *light*. He sleeps on a *hard* park bench and a *soft* couch. One word on each page names the concept shown.

93. Burningham, John. **Just Cats: Learning Groups.** Illus.: Burningham, John. Viking, 1983.
ISBN: 0-670-41094-2 (board); LC: 82-051280. Series: Viking Number Play. Wordless - symbols, Format - accordion fold.

In an unusual format, designed to fold out in two ways, each set of pages shows a new cat joining a group of cats going on a picnic. Mishaps occur as the cats try different forms of transportation and meet other groups of animals in sets of five.

94. Burningham, John. **Pigs Plus: Learning Addition.** Illus.: Burningham, John. Viking, 1983.
    ISBN: 0-670-55508-8 (board); LC: 82-51283. Series: Viking Number Play. Wordless - symbols, Format - board; accordion.

    A long foldout is divided into five sections, each of which unfolds further to complete a mini-sequence. Each sequence shows a pig, out tor a ride in an old red car, being joined by five other pigs. As each one joins the group, a different problem is solved.

95. Burningham, John. **Read One: Numbers as Words.** Illus.: Burningham, John. Viking, 1983.
    ISBN: 0-670589-86-1 (board); LC: 82-51281. Series: Viking Number Play. Almost wordless - labels, Format - board; accordion.

    Cheerfully drawn bears in a variety of activities demonstrate the words for numbers. The accordion-folded pages unfold twice again.

96. Burningham, John. **Ride Off: Learning Subtraction.** Illus.: Burningham, John. Viking, 1983.
    ISBN: 0-67059798-8 (board); LC: 82-51278. Series: Viking Number Play. Wordless - symbols, Format - board; accordion.

    Simple line with soft color illustration demonstrates subtraction as a horse loses its riders one by one. Each of five sections unfolds to reveal the story sequence.

97. Burningham, John. **Time to Get Out of the Bath, Shirley.** Illus.: Burningham, John. Thomas Y. Crowell, 1978.
    ISBN: 0-690-01378-7; 0-690-01379-5 (lib.); LC: 76-58503. Wordless sequence in book.

    While her mother straightens up the bathroom on the left-hand pages, the right-hand pages show a girl's fantasy adventures. She becomes tiny and slips through the pipes into a medieval countryside where she is befriended by knights and a king and queen. The mother fusses while Shirley's adventure unfolds wordlessly.

98. Burton, Marilee Robin. **Elephant's Nest: Four Wordless Stories, The.** Illus.: Burton, Marilee Robin. Harper and Row, 1978.
    ISBN: 0-06-020905-4; 0-06-020906-2 (lib.); LC: 78-20263. Wordless - titles.

    Animals are portrayed humorously in four short stories. Black line drawings with limited colors of gold, lavender, and brown tell of a bird hatching flying elephants, mice going to the moon for cheese, a lion covered by a flock of overly friendly birds, and a mother kangaroo with a surprisingly full pocket.

99. Butterworth, Nick. **Amanda's Butterfly.** Illus.: Butterworth, Nick. Delacorte, 1991.
    ISBN: 0-385-30433-1; 0-385-30434-X (lib.); LC: 90-48741. Wordless - no print.

    After reading a book which shows someone catching butterflies, a girl decides to try catching some herself. Disappointed when it begins to rain, she goes into a garden shed and there discovers a tiny fairy with an injured wing. The elaborate storyline is developed in panel sequences and full-page color illustrations.

100. Cannon, Beth. **Cat Had a Fish about a Dream, A.** Illus.: Cannon, Beth. Pantheon, 1976. ISBN: 0-394-83255-8; 0-394-93255-2 (lib.). Wordless - no print.

A peaceful room with sleeping cat and sun shining through the window becomes the stage for a surreal sequence in which each scene fragments to slowly form another scene. In dream-like fashion, the transformation of the cat, the fish, and the clouds is shown in each softly colored drawing.

101. Capdevila, Roser. **At the Farm.** Illus.: Capdevila, Roser. Annick Press, 1985. ISBN: 0-920303-08-0 (board). Series: Books about Us, 1. Wordless - no print, Format - board pages.

In large format, this sturdy board book presents double-page spreads detailing life in the farmyard, garden, field, barn, and the spacious farm kitchen. Daily activities for three generations and the common tools of a largely unmechanized farm are depicted in muted color and amusing vignettes.

102. Capdevila, Roser. **City, The.** Illus.: Capdevila, Roser. Annick Press, 1986. ISBN: 0-920303-45-5 (board). Series: Books about Us, 5. Wordless - no print, Format - board pages.

This European city is a bustling, active place full of all ages of people. From the city park and downtown streets to the train station and harbor, each double-page spread is packed with detail and mini-dramas as people play, work, and travel.

103. Capdevila, Roser. **Our House.** Illus.: Capdevila, Roser. Annick Press, 1985. ISBN: 0-920303-10-2 (board). Series: Books about Us, 2. Wordless - no print, Format - board pages.

Each room of a large city apartment is filled with details of furniture and household objects as well as with the activities of three children and their parents. Large double-page spreads drawn in flat outlines with watery color show both familiar and unfamiliar aspects of the family's lifestyle.

104. Capdevila, Roser. **Shopping.** Illus.: Capdevila, Roser. Annick Press, 1986. ISBN: 0-920303-43-9 (board). Series: Books about Us, 3. Wordless - signs, Format - board pages.

Flat, cartoon-like drawings fill each double-page spread with the details of each type of shop: the bakery, outdoor market, department store, sporting goods store, grocery store, and butcher shop. A woman in a fur-collared coat appears in each store, becoming more exhausted with each purchase and collapsing in the end.

105. Capdevila, Roser. **Weekend, The.** Illus.: Capdevila, Roser. Annick Press, 1986. ISBN: 0-920303-44-7 (board). Series: Books about Us, 4. Wordless - no print, Format - board pages.

A family with mustached father, pregnant mother, and twin boys is shown in a series of weekend activities—hiking in the country, swimming at a beach, playing in the snow, and having company over on a summer day. The final two-page spread of a festival with carnival rides reveals new twin girls in a stroller.

106. Capdevila, Roser. **What We Do.** Illus.: Capdevila, Roser. Annick Press, 1986. ISBN: 0-920303-46-3 (board). Series: Books about Us, 6. Wordless - signs, Format - board pages.

A family leaves their apartment house in the morning, and in each double-page spread the activities of the day are shown. The girl is shown in a nursery school playground, the family together at the zoo, in the park, and dining with grandparents at a restaurant. The final spread shows the children at the doctor's.

107. Carle, Eric. **1,2,3 to the Zoo.** Illus.: Carle, Eric. Philomel Books, 1968. ISBN: 0-399-61172-X (lib.); 0-399-20847-X (pbk.); LC: 81-8609. Wordless - signs.

As the zoo train passes, each brightly colored car has one animal more than the previous car, from one elephant to ten exotic birds. Large, bright two-page spreads show each car, with the cumulative train in miniature below. Each animal page has a tiny mouse to find. When the train ends, the full zoo is seen in a foldout page.

108. Carle, Eric. **Do You Want to Be My Friend?** Illus.: Carle, Eric. Thomas Y. Crowell, 1971. ISBN: 0-690-24276-X; 0-690-24277-8 (lib.); LC: 70-140643. Wordless - frame.

A mouse asks "do you want to be my friend?" to a succession of animals, which are shown first by their tail only and then in full on the next page, making a guessing game of each animal. In the end, when mouse finds a mouse friend, the green line at the bottom of each page is revealed to be a snake.

109. Carle, Eric. **I See a Song.** Illus.: Carle, Eric. Thomas Y. Crowell, 1973. ISBN: 0-690-43306-9; 0-690-43307-7 (lib.); LC: 72-9249. Wordless - frame.

Shown in a black block print, a violinist enters and invites the readers to use their imagination to see their own song while he plays. As he begins, colorful blobs dance across the pages to create shapes and pictures. As the musician finishes and bows, he has absorbed the colors and designs of his music.

110. Carle, Eric. **My Very First Book of Colors.** Illus.: Carle, Eric. Crowell (reissue 1991 HarperCollins), 1974. ISBN: 0-694-0011-6 (board). Wordless - no print, Format - mix-and-match.

The top half of each split page contains a solid color rectangle and the bottom half an object featuring one primary color. The objects on the bottom can be matched with the colors on the top.

111. Carle, Eric. **My Very First Book of Numbers.** Illus.: Carle, Eric. Crowell (reissue 1991 HarperCollins), 1974. ISBN: 0-694-0012-4 (board); LC: 72-83777. Wordless - symbols, Format - mix-and-match.

Fruits such as bananas, cherries, lemons, and pineapples are painted in color on the bottom half of these split pages. The top half bears a numeral and a corresponding number of black squares to match with the appropriate number of fruits.

112. Carle, Eric. **My Very First Book of Shapes.** Illus.: Carle, Eric. Crowell (reissue 1991 HarperCollins), 1974.
ISBN: 0-694-00013-2 (board); LC: 72-83778. Wordless - no print, Format - mix-and-match.

Solid black shapes on the top half of these split pages reflect the shapes of objects featured on the bottom half. Colorful pictures of such varied things as a bug, a train car, or a watermelon slice are built from simple forms.

113. Carrick, Donald. **Drip, Drop.** Illus.: Carrick, Donald. Macmillan, 1973.
ISBN: 0-02-717340-2; LC: 73-4056. Wordless - no print.

Blue backgrounds with bled ink line drawings and a white line for the rain enhance the watery theme of this tale. Late at night a storm blows a bit of the roof off, and water drip, drops in. It falls through the attic, by baby's bed, on the dog, into a boy's room, and on to the basement. Details with boats add to the theme of wetness.

114. Carrier, Lark. **Snowy Path: A Christmas Journey, The.** Illus.: Carrier, Lark. Picture Book Studio, 1989.
ISBN: 0-88708-121-5; LC: 89-8449. Wordless - no print, Format - flaps.

In snowy woods, a girl follows the tracks of wild animals. Each set of tracks ends with a cut-out to turn over and discover the animal, which then joins the girl on her walk. Soft, pastel color and rounded forms give the impression of twilight and snowfall. The final set of tracks leads to Santa and reindeer.

115. Carroll, Ruth. **Chimp and the Clown, The.** Illus.: Carroll, Ruth. Henry Z. Walck, 1968.
LC: 68-29029. Wordless - no print.

Lively colored pencil drawings convey a circus atmosphere as the chimp becomes tired of the parade and runs away; the clown searches for her and finally rescues her from a capsized boat.

116. Carroll, Ruth. **Dolphin and the Mermaid, The.** Illus.: Carroll, Ruth. Henry Z. Walck, 1974.
ISBN: 0-8098-1219-3; LC: 74-5452. Wordless - no print.

The peaceful underwater world of a mermaid and her friends is shown in watercolor pencil sketches and washes of blue, green, and pink. When first a diver and then a family fishing threaten their existence, the sea creatures rescue one another and clean their environment of human trash.

117. Carroll, Ruth. **Rolling Downhill.** Illus.: Carroll, Ruth. Henry Z. Walck, 1973.
ISBN: 0-8098-1201-0; LC: 72-10649. Wordless - no print.

A frisky kitten and puppy playfully become entangled in a ball of yarn near their mountain cabin home. They roll downhill to a pond and encounter water and woodland creatures. Wearily they return home to nap before getting into more mischief. Charcoal drawings in three colors convey energy and warmth.

118. Carroll, Ruth. **What Whiskers Did.** Illus.: Carroll, Ruth. Henry Z. Walck, 1932. LC: 65-19730. Wordless - no print.

Whiskers, a rambunctious puppy, runs after rabbit tracks when his rope breaks. Alone in the woods, he misses the rabbit and finds a fox. The puppy is saved by running into the rabbit hole, where he becomes friends with the bunnies before returning to his own home. Sketches in gray and brown convey the wintry adventure.

119. Carroll, Ruth. **Witch Kitten, The.** Illus.: Carroll, Ruth. Henry Z. Walck, 1973. ISBN: 0-8098-1206-1; LC: 73-7391. Wordless - no print.

While the witch sleeps, her kitten unties the broom to go on an unauthorized ride by daylight. The broom seems to have a mind of its own as they disturb people and animals in the wood, causing humorous mishaps. When a large bird attacks them, kitten is glad to be rescued by the witch. Orange, brown and green pencil sketches.

120. Carroll, Ruth, and Latrobe Carroll. **Christmas Kitten, The.** Illus.: Carroll, Ruth and Latrobe Carroll. Henry Z. Walck, 1970. ISBN: 0-8098-1164-2; LC: 75-109123. Wordless - no print.

The children in a gingerbread Victorian house are delighted with the offer of a kitten, but their mother shoos them back inside. The kitten proceeds to try various ways to get inside, and at last is discovered in the Christmas tree and allowed to stay. The line drawings have an old-fashioned charm.

121. Cartwright, Stephen, and Claudia Zeff. **Find the Duck.** Illus.: Cartwright, Stephen. Usborne/EDC Publishing, 1983. ISBN: 0-86020-714-5 (board). Series: Find It Board Books. Wordless - no print, Format - board pages.

The yellow duck toy can be found in each picture of a toddler's bathtime. Tangled in the unrolled toilet paper, tucked under clothes or behind the potty, the duck takes a bathroom tour that ends when the toddler, clad in pajamas, carries it off to bed.

122. Cartwright, Stephen, and Claudia Zeff. **Find the Puppy.** Illus.: Cartwright, Stephen. Usborne/EDC Publishing, 1983. ISBN: 0-86020-717-X (board). Series: Find It Board Books. Wordless - no print, Format - board pages.

Puppy's in the kitchen, hiding under the high chair before breakfast. While the toddler eats, helps put things away, and washes dishes, the puppy is knocking things over, getting into the trash, and spoiling the clean laundry with dirty footprints.

123. Catalanotto, Peter. **Dylan's Day Out.** Illus.: Catalanotto, Peter. Orchard Books, 1989. ISBN: 0-531-05829-8; 0-531-08429-9 (lib.); LC: 88-36440. Wordless sequence in book.

Dylan, a dalmation dog, dreams black-and-white dreams all day after his owner leaves. One day the back door is open and Dylan is free to run into the countryside where he is the hero of a soccer game featuring penguins and skunks. The bright watercolors include all sorts of black-and-white objects and animals.

124. Charlip, Remy, and Jerry Joyner. **Thirteen.** Illus.: Charlip, Remy and Jerry Joyner. Parents Magazine Press, 1975. Wordless sequence in book.

Thirteen simultaneous stories include five wordless sequences: "The Leaf and the Caterpillar"; "The Mystery of the Pyramid"; "Getting Thin and Getting Fat Again Dance"; "Paper Magic"; and "The Rise and Fall of Civilization." Unusual and playful illustrations in soft colors.

125. Charlot, Martin. **Once upon a Fishhook.** Illus.: Charlot, Martin. Island Heritage, 1972.
ISBN: 0-8348-3025-6; LC: 74-152567. Wordless - no print.

A boy fishing in a small pool is shown in black-and-white line drawings. The tiny fish he catches is in color, as are the series of ever-larger fish and monsters that appear. Each new creature swallows the creature before it along with the fishing line. The final fish is the first tiny one, which the boy tosses back in.

126. Charlot, Martin. **Sunnyside Up.** Illus.: Charlot, Martin. Weatherhill, 1972.
ISBN: 0-8348-3000-0; LC: 73-173473. Wordless - no print.

In a pioneer cabin, a young man wakes to a sunny morning. His clearing is full of farm animals, while a gun and traps can be seen in his house and barn. His life changes when a giant chick comes from his morning egg, beginning a journey of exploration and rebirth. Colorful, cross-hatched drawings chart his changes.

127. Chochola, Frantisek. **Farm, The.** Illus.: Chochola, Frantisek. Floris Books, 1988.
ISBN: 0-86315-051-9 (board). Wordless - no print, Format - board pages.

Clear paintings show farm animals on a European farm. Both horse-drawn and tractor-drawn hay wagons are used to gather hay, a boy leads a goat from a field of sheep and cattle, and inside the barn, cows are milked by hand.

128. Chochola, Frantisek. **Forest, The.** Illus.: Chochola, Frantisek. Floris Books, 1988.
ISBN: 0-86315-073-X (board). Wordless - no print, Format - board pages.

From a meadow at wood's edge to treetops and a small forest pond, the wildlife and vegetation typical of European woodlands are painted in double-page spreads. The leafy green of a sunny day in spring or summer is the dominant color. Rabbits, deer, fox, and hedgehog are accompanied by smaller wildlife in each scene.

129. Chwast, Seymour, and Martin Stephen Moskof. **Still Another Number Book.**
Illus.: Chwast, Seymour, and Martin Stephen Moskof. McGraw-Hill, 1971.
LC: 74-141916. Almost wordless - labels.

Each set of objects leads to the next as numbers accumulate from one to ten. Each slightly surreal illustration contains groups of objects to count as well as one object to add to the set being accumulated.

130. Coker, Gylbert. **Naptime.** Illus.: Coker, Gylbert. Delacorte, 1978.
ISBN: 0-440-06303-5; 0-440-06304-3 (lib.); LC: 78-50415. Almost wordless - dialog.

In a multi-ethnic preschool, seven children and their male teacher have a snack and prepare for naptime. The active children have difficulty settling down until the teacher pulls out a book to read aloud, and succeeds in putting all to sleep—including himself. Black ink drawings in a red line frame.

131. Collington, Peter. **Angel and the Soldier Boy, The.** Illus.: Collington, Peter. Alfred A. Knopf, 1987.
ISBN: 0-394-88626-7; 0-394-98626-1 (lib.). Wordless - signs.

After a bedtime story about pirates, a little girl sleeps with her angel and soldier dolls on her pillow. A coin is stolen from her piggy bank by pirates, who kidnap the soldier boy. The brave angel rescues him and together they return the coin. Panels of softly colored pencil drawings convey their perilous adventure.

132. Collington, Peter. **Little Pickle.** Illus.: Collington, Peter. Dutton, 1986.
ISBN: 0-525-44230-8. Wordless - no print.

A toddler awakens her parents and they prepare for the day. Later, mother takes her in a stroller. The child dreams that her mother has fallen asleep in the stroller while she has adventures with trains and boats and is rescued at sea. Softly colored pencil and line drawings fill variously sized panels on each page.

133. Collington, Peter. **My Darling Kitten.** Illus.: Collington, Peter. Alfred A. Knopf, 1988. ISBN: 0-394-89924-5; LC: 87-31002. Almost wordless - dialog.

A soft gray kitten wakes, then runs upstairs to wake its sleeping owner, a little girl. Delicate drawings in early morning colors are framed in pastel borders. The kitten's "Meow" and the girl's response "My darling kitten!" are the only words.

134. Collington, Peter. **On Christmas Eve.** Illus.: Collington, Peter. Alfred A. Knopf, 1990.
ISBN: 0-679-80830-2; 0-679-90830-7 (lib.); LC: 90-4202. Wordless - signs.

A magical story for "chimneyless children everywhere" shows tiny angelic fairies opening the door to the house and lighting the way for Santa Claus to find a little girl on Christmas Eve. In soft color and delicate detail, panels show the snowy journey and shadowy house as the child's wishes are fulfilled.

135. Corbett, Grahame. **Who Is Next?** Illus.: Corbett, Grahame. Dial, 1982.
ISBN: 0-8037-9759-1 (board); LC: 82-70036. Series: Very First Books. Wordless - no print, Format - board pages.

A parade of colorful mechanical characters goes by, with part of the next character appearing on the page to indicate what will follow. The humorously drawn creatures include a hippo on wheels, penguins, a caterpillar, and an octopus. The final spread shows all the characters revolving on a carousel.

136. Craig, Helen. **Mouse House 1,2,3, The.** Illus.: Craig, Helen. Random House, 1980. ISBN: 0-394-84345-2 (cased); LC: 79-66702. Series: Mouse House. Wordless - symbols, Format - accordion fold.

From zero to ten, busy mice create numerals and provide counting opportunities. From 10 to 100, mice gather on the beach in groups of ten. The lightly colored illustrations have a surprising amount of detail for a miniature (2" x 2") format.

137. Craig, Helen. **Mouse House ABC, The.** Illus.: Craig, Helen. Random House, 1978. ISBN: 0-394-84218-9 (cased); LC: 78-20715. Series: Mouse House. Wordless - symbols, Format - accordion fold.

Busy mice create the letters of the alphabet in the fold-out pages of this miniature book. The activities of the mice involve something beginning with the letter, for example, two mice nail 'N' and a gardener mouse prunes a bush shaped as 'P.'

138. Craig, Helen. **Mouse House Months.** Illus.: Craig, Helen. Random House, 1981. ISBN: 0-394-84580-3 (cased); LC: 79-93307. Series: Mouse House. Almost wordless - labels, Format - accordion fold.

A tiny (2" x 2") accordion-fold book features delicately colored scenes in which mice are engaged in seasonal activities. A white mouse looks at a tree in the four seasons, followed by a scene for each month. Mice make a snow mouse and ice skate in January, rake leaves and roast marshmallows in November, for example.

139. Crews, Donald. **Truck.** Illus.: Crews, Donald. Greenwillow, 1980. ISBN: 0-688-80244-3; 0-688-84244-5 (lib.); LC: 79-19031. Wordless - signs.

Strong graphic design and bold colors show a large red trailer truck from loading dock to destination. Along the way, typical road signs and sights accompany the truck through traffic, on the highway, through rain and fog, during a nighttime stop for fuel, and on the freeway approach to a large city.

140. Cristini, Ermanno, and Luigi Puricelli. **Il Papavero.** Illus.: Cristini, Ermanno, and Luigi Puricelli. Emme Edizioni, 1977. Wordless - no print.

Bright red poppies bloom in a vivid green wheat field. A bee flies from flower to flower carrying pollen. As the wheat turns golden the poppy seeds fall to the ground. The simplicity of the form allows the development from flower to seed to be clearly presented in beautifully designed prints.

141. Cristini, Ermanno, and Luigi Puricelli. **In My Garden.** Illus.: Cristini, Ermanno, and Luigi Puricelli. Neugebauer Press, 1981. ISBN: 0-907234-05-4. Wordless - no print.

Simple graphics with boldly painted colors show the many lifeforms in a rural garden. As in a real garden, patience and careful observation will reveal the variety of plants, animals, and insects that share the habitat.

142. Cristini, Ermanno, and Luigi Puricelli. **In the Pond.** Illus.: Cristini, Ermanno, and Luigi Puricelli. Picture Book Studio/ Neugebauer Press, 1984.
ISBN: 0-907234-43-7. Wordless - no print.

Bright, realistic paintings show a slice of pond life from one bank to the next. The separate pages are each part of a diorama with a view of plant and animal life above and below water.

143. Cristini, Ermanno, and Luigi Puricelli. **In the Woods.** Illus.: Cristini, Ermanno, Luigi Puricelli, and Renato Pegoraro. Picture Book Studio USA, 1983.
ISBN: 0-907234-31-3; 0-88708-008-1; LC: 83-8153. Wordless - no print.

Richly colored paintings show the wealth of life on the forest floor. In panoramic fashion, each page continues the picture from the page before, as if the whole would create a mural of the animals and plants found from ground to about a foot up.

144. d'Este, Alessandra. **Arctic Fox, The.** Illus.: d'Este, Alessandra. The Wright Group, 1986.
ISBN: 1-55624-067-8 (set, pbk.). Series: First Nature Watch. Wordless - no print.

As snow falls, two arctic foxes meet. Buds bloom and pups are born. The role of the fox as a predator is seen as the mother shows the pups how to hunt. In winter an arctic fox's coat changes color, although the completely white fox is not shown here.

145. d'Este, Alessandra. **Bluetit, The.** Illus.: d'Este, Alessandra. The Wright Group, 1986.
ISBN: 1-55624-000-7 (set, pbk.). Series: First Nature Watch, Set 1. Wordless - no print.

The bluetit is a common woodland bird of Europe. Over the course of a year, a pair is shown nesting, raising young, and feeding. Stylized illustrations in harmonious colors show the birds and their park-like environment.

146. Daughtry, Duanne. **What's Inside?** Illus.: Daughtry, Duanne. Alfred A. Knopf, 1984.
ISBN: 0-394-86249-X; 0-394-96249-4 (lib.). Wordless - signs.

A close-up view of an object invites the reader to guess what might be inside, and the following page shows the answer: an invitation in an envelope, peas in a pod, coins in a purse, eggs in a carton, "Jack" in a box, cat in a carrier, yolk in an egg, lunch in a lunch box, toes inside socks, and so on.

147. Davis, Annelies. **This Is My Garden.** Illus.: Davis, Annelies. Hayes Publishing/CHP books, 1987.
ISBN: 0-88625-138-9 (board). Series: Smalltalk. Wordless - no print, Format - board pages.

A child and puppy explore a backyard which includes a swing set, a tree house, a garden shed, a wading pool, a sandbox, and a vegetable garden.

148. Davis, Annelies. **This Is My Pet.** Illus.: Davis, Annelies. Hayes Publishing/CHP books, 1987.
ISBN: 0-88625-139-7 (board). Series: Smalltalk. Wordless - no print, Format - board pages.

Drawn in a blocky cartoon style, a child in overalls enjoys eight different pets, interacting with each one separately and then lining them all up together.

149. Davis, Annelies. **This Is My Playworld.** Illus.: Davis, Annelies. Hayes Publishing/CHP books, 1987.
ISBN: 0-88625-141-9 (board). Series: Smalltalk. Wordless - no print, Format - board pages.

A toddler finds floor-level playthings while exploring indoors. Unrolling toilet tissue, standing in a shoe box, trying on caps and clothes, and looking at a jumble of sports equipment occupies the curious child, who finally hugs a worn, one-eyed teddy bear.

150. Day, Alexandra. **Carl Goes Shopping.** Illus.: Day, Alexandra. Farrar, Straus, & Giroux, 1989.
ISBN: 0-374-31110-2; LC: 88-462162. Wordless - frame.

Carl, a Rottweiler, is left in charge of the baby in a large department store, and together they visit various areas, leaving chaos in their wake. The richly detailed paintings show the effect of a large dog and a baby on the structured displays of goods. Mother returns to find the two seemingly as she left them.

151. Day, Alexandra. **Carl's Christmas.** Illus.: Day, Alexandra. Farrar, Straus, & Giroux, 1990.
ISBN: 0-374-31114-5; LC: 90-55164. Wordless - signs.

Carl, a Rottweiler, is left in charge of baby on Christmas Eve. They go for a winter walk, past shops and carolers, before returning home to wait by the fire for a visit from Santa. Carl helps Santa before putting the sleeping baby to bed. Full color oil paintings with the flavor of the 1940s.

152. Day, Alexandra. **Good Dog, Carl.** Illus.: Day, Alexandra. Green Tiger Press, 1985.
ISBN: 0-88138-062-8; LC: 85-070419. Wordless - frame.

In beautifully realized paintings with an old-fashioned flavor, a responsible Rottweiler, Carl, is left in charge of the baby. Their exploration of the house includes dancing to the radio and fixing a very messy snack. Carl dumps baby back in bed and cleans the house just in time for mother to arrive and praise him.

153. de Groat, Diane. **Alligator's Toothache.** Illus.: de Groat, Diane. Crown, 1977.
ISBN: 0-517-52-805-3; LC: 76-22780. Wordless - no print.

Alligator is getting ready for a party and animals are arriving—but poor Alligator can't enjoy it, because of a terrible toothache. Friends try bringing in a dentist, but alligator won't see him. They play a trick by putting the dentist on a lidded tray, the tooth is pulled, and all ends in a humorously drawn party.

154. Degen, Bruce. **Aunt Possum and the Pumpkin Man.** Illus.: Degen, Bruce. Harper and Row, 1977.
ISBN: 0-06-021412-0; 0-06-021413-9 (lib.); LC: 76-58685. Almost wordless - sounds.

Aunt Possum has settled in for a comfortable Halloween night when the door bangs open—and only a pair of boots is there. A shirt flaps up; the pumpkin head goes "oooooo." She lets fly with a broom and reveals small tricksters, who come in to carve a jack-o-lantern and eat pie. Drawings reveal a dry folk humor.

155. Delon-Boltz, Mireille. **Polar Bear, The.** Illus.: Delon-Boltz, Mireille. The Wright Group, 1986.
ISBN: 1-55624-067-8 (set, pbk.). Series: First Nature Watch. Wordless - no print.

As the Arctic sun sets for the long winter, two polar bears are seen on the ice. The female then is seen in a snow cave holding twin cubs, and when spring comes she shows the cubs around the still snow-covered environment.

156. Demarest, Chris L. **Orville's Odyssey.** Illus.: Demarest, Chris L. Prentice-Hall, 1986. ISBN: 0-13-642851-7; LC: 86-8439. Wordless - signs.

Orville is ready to go fishing and casts his line into a puddle on the sidewalk in front of his apartment house. He is pulled into the puddle and into an underwater world where the giant fish he hooked hunts him. Simple line and watercolor illustration show the cartoon-like character's inventive escape.

157. Demi. **Follow the Line.** Illus.: Demi. Holt, Rinehart and Winston, 1981.
ISBN: 0-03-059112-0; LC: 81-4072. Almost wordless - labels.

Embellished with all manner of visual and verbal puns, a line travels through the book. Tiny, colorful illustrations show a great variety of things a line can do or be, from outline to ABC. Playful and sophisticated, the line changes perspective and character as it moves through space to the "end of the line."

158. Demi. **Where Is It? A Hide-and-Seek Puzzle Book.** Illus.: Demi. Doubleday, 1979.
ISBN: 0-385-14846-1; 0-385-14847-X (lib.); LC: 78-22634. Almost wordless - sentences.

In a small box at the top of each page appears a creature or object which can be found in the illustration on that page. Pages filled with many small objects, and imaginative pages of people and animals made into letters and numbers challenge the reader.

159. dePaola, Tomie. **Flicks.** Illus.: dePaola, Tomie. Harcourt, Brace, Jovanovich, 1979.
ISBN: 0-15-228487-7; LC: 79-87514. Wordless - titles.

In an old-fashioned theater, five short silent films are shown, each preceded by a title slide. An audience of children buys tickets and popcorn, enters the theater, and forms the bottom frame for the screen. Pastels in a limited range give a feeling of the dark theater and the old time "flicks."

160. dePaola, Tomie. **Hunter and the Animals, The.** Illus.: dePaola, Tomie. Holiday House, 1981.
ISBN: 0-8234-0397-1; 0-8234-0428-5 (pbk.). Wordless - no print.

In the style of Hungarian folk art, a hunter is shown entering a forest to shoot game. However, the animals are all hidden and he becomes lost. While he sleeps, the animals take away his gun, and when he wakes they make friends with him and show him to his home. Heavy line and bold color give effect to a gentle tale.

161. dePaola, Tomie. **Knight and the Dragon, The.** Illus.: dePaola, Tomie. G.P. Putnam's Sons, 1980.
ISBN: 0-399-20707-4; 0-399-20708-2 (pbk.); LC: 79-18131. Wordless sequence in book.

In whimsical watercolor illustrations, a young knight and a dragon read about how to fight the other and prepare to do battle. When their fighting ends with both of them losers, the princess-librarian brings them new books which show them how to be winners by cooperating and they open a successful Bar-B-Q Restaurant.

162. dePaola, Tomie. **Pancakes for Breakfast.** Illus.: dePaola, Tomie. Harcourt, Brace, Jovanovich, 1978.
ISBN: 0-15-259455-8; 0-15-6707683 (pbk.); LC: 77-15523. Wordless - signs.

A little old lady wakes up on a snowy morning thinking about hot pancakes. She checks the recipe, then gathers ingredients—eggs from the hens, milk from the cow, butter which she churns. While she hikes to buy maple syrup, her pets eat the ingredients, and she must find pancakes at a neighbor's table.

163. dePaola, Tomie. **Sing, Pierrot, Sing: A Picture Book in Mime.** Illus.: dePaola, Tomie. Harcourt, Brace, Jovanovich, 1983.
ISBN: 0-15-274988-8; 0-15-274989-6 (pbk.); LC: 83-84032. Wordless - no print.

Poor Pierrot dreams of the lovely Columbine, who is with the handsome Harlequin when he comes to serenade her under the balcony. His music draws a crowd, who laugh at his humiliation, and Pierrot escapes to the moon in embarrassment. The children draw him back to be with them in softly colored pastel pictures.

164. Dinardo, Jeffrey. **Day at the Circus, A.** Illus.: Dinardo, Jeffrey. Modern Publishing, 1988. ISBN: 0-87449-416-8. Series: Honey Bear Books. Wordless - no print.

A grinning girl pig follows a clown into a circus tent, where she finds herself becoming part of each act: overbalancing the acrobats, replacing the trapeze artist, causing the lion to roar, and being shot from a cannon. Although poorly reproduced, the illustration is colorful.

165. Dinardo, Jeffrey. **Day in Space, A.** Illus.: Dinardo, Jeffrey. Modern Publishing, 1988. ISBN: 0-87449-417-6. Series: Honey Bear Books. Wordless - no print.

A little girl rabbit blasts off from her backyard in a rocket and rides through space to a purple planet, where she finds small, friendly, furry creatures. They are frightened by a monster, and she shows them how to frighten the monster in return. Garish color detracts somewhat from the imaginative storyline.

166. Dinardo, Jeffrey. **Day in the Park, A.** Illus.: Dinardo, Jeffrey. Modern
     Publishing, 1988.
     ISBN: 0-87449-414-1. Series: Honey Bear Books. Wordless - no print.

   A father cat takes his son to the park. While dad sits on a bench and reads, the
small cat embarks on a series of adventures: being carried away by a balloon, sailing
off to escape a dog, finding a sea monster, being rescued by a hot-air balloon, and
finally floating down with an umbrella to sit quietly beside his father.

167. Dinardo, Jeffrey. **Day on the Farm, A.** Illus.: Dinardo, Jeffrey. Modern Pub-
     lishing, 1988.
     ISBN: 0-87449-415-X. Series: Honey Bear Books. Wordless - no print.

   A small bear's cap is blown off his head toward a barn. As he chases it, it is
blown from one farm animal to another and finally returns to him. The scarecrow,
cornfield, pumpkin, and turkey provide autumn touches in this simply drawn story. A
spectator mouse can be found throughout.

168. Donnelly, Liza. **Dinosaur Day.** Illus.: Donnelly, Liza. Scholastic, 1987.
     ISBN: 0-590-41800-9 (pbk.). Almost wordless - dialog.

   A boy who loves dinosaurs goes dinosaur hunting with his dog on a winter day.
They find various snow-covered shapes which the boy identifies as various dinosaurs,
but which are garbage cans, cars, and so on. Finally, one shakes off the snow and is
real, chasing them home again. Funny flat drawings with color.

169. Drescher, Henrick. **Yellow Umbrella, The.** Illus.: Drescher, Henrick. Bradbury
     Press, 1987.
     ISBN: 0-02-733240-3. Wordless - signs.

   The story of two monkeys escaping from a zoo is told in black ink drawings
with yellow highlights. A yellow umbrella, dropped into the enclosure, opens and carries the monkeys away to sea. Through a series of adventures, they return at last to the
jungle and are welcomed by their family.

170. Dubois, Claude K. **He's MY Jumbo!** Illus.: Dubois, Claude K. Viking Kestrel,
     1989. ISBN: 0-670-83029-1. Wordless - no print.

   Brother bear jealously wants his little sister's special toy elephant, Jumbo, and
takes it while she sleeps. Upon waking, he finds Jumbo gone and discovers sister and
Jumbo in the kitchen. His sadness leads sister to share with him. Soft, rounded shapes
in delicate watercolor tones convey the loving feeling of the tale.

171. Dubois, Claude K. **Looking for Ginny.** Illus.: Dubois, Claude K. Viking
     Kestrel, 1989.
     ISBN: 0-670-83030-5. Wordless - no print.

   As two siblings quarrel, their guinea pig escapes from her cage and scampers
about the house, appearing in unusual places as the young bears look for her. Just as
the youngsters give up the search, the pet is discovered sleeping in her cage. Soft
watercolors convey warmth and caring.

172. Duke, Kate. **Guinea Pig ABC, The.** Illus.: Duke, Kate. Dutton, 1983.
      ISBN: 0-525-44058-5; LC: 83-1410. Almost wordless - labels.

Personable guinea pigs act out unusual words such as *vain, greedy, ferocious, itchy,* and *juicy* for each letter of the alphabet. A large letter is incorporated into each watercolor scene. The word appears in large print in a box below each picture.

173. Duke, Kate. **Guinea Pigs Far and Near.** Illus.: Duke, Kate. Dutton, 1984.
      ISBN: 0-525-44112-3; LC: 84-1580. Almost wordless - labels.

Brightly watercolored, comical guinea pigs are shown in outdoor sequences that illustrate concepts such as *apart, together, far, near, around,* and *through.* The word for each concept appears in large print beneath each picture. The two main characters begin by catching a train to the country and are featured throughout.

174. Dupasquier, Philippe. **Great Escape, The.** Illus.: Dupasquier, Philippe.
      Houghton Mifflin, 1988.
      ISBN: 0-395-46806-X; LC: 87-21500. Wordless - signs.

Told in panels and large busy spreads, the complicated escape of a prisoner and the resulting chase through town, in and out of buildings, and on to the circus and the countryside unfolds in humorous details. The police remind one of the Keystone Cops. The prisoner is inventive in his evasive techniques.

175. Dupasquier, Philippe. **I Can't Sleep.** Illus.: Dupasquier, Philippe. Orchard
      Books, 1990.
      ISBN: 0-531-05874-3; 0-531-08474-4 (lib.); LC: 89-26599. Wordless - no print.

A full moon shines above a sleeping town, but one person lies in bed wide awake. He gets up, goes to his drawing table to work, and one by one the other members of the family get up. They have a midnight snack, go outside to see the stars, and finally all fall asleep in the same bed. Humorous full color drawings.

176. Dupasquier, Philippe. **Our House on the Hill.** Illus.: Dupasquier, Philippe.
      Viking Kestrel, 1987.
      ISBN: 0-670-81971-9; LC: 87-40230. Almost wordless - labels.

On each double-page spread, the artist's house and its surrounding countryside are shown in a large, softly colored illustration, while small strips to the right show the family's activities. Seasonal activities show a close family chasing cows out of the yard, acquiring a kitten, and celebrating the father's birthday.

177. Ehlert, Lois. **Color Farm.** Illus.: Ehlert, Lois. J.B. Lippincott, 1990.
      ISBN: 0-397-32446-5; 0-397-32441-3 (lib.). Almost wordless - labels, Format
      - die-cut windows.

Using the same technique as the earlier *Color Zoo,* farm animal faces are created with die-cut pages. Rooster, sheep, cow, and pig, as well as other animals, are made up of squares, circles, rectangles, and other shapes. Vivid colors.

178.   Ehlert, Lois. **Color Zoo.** Illus.: Ehlert, Lois. J.B. Lippincott, 1989.
       ISBN: 0-397-32259-3; 0-397-32260-7 (lib.). Almost wordless - labels, Format
       - die-cut windows.

       Die-cut shapes are superimposed to create the geometric forms of animal faces.
As the page is turned, the shape is seen clearly against a bright solid color, and the
word for the shape appears. Saturated colors and cleverly designed animal faces make
the unusual format work. Final pages review shapes, colors, and animals.

179.   Eindhoven Druk BV. **Airplane, The.** Larousse, 1981.
       ISBN: 0-88332-274-9 (board). Series: Larousse Panorama Books. Wordless -
       no print, Format - board pages; accordion fold.

       A panorama of objects is presented, one per page, on a white background. The
designs look like stencils. Toys such as a wooden train and building blocks, animals
such as a seal and three bees with a hive, and objects such as the airplane of the title
appear in no apparent order.

180.   Eindhoven Druk BV. **Dog, The.** Larousse, 1981.
       ISBN: 0-88332-273-0 (board). Series: Larousse Panorama Books. Wordless -
       no print, Format - board pages; accordion fold.

       The dog in his house on the cover is followed by a series of objects and animals,
each pictured in deep colors in a stenciled graphic design.

181.   Eindhoven Druk BV. **Truck, The.** Larousse, 1981.
       ISBN: 0-88332-271-4 (board). Series: Larousse Panorama Books. Wordless -
       no print, Format - board pages; Format - accordion fold.

       Rich colors show such objects as a dump truck, jumping jack, drum, or mush-
room on each side of the accordion folded board pages.

182.   Eindhoven Druk BV. **Tugboat, The.** Larousse, 1981.
       ISBN: 0-88332-272-2 (board). Series: Larousse Panorama Books. Wordless -
       no print, Format - board pages; Format - accordion fold.

       The tugboat on the cover is typical of the objects and animals pictured on both
sides of an accordion fold board book. On each panel, a single stylized object is centered on a white background.

183.   Elzbieta. **Little Mops and the Butterfly.** Illus.: Elzbieta. Doubleday, 1972.
       ISBN: 0-385-06793-3; 0-385-02670-6 (lib.); LC: 73-10373. Wordless - no
       print.

       Little Mops is a round-eared, long-nosed small animal carrying a bundle on a
stick. After unsuccessfully chasing a butterfly, he finds a shoe, then a pile of shoes,
then the caterpillar to whom the shoes belong. The caterpillar becomes a butterfly, flies
off, and Little Mops chases after. Simple outline drawings.

184. Elzbieta. **Little Mops and the Moon.** Illus.: Elzbieta. Doubleday, 1972.
    ISBN: 0-385-06797-6; 0-385-02684-6 (lib.); LC: 73-10374. Wordless - no print.

    After his dog runs away from his bath, Little Mops notices the reflection of the crescent moon in the water and tries to capture it. He rows across a lake and climbs a mountain but cannot touch the moon. When he returns, the dog is waiting, and both playfully bathe. Simple black line drawings.

185. Elzbieta. **Little Mops at the Seashore.** Illus.: Elzbieta. Doubleday, 1972.
    ISBN: 0-385-06792-5; 0-385-02654-4 (lib.); LC: 73-10375. Wordless - no print.

    While at the beach, Little Mops chases and scares away a nesting bird, then decides to cook the egg. The mother tearfully returns, and Little Mops helps to hatch the egg instead. When the baby and mother fly away, they take their new friend with them. Simple black outline drawings convey many feelings.

186. Emberley, Ed. **Birthday Wish, A.** Illus.: Emberley, Ed. Little Brown, 1977.
    ISBN: 0-316-23409-5; LC: 77-5147. Wordless - signs.

    As a small mouse child blows out the candles on his birthday cheese, he wishes for strawberry ice cream. He blows a party hat out the window, starting a seemingly unrelated chain of events that make his wish come true. The illustrations are small and action-packed, with a variety of comical animals in dull shades.

187. Emberley, Ed. **Ed Emberley's ABC.** Illus.: Emberley, Ed. Little Brown, 1978.
    ISBN: 0-316-23408-7; LC: 77-28099. Almost wordless - labels.

    Four panel vignettes show whimsical animals forming letters of the alphabet. The word for the animal appears on the page which contains that letter. Each humorous mini-story is told with line drawings and color overlays. Numerous objects and animals are incorporated in each alphabetical sequence.

188. Emberley, Ed. **Ed Emberley's Christmas Drawing Book.** Illus.: Emberley, Ed. Little Brown, 1989.
    ISBN: 0-316-23438-9; LC: 89-2684. Almost wordless - labels.

    A simple drawing "alphabet" of shapes and lines is used to make a variety of Christmas symbols and scenes. Instructions are given visually by presenting the piece to be added below a sample of the developing drawing. Red, green, and black marker and pencil create a wintry holiday world in basic shapes.

189. Emberley, Edward R. **Butterfly/The Dandelion, The.** Illus.: Emberley, Edward R. Little Brown, 1982.
    LC: 82-236160 (pbk.). Series: Emberley Flip Books. Wordless - frame, Format - flip book; back-to-back.

    Two natural sequences are seen in this small flip books in detailed color illustrations. The caterpillar crawls up a branch, forms a chrysalis, and emerges as a monarch butterfly. From the opposite side, a dandelion buds, blooms, forms a blowball, and the seeds are carried away by the wind.

190. Emberley, Edward R. **Chicken/The Chameleon, The.** Illus.: Emberley, Edward R. Little Brown, 1982.
LC: 82-236160 (pbk.). Series: Emberley Flip Books.Wordless - frame, Format - flip book; back-to-back.

The scraggly chick that struggles from a brown egg grows into a plump red hen and lays an egg of her own in the first sequence of this small paperback flip book. Turn the book around and a brown chameleon turns green as it moves along a branch and snags an insect with its long sticky tongue.

191. Emberley, Edward R. **Frog/The Hare, The.** Illus.: Emberley, Edward R. Little Brown, 1982.
LC: 82-236160 (pbk.). Series: Emberley Flip Books. Wordless - frame, Format - flip book; back-to-back.

Two back-to-back stories are featured in this small paper flip book utilizing a pointillist style with delicate colors. A tiny egg develops into a tadpole which turns into a frog. Turn over the book and a snowshoe hare is seen changing from white to brown as the seasons and its habitat change.

192. Emberley, Rebecca. **City Sounds.** Illus.: Emberley, Rebecca. Little Brown, 1989.
ISBN: 0-316-23635-7; LC: 88-81191. Almost wordless - sounds.

This city is full of interesting sights and noises. Colorful papercuts illustrate diverse city scenes with the noises printed next to the objects making the sounds. The reader is challenged to make sounds representing morning, sirens, traffic, feet, subways, construction, radios, and night activities.

193. Emberley, Rebecca. **Jungle Sounds.** Illus.: Emberley, Rebecca. Little Brown, 1989.
ISBN: 0-316-23636-5; LC: 88-81192. Almost wordless - sounds.

Dark, grey-blue pages give the impression of the darkness of the jungle while bright papercuts show the many life forms. The jungle sounds are printed next to the animal that makes the sound and include the tiger's "grrrr," the "tromp clomp" of the elephant's feet, and the "snap snap" of the crocodile's jaws.

194. Endersby, Frank. **Baby Sitter, The.** Illus.: Endersby, Frank. Child's Play, 1986.
ISBN: 0-85953-271-2 (board). Series: All in a Day. Wordless - no print, Format - board pages.

A welcome babysitter arrives to a hug from a toddler and holds the child up for a cheerful wave goodbye as parents go out. The sitter entertains with puppets and games, gives a bedtime snack, takes the toddler through bedtime rituals, and tucks the covers around the sleeping child as parents return.

195. Endersby, Frank. **Holidays.** Illus.: Endersby, Frank. Child's Play, 1984.
ISBN: 0-85953-189-9 (board). Series: Choices, Book 2. Wordless - no print, Format - board pages; accordion fold.

Colored pencil drawings show a family visiting a travel agency, selecting brochures, and deciding together on a vacation site. Reservations are phoned in, bags are packed, and they fly off in an airplane for an enjoyable holiday.

196. Endersby, Frank. **Jasmine and the Cat.** Illus.: Endersby, Frank. Child's Play, 1984. ISBN: 0-85953-183-X (board). Series: Tantrums, Book 1. Wordless - no print, Format - board pages; accordion fold.

A little girl chases the marmalade cat under a wheelbarrow on an autumn day, catches it by the tail, and is scolded by her mother. In her tantrum, Jasmine overturns the wheelbarrow and throws herself around in the leaves. A dog comes to lick her face and play ball with her as she recovers from her tantrum.

197. Endersby, Frank. **Jasmine and the Flowers.** Illus.: Endersby, Frank. Child's Play, 1984. ISBN: 0-85953-184-8 (board). Series: Tantrums, Book 2. Wordless - no print, Format - board pages; accordion fold.

Mother is upset when she finds Jasmine uprooting the flowers, and Jasmine is upset after she is scolded. An older child, rollerskating by, stops to help Jasmine make a bouquet and suggests a way to make both mother and Jasmine feel better.

198. Endersby, Frank. **Jasmine's Bath Time.** Illus.: Endersby, Frank. Child's Play, 1984. ISBN: 0-85953-185-6 (board). Series: Tantrums, Book 3. Wordless - no print, Format - board pages; accordion fold.

A young girl prepares to bathe with her rubber duck as her mother fills the tub with water. Colored pencil illustrations show her playing with the bubbles, crying when her hair is washed, and being comforted by her mother. A realistic portrayal of a young child's bathtime routine.

199. Endersby, Frank. **Jasmine's Bedtime.** Illus.: Endersby, Frank. Child's Play, 1984. ISBN: 0-85953-186-4 (board). Series: Tantrums, Book 4. Wordless - no print, Format - board pages; accordion fold.

Jasmine, a little girl, is playing ball with two older children when her mother calls her in. As mother points out the time and takes Jasmine inside, Jasmine has a temper tantrum. Mother helps her into pajamas, and she sleeps peacefully, waking in the morning to wave to her friends outside the window.

200. Endersby, Frank. **Man's Work.** Illus.: Endersby, Frank. Child's Play, 1986. ISBN: 0-85953-270-4 (board). Series: All in a Day. Wordless - no print, Format - board pages.

In colorful pencil sketches a young boy and his father are shown cleaning the house. Together they mop the floor, wax furniture, clean windows, dust, vacuum, and clean the bathtub. While making the bed they take time to play peekaboo.

201. Endersby, Frank. **My Baby Sister.** Illus.: Endersby, Frank. Child's Play, 1985. ISBN: 0-85953-231-3 (board). Series: New Baby, Book 2. Wordless - no print, Format - board pages; accordion fold.

In soft, colored pencil sketches, a little girl welcomes her new sister and interacts with the baby in five outside and five inside scenes. Whether watching mother nurse or father bathe the baby, the older sister is delighted with her role.

202. Endersby, Frank. **Nuisance, The.** Illus.: Endersby, Frank. Child's Play, 1985.
ISBN: 0-85953-233-X (board). Series: New Baby, Book 4. Wordless - no print,
Format - board pages; accordion fold.

A crawling baby wants to be with her big sister and gets into whatever the older
girl is doing. With mother's support, the older child good-naturedly allows the little
one to join in her activities even when a friend comes over. Softly colored pencil
sketches illustrate sisterly caring.

203. Endersby, Frank. **Pet Shop, The.** Illus.: Endersby, Frank. Child's Play, 1984.
ISBN: 0-85953-191-0 (board). Series: Choices, Book 4. Wordless - no print,
Format - board pages; accordion fold.

A family eagerly enters a pet shop and examines different animals before finding a basket of kittens. Each child picks a different kitten, but the choice is finally
made when one kitten crawls into their shopping bag and chooses them.

204. Endersby, Frank. **Plumber, The.** Illus.: Endersby, Frank. Child's Play, 1986.
ISBN: 0-85953-272-0 (board). Series: All in a Day. Wordless - no print, Format
- board pages.

When two early-rising children discover the kitchen floor full of water and
waken their parents, the whole family becomes involved in dealing with the crisis.
Everyone works to remove the water, and a female plumber arrives to deal with the
leaky pipe. Lightly colored pencil drawings show a pleasant response to the situation.

205. Endersby, Frank. **Pocket Money.** Illus.: Endersby, Frank. Child's Play, 1984.
ISBN: 0-85953-190-2 (board). Series: Choices, Book 3. Wordless - no print,
Format - board pages; accordion fold.

Four neighborhood children with money to spend visit a toy store and a candy
store offering many choices. They help each other make selections, and take their purchases to the park to enjoy. Pencil drawings in light color show a friendly multi-ethnic
neighborhood.

206. Endersby, Frank. **Waiting for Baby.** Illus.: Endersby, Frank. Child's Play, 1985.
ISBN: 0-85953-230-5 (board). Series: New Baby book 1. Wordless - no print,
Format - board pages; accordion.

A little girl helps pack a hospital bag and put together a crib for the expected
new baby. Grandmother comes to stay with the child while her parents go to the hospital, then takes her to see the new baby the next day.

207. Endersby, Frank. **Wallpaper.** Illus.: Endersby, Frank. Child's Play, 1984.
ISBN: 0-85953-188-0 (board). Series: Choices, Book 1. Wordless - no print,
Format - board pages; accordion fold.

Father and son visit a wallpaper store to find the perfect paper for the little boy's
room. They purchase rolls, and the boy helps as his father works to paper the room. He
happily rides his rocking horse in front of his new Wild West wallpaper.

208. Endersby, Frank. **Wash Day.** Illus.: Endersby, Frank. Child's Play, 1986.
ISBN: 0-85953-273-9 (board). Series: All in a Day. Wordless - no print, Format - board pages.

The mother of a muddy toddler removes his overalls and pants in front of the washing machine. Together the bare-bottomed boy and his mother go through the steps of washing, drying, and ironing until he is cleanly dressed and ready to go out and play again.

209. Endersby, Frank. **What about Me?** Illus.: Endersby, Frank. Child's Play, 1985.
ISBN: 0-85953-232-1 (board). Series: New Baby, Book 3. Wordless - no print, Format - board pages; accordion fold.

A young girl cheerfully helps her mother feed and clean the baby and then plays with her sibling. When the whole family goes to the park, she becomes jealous of the attention given the baby by strangers. She's happy again when she gets extra attention by playing ball with dad.

210. Epenscheid, Gertrude. **OH Ball, The.** Illus.: Epenscheid, Gertrude. Harper and Row, 1966.
LC: 66-10517. Wordless - exclamations.

A young prince awakens and joyfully skips across the castle yard with his dog. Coming across a ball, he bends to pick it up, but the ball goes flying mischievously around the courtyard. Trying to restrain it, the boy discovers that balls, like birds, are happiest free. Humorous line drawings portray action and emotion.

211. Ernst, Lisa Campbell. **Colorful Adventure of the Bee Who Left Home One Monday, A.** Illus.: Ernst, Lisa Campbell. Lothrop Lee and Shepard, 1986.
ISBN: 0-688-05563-X; 0-688-05564-8 (lib.); LC: 85-23673. Almost wordless - labels.

A honeybee leaves the dark inside of its hive on a color-filled flight to gather pollen from different flowers. Each two-page spread has large boldly colored silk-screened illustrations. One large print color word appears on an item of that color.

212. Ernst, Lisa Campbell. **Up to Ten and Down Again.** Illus.: Ernst, Lisa Campbell. Lothrop Lee and Shepard, 1986.
ISBN: 0-688-04541-3; 0-688-04542-1 (lib.); LC: 84-21852. Almost wordless - labels.

As one Duck enjoys swimming, two cars full of children arrive at the pond for a picnic. Activities and play push the shy duck out of the picture, until ten clouds bring wind and rain; as the numbers count down, all pack up and leave one duck in the rain. Illustrations resemble snapshots in an album.

213. Euvremer, Teryl. **Sun's Up.** Illus.: Euvremer, Teryl. Crown, 1987.
ISBN: 0-517-56432-7; LC: 86-24248. Wordless - no print.

The sun, a congenial gentleman, is sleeping behind the hills when morning comes. He wakes, breakfasts, combs his rays, and goes about his daily work until evening when he prepares for bed and falls back to sleep. As the sun's activity is shown in the sky, people and animals go about their day in a pleasant countryside.

214. Feldman, Judy. **Alphabet in Nature, The.** Illus.: Feldman, Judy. Children's Press, 1991. ISBN: 0-516-05101-6; LC: 90-22315. Series: Wordless Concept Books. Wordless - symbols.

Each letter of the alphabet is accompanied by a large, full-color photograph of a natural object or animal in which the shape of the letter can be found. For example, the tail of a diving humpback whale forms the letter *Y.*

215. Feldman, Judy. **Shapes in Nature.** Illus.: Feldman, Judy. Children's Press, 1991. ISBN: 0-516-05102-4; LC: 90-23091. Series: Wordless Concept Books. Wordless - titles.

Full-color nature photographs are placed on a page with a shape outlined above. The circle of the moon, the spiral of a snail's shell, the oval of a robin's egg are among the more familiar shapes to be found. The square shape of a diatom and the heart shape of a growing sponge are among the less familiar.

216. Felix, Monique. **Further Adventures of the Little Mouse Trapped in a Book, The.** Illus.: Felix, Monique. Green Tiger Press, 1983. ISBN: 0-88138-009-1. Wordless - no print.

A delicately drawn mouse chews through the page of a book to find an ocean on the other side. As the water flows through, he hastens to fashion a folded paper boat from the piece of page he chewed off. Just in time, he jumps aboard his boat and floats off on the watercolor waves.

217. Felix, Monique. **Story of a Little Mouse Trapped in a Book, The.** Illus.: Felix, Monique. Green Tiger Press, 1980. ISBN: 0-914676-52-0. Wordless - no print.

A small mouse trapped inside the white pages of a book anxiously looks for a way to escape. As he gnaws at a page, he glimpses a farm below. He carefully removes a square from the page, folds it into an airplane, climbs aboard, and sails out of the book into the farm. Delicate watercolor mouse and vigorous color in farm.

218. Florian, Douglas. **Airplane Ride.** Illus.: Florian, Douglas. Thomas Y. Crowell, 1984. ISBN: 0-690-04364-3; 0-690-04365-1 (lib.); LC: 83-45048. Wordless - titles.

After checking his map, a pilot starts his biplane by turning the propeller, goes down the runway, and takes off into the sky. As he flies over a city, beach, forest, farms, mountains, and desert, he does tricks and encounters a variety of weather. The comical drawings have short descriptive captions on them.

219. Florian, Douglas. **Beach Day, A.** Illus.: Florian, Douglas. Greenwillow, 1990. ISBN: 0-688-09104-0; 0-688-09105-9 (lib.); LC: 89-1933. Almost wordless - labels.

As the sun rises, a family of four packs and drives to the beach for a day of swimming and playing. After sunset, Fourth of July fireworks fill the sky. Each double-page spread contains a few rhyming words, and there is a guide page to seashells in the back. Illustrations are energetic, dark outlines filled with color.

220. Florian, Douglas. **City, The.** Illus.: Florian, Douglas. Crowell, 1982.
ISBN: 0-690-04166-7; LC: 81-43312. Wordless - signs.

City scenes are shown in double-page illustrations utilizing black lines and colored markers. A woman buys a painting from an outdoor artist and carries it home across the city, walking by traffic, construction, shops, a park, and a museum. She takes a subway and when she arrives home, hangs up a picture of the city.

221. Florian, Douglas. **Nature Walk.** Illus.: Florian, Douglas. Greenwillow, 1989.
ISBN: 0-688-08266-1; 0-688-08269-6 (lib.); LC: 88-39430. Almost wordless - labels.

A walk becomes an exploration of nature as two children and an accompanying adult hike through the woods. A few words at the bottom of each picture provide a rhyming chant of the things they observe: "rotting log" "bullfrog", for example. Small pictures in the back show details that can be found in the colorful pages.

222. Florian, Douglas. **Summer Day, A.** Illus.: Florian, Douglas. Greenwillow, 1988.
ISBN: 0-688-07564-9; 0-688-07565-7 (lib.); LC: 87-8484. Almost wordless - labels.

A city family awakens and prepares for a picnic. They drive to the countryside where they swim, fish, and enjoy the sunset before returning home to their apartment. Watercolor and markers with simple drawings, and a rhyming phrase on each page.

223. Florian, Douglas. **Winter Day, A.** Illus.: Florian, Douglas. Greenwillow, 1987.
ISBN: 0-688-07351-4; 0-688-07352-2 (lib.); LC: 86-33524. Almost wordless - labels.

The weather changes and it begins snowing. A family eats, dresses warmly, and goes outside to ice skate, sled, and make a snowman. Once inside, they warm in front of a fire, eat soup, and look out at the beauty of winter. Simple drawings colored with pencil and markers, with a rhyming phrase on each page.

224. Florian, Douglas. **Year in the Country, A.** Illus.: Florian, Douglas. Greenwillow, 1989.
ISBN: 0-688-08186-X; 0-688-08187-8 (lib.); LC: 88-16026. Almost wordless - labels.

A house and barn in the country are shown from the same view month-by-month throughout the year. The family works and plays outdoors as appropriate for each season. Their chores include the care of farm animals. Two-page illustrations for each month are shown in warm colors with the name of the month in large print.

225. Floyd, Lucy, and Kathryn Lasky. **Agatha's Alphabet: With Her Very Own Dictionary.** Illus.: Leder, Dora. Rand McNally, 1975.
ISBN: 0-528-82145-8; 0-528-80149-X (lib.); LC: 75-13951. Wordless - symbols.

Monochromatic spreads alternate with full-color ones as Agatha has adventures through the alphabet. Each large, two-page picture shows the red-haired Agatha with other children interacting with objects beginning with the letters shown in capital and lowercase forms. A seven-page dictionary gives the meanings of words pictured.

226. Francis, Anna B. **Pleasant Dreams.** Illus.: Francis, Anna B. Holt, Rinehart and Winston, 1983.
     ISBN: 0-03-060574-1; LC: 83-6171. Almost wordless - dialog.

     Within a pale blue border, detailed line drawings in pastel color show a child's bedroom late at night. Slowly the door creaks open, and a green monster quietly enters. Another monster joins the first by the bed—and their green monster child pops up with BOO! A deliberately scary buildup to a "pleasant dreams" ending.

227. Fromm, Lilo. **Muffel and Plums.** Illus.: Fromm, Lilo. Macmillan, 1972.
     LC: 72-85184. Wordless - titles.

     A whiskery lion and his small friend, who resembles a piglet, share a house and many humorous times. Nine short chapters show their activities with black-and-white line drawings in numbered panels.

228. Fuchs, Erich. **Journey to the Moon.** Illus.: Fuchs, Erich. Delacorte, 1969.
     LC: 74-103151. Wordless - signs.

     The historic flight of the Apollo II to the moon is shown from launch to splash-down. Pages washed with dark shades form a background for simple, geometrical pictures illustrating the landing on the moon and the astronauts' activity there.

229. Gardner, Beau. **Guess What?** Illus.: Gardner, Beau. Lothrop Lee and Shepard, 1985.
     ISBN: 0-688-04982-6; 0-688-04983-4 (lib.); LC: 85-242. Almost wordless - labels.

     Bright graphics show a part of an animal's body. When the page is turned, the entire animal is shown in gray with a box around the portion shown on the previous page. The name of the animal is printed in small letters by the silhouette of the entire animal.

230. Gardner, Beau. **Look Again...and Again, and Again, and Again Book, The.**
     Illus.: Gardner, Beau. Lothrop Lee and Shepard, 1984.
     ISBN: 0-688-03805-0; 0-688-03806-9 (lib.); LC: 84-748. Almost wordless - labels.

     Bold graphics in two or three bright colors form a design in which four different pictures can be seen as the book is turned around. The various interpretations of each picture are printed on each side. The number 4 is seen as a road intersection, a chair, and the letter J, for example.

231. Geisert, Arthur. **Oink.** Illus.: Geisert, Arthur. Houghton Mifflin, 1991.
     ISBN: 0-395-55329-6; LC: 90-46123. Almost wordless - sounds.

     As the sun rises, a sow wakes her piglets with an "oink" and they "oink" their way through the day, visiting the pond to splash and play until the sow leads them back for a nap. While she sleeps, the piglets climb a haystack and leap into an apple tree, much to mother's dismay when awakened. Etchings on gray with pink touches.

232.   Generowicz, Witold. **Train, The.** Illus.: Generowicz, Witold. Dial, 1982.
       ISBN: 0-8037-8834-7; LC: 82-73216. Wordless - signs, Format - accordion fold.

Two thieves jump aboard a train and are chased from car to car by two policemen. The cars are filled with humorously drawn details of unlikely cargo. Visual jokes and slapstick situations abound as the chase goes on. Counting and alphabet are included. This accordion fold book unfolds to an eighteen foot frieze.

233.   Gibson, Barbara Leonard. **Pile of Puppies.** Illus.: Gibson, Barbara Leonard.
       National Geographic Society, 1990.
       ISBN: 0-7922-1834-5 (board). Almost wordless - labels, Format - board pages; die-cut pages.

A die cut hole on the right hand page spotlights first one, then additional puppies up to ten, as they build a pyramid standing on each others shoulders. When all ten are in place a cat with a camera arrives to take their picture and brings the pyramid down. Ten breeds of dogs represented are identified on the back cover.

234.   Gibson, Barbara Leonard. **Rainbow Books.** Illus.: Gibson, Barbara Leonard.
       National Geographic Society, 1990.
       ISBN: 0-7922-1831-0 (board, cased). Wordless - no print, Format - board pages.

A set of six small books is packed in a box decorated with blue sky and clouds. Each book is labeled with the name of the cover color and features a short, four-page story with characters in that color. A different natural habitat forms the background for each story, from a garden in *Orange* to underwater in *Blue.*

235.   Gibson, Barbara Leonard. **Who's There?** Illus.: Gibson, Barbara Leonard.
       National Geographic Society, 1990.
       ISBN: 0-7922-1833-7 (board). Wordless - hidden print, Format - pull tab.

A curious lion cub spots ears in foliage, and when a tab is pulled, the animal hiding there is seen. Zebras, antelopes, rhinoceroses, and finally, the lion cub's own family appears. When the pull tab reveals the hidden animal, the word for that animal also appears.

236.   Gilbert, Elliott. **Cat Story, A.** Illus.: Gilbert, Elliott. Holt, Rinehart and Winston, 1963. LC: 63-9088. Wordless - no print.

A striped mother cat with four variously marked and colored kittens introduces them to the world. One finds a mouse, another a bird, and a third a dog—and mother chases each animal away. The curious kittens and their mother are drawn in an unanatomical fashion, with green, blue, and gray washes over ink.

237.   Giovannetti. **Max.** Illus.: Giovannetti. Atheneum, 1954.
       ISBN: 0-689-50082-3; LC: 76-50008. Wordless - no print.

Charmingly comic sketches show a very human hamster as he deals with life in short cartoon sequences. Situations from playing the violin to eating spaghetti all end with a humorous and unexpected twist. The engaging little animal is sketched in black and white with a style reminiscent of Walt Kelly's work.

238. Goodall, John S. **Above and Below Stairs.** Illus.: Goodall, John S. Atheneum, 1983. ISBN: 0-689-50238-9; LC: 82-48528. Almost wordless - labels, Format - half pages; sideways.

Sixteen well-researched and richly detailed watercolor scenes explore the contrasts between the lives of British servants and their masters from the Middle Ages to today. Held sideways, the split pages show changes in locale and activity as different classes work and play. Each time period is labeled.

239. Goodall, John S. **Adventures of Paddy Pork, The.** Illus.: Goodall, John S. Harcourt, Brace, Jovanovich, 1968. ISBN: 0-15-201589-2. Wordless - signs, Format - half pages.

Young Paddy Pork, in a shop with his mother, sees the circus wagon go by. He follows, becomes lost in the woods, and is almost cooked by a sly wolf. Paddy finds the circus, and the bears try to teach him tricks, but his clumsiness causes problems. Tossed out, he finds the way home. Black line drawings with split pages.

240. Goodall, John S. **Ballooning Adventures of Paddy Pork, The.** Illus.: Goodall, John S. Harcourt, Brace, Jovanovich, 1969. ISBN: 0-15-205693-9; LC: 69-18625. Wordless - signs, Format - half pages.

Aloft for adventure, Paddy lands his hot-air balloon on an island to rescue a female pig. On the way home, they run into a storm at sea, a threatening leviathan, and a mountaintop encounter with bears, from whom Paddy is rescued by the lady pig. They return to a British hero's welcome. Detailed black line drawings.

241. Goodall, John S. **Before the War: 1908-1939: An Autobiography in Pictures.** Illus.: Goodall, John S. Atheneum, 1981. ISBN: 0-689-50203-6; LC: 81-65810. Almost wordless - labels.

This very personal collection of affectionate memories was painted for the artist's wife rather than for publication. Each detailed spread is identified with a year or place name, and skillful representations of old photographs are set over the illustrations in a scrapbook fashion.

242. Goodall, John S. **Creepy Castle.** Illus.: Goodall, John S. Atheneum, 1975. ISBN: 0-689-50027-0; LC: 74-16836. Wordless - signs, Format - half pages.

In charming detail a medieval scene is set in watercolor. A mouse and his lady leave their gates and explore a deserted castle, unknowingly followed by a roguish rat. When locked in the cellar, they must battle bats and a monster before escaping across the moat with the help of a frog. On the way home they trick the rat.

243. Goodall, John S. **Edwardian Christmas, An.** Illus.: Goodall, John S. Atheneum, 1978. ISBN: 0-689-50106-4; LC: 77-4580. Wordless - signs.

The Christmas season of a bygone era is depicted in beautifully detailed watercolor paintings, showing the transportation, homes, clothing, shops, customs, and parties of the English upper class of the time realistically. A family visiting a country estate takes part in traditional entertainments, assisted by servants.

244.   Goodall, John S. **Edwardian Entertainments.** Illus.: Goodall, John S.
       Atheneum, 1982.
       ISBN: 0-689-50220-6; LC: 81-67668. Wordless - signs.

Careful research underlies this collection of entertainments of a bygone era. The theatre, the music hall, street performers, and various spots to visit are painted in rich color. Balls and races, the circus and the waxworks, show the enjoyment of the crowds, while specific performers appear on scrapbook-style pages.

245.   Goodall, John S. **Edwardian Holiday, An.** Illus.: Goodall, John S. Atheneum, 1979.
       ISBN: 0-689-501358; LC: 78-64773. Wordless - signs.

The boy and girl of the other "Edwardian" books go with their parents on a seaside vacation and are seen in all the usual beach activities of the day: watching open air shows, riding donkeys, fishing and wading, and going for a day trip across the channel to France. Sunny watercolor with elaborate detail.

246.   Goodall, John S. **Edwardian Season, An.** Illus.: Goodall, John S. Atheneum,
       1980. ISBN: 0-689-50155-2; LC: 79-89497. Wordless - signs.

The activities of the English upper class during the three months of "The Season" in London are shown in sumptuous watercolors. The various fashionable entertainments which occupied their time are documented with an emphasis on the elegant clothing of the era.

247.   Goodall, John S. **Edwardian Summer, An.** Illus.: Goodall, John S. Atheneum,
       1976. ISBN: 0-689-50062-9; LC: 76-336. Wordless - signs.

The security and peace of the brief era of Edward VII (1901-1910) is depicted in scenes of an English village. Each detailed two-page watercolor spread follows a young brother and sister as they wander past shops, visit neighbors, go to school, attend a flower show and a wedding, and participate in the pastimes of the day.

248.   Goodall, John S. **Jacko.** Illus.: Goodall, John S. Harcourt Brace Jovanovich, 1971.
       ISBN: 0-15-239493-1; LC: 72-149750. Wordless - no print, Format - half pages.

Jacko is an organ-grinder's monkey in a seaport town of the past. He escapes and stows away on a sailing ship. When pirates attack the ship, Jacko and his parrot friend take the pirate ship and head for an island where Jacko is reunited with his family and the parrot meets a friend. Detailed paintings with subdued color.

249.   Goodall, John S. **John S. Goodall's Theatre: The Sleeping Beauty.** Illus.:
       Goodall, John S. Atheneum, 1979.
       ISBN: 0-689-50161-7 (pbk.). Wordless - signs, Format - half pages.

A slender greeting card size book presents an elaborate theater. At the entrance, a variety of well-dressed animals pour in past a poster listing a "stupendous cast." Inside, the red curtain conceals half-pages which show scenes from the traditional story of "Sleeping Beauty" as acted by an all-animal cast.

250. Goodall, John S. **Lavinia's Cottage: Imagined by Her Devoted Grandfather.**
Illus.: Goodall, John S. Atheneum, 1982.
ISBN: 0-689-50257-5; LC: 82-71160. Wordless - signs, Format - pop-up.

Two little girls in old-fashioned clothes go visiting with their mother or nanny
to an English country cottage. With their young hostess, they explore the cottage and
yard. Doors open, revealing the interiors of cabinets, stalls, stairways, and sheds. The
details inside and out give a glimpse of a bygone way of life.

251. Goodall, John S. **Midnight Adventures of Kelly, Dot, and Esmeralda, The.**
Illus.: Goodall, John S. Atheneum, 1972.
LC: 75-190555. Wordless - no print, Format - half pages.

At midnight three toys come to life: a doll, a koala bear, and a tiny mouse.
Entering a picture frame, they row along a river and into adventure. Dark-toned watercolors create old-fashioned countryside, with half-pages changing each scene. The
toys are glad to return home after encountering evil cats at a carnival.

252. Goodall, John S. **Naughty Nancy.** Illus.: Goodall, John S. Atheneum, 1975.
ISBN: 0-689-50000-7; LC: 73-94153. Wordless - no print, Format - half pages.

Nancy, a small mouse dressed in pink ruffles, creates mischief as part of a large
wedding party. She rides down the aisle on the bride's train, sits on the wedding cake,
and otherwise causes disruption of the proper proceedings, even hiding in the bride's
trunk and leaving for the honeymoon with the unsuspecting couple.

253. Goodall, John S. **Naughty Nancy Goes to School.** Illus.: Goodall, John S.
Atheneum, 1985.
ISBN: 0-689-50329-6; LC: 85-70230. Wordless - signs, Format - half pages.

Nancy, an active young mouse, is reluctant to go to school and does not stay in
her seat long. Her wild behavior in class and on the playground amuses her fellow students. On a field trip to the beach, her mischievous antics end when she rescues a rafter
and becomes a heroine. A half-page shows action in the bright scenes.

254. Goodall, John S. **Paddy Finds a Job.** Illus.: Goodall, John S. Atheneum, 1981.
ISBN: 0-689-50213-3; LC: 81-43103. Wordless - signs, Format - pop-up.

The action in this brief Paddy Pork story is shown with various devices, including pop-ups, flaps, and half pages. Paddy's job as a waiter comes to a dramatic ending
when he trips over the fur piece of an elegant dog diner. The resultant chaos is reminiscent of slapstick comedy. Watercolor in Goodall's characteristic style.

255. Goodall, John S. **Paddy Goes Traveling.** Illus.: Goodall, John S. Atheneum, 1982.
ISBN: 0-689-50239-7; LC: 82-71159. Wordless - signs, Format - half pages.

Paddy Pork, the pig, goes on holiday by boat and train to Monte Carlo. He
relaxes on the beach until a kite flies loose and he tries to retrieve it—ending up in the
Swiss Alps. A bear family provides him with proper clothing, and he wins a sled race.
Paddy's vacation is shown in watercolor with half-pages to show events.

256. Goodall, John S. **Paddy Pork's Holiday.** Illus.: Goodall, John S. Atheneum, 1976. ISBN: 0-689-50043-2; LC: 75-28278. Wordless - signs, Format - half pages.

Paddy's camping trip is ruined when his tent is blown away and dogs take his clothes. Wearing a scarecrow's tuxedo he is taken for a famous pianist and thrust unwilling on stage. He escapes and joins a gypsy family who takes him home. Animals and countryside are shown in watercolor spreads with half pages.

257. Goodall, John S. **Paddy Pork—Odd Jobs.** Illus.: Goodall, John S. Atheneum, 1983.
ISBN: 0-689-50293-1; LC: 83-70453. Wordless - signs, Format - half pages.

Paddy is willing to try any type of odd job. However, each job he takes ends up a mess as he wallpapers over a doorway, falls from a roof, and smashes the village water pump. All is forgiven when he finds a missing baby. Soft watercolors, with half-pages that change the scene when turned show a village of various animals.

258. Goodall, John S. **Paddy to the Rescue.** Illus.: Goodall, John S. Atheneum, 1985. ISBN: 0-689-50330-X; LC: 85-70231. Wordless - exclamations, Format - half pages.

On a rainy day Paddy, a dapper pig, hears a call for help and finds a thief robbing a female pig. In bright, full-page watercolor illustrations with half pages that forward the action, Paddy, with his trusty umbrella, pursues the thief. The chase goes over rooftops, out to sea, and through town before the thief is caught.

259. Goodall, John S. **Paddy under Water.** Illus.: Goodall, John S. Atheneum, 1984. ISBN: 0-689-50297-4; LC: 83-71901. Wordless - no print, Format - half pages.

When Paddy Pork goes scuba diving, he encounters numerous sea creatures. He gallantly rescues a baby sea monster and meets King Neptune, whose mermaids show Paddy a sunken ship and its treasure chest. Watercolors in sea shades with half pages that show the action.

260. Goodall, John S. **Paddy's Evening Out.** Illus.: Goodall, John S. Atheneum, 1973. ISBN: 0-689-30412-9; LC: 72-98006. Wordless - signs, Format - half pages.

At a vaudeville theater, Paddy Pork creates havoc and steals the show. He falls out of his theater box into a tuba, wrecks a magician's act, lands on an acrobatic team, and ends up center stage for a bow. Richly colored illustrations have half pages that change the scene.

261. Goodall, John S. **Paddy's New Hat.** Illus.: Goodall, John S. Atheneum, 1980. ISBN: 0-689-50172-2; LC: 80-80129. Wordless - signs, Format - half pages.

Proud Paddy Pork's new straw boater is blown into the police office, where he is outfitted as a policeman. During training he has many mishaps, culminating in a traffic jam during a royal visit. He catches a thief, and the royal couple present him with a medal. He struts off wearing the medal and the new hat.

262. Goodall, John S. **Shrewbettina Goes to Work.** Illus.: Goodall, John S. Atheneum, 1981.
ISBN: 0-689-50214-1; LC: 81-43104. Wordless - signs, Format - pop-up.

Pop-ups, flaps, and pull-tabs create the action as Shrewbettina applies for a job as an assistant in a large store and becomes involved in chasing and capturing a sneaky rat purse-snatcher. A population of assorted small animals dressed in old-fashioned clothing are humorously sketched and delicately colored.

263. Goodall, John S. **Shrewbettina's Birthday.** Illus.: Goodall, John S. Harcourt, Brace, Jovanovich, 1970.
ISBN: 0-15-274080-5. Wordless - signs, Format - half pages.

Shrewbettina wakes and leaves her cosily furnished burrow to shop for her party. A thief takes her purse but is apprehended by a gentleman mouse, who assists Shrewbettina in her marketing and sees her home. After her busy preparations, friends attend a lively birthday party. Warm watercolors with half pages.

264. Goodall, John S. **Story of a Castle, The.** Illus.: Goodall, John S. Margaret K. McElderry Books, 1986.
ISBN: 0-689-50405-5; LC: 86-70130. Wordless - signs, Format - half pages.

In the 13th century, Normans carefully chose an easily defended site for their castle. As the centuries pass, interior and exterior views show the changes time brings to the architecture and the life of the castle. Watercolors with half pages to change each scene represent historically accurate details.

265. Goodall, John S. **Story of a Farm, The.** Illus.: Goodall, John S. Margaret K. McElderry Books, 1989.
ISBN: 0-689-50479-9; LC: 88-3398. Wordless - signs, Format - half pages.

Sketchy, impressionist watercolors show the history of a British farm from the early Middle Ages to the countryside of today. The bucolic scenes show farm activities at various seasons and the relationship of the farm to the small town nearby. As each half page alters the scene, aspects of change over time are revealed.

266. Goodall, John S. **Story of a Main Street, The.** Illus.: Goodall, John S. Margaret K. McElderry Books, 1987.
ISBN: 0-689-50436-5; LC: 87-60644. Wordless - signs, Format - half pages.

The evolution of an English main street is shown in historically accurate, colorful watercolors, with half pages that change the scene. Street and market scenes from medieval days to the present mark the changing centuries. Interior scenes of shops, coffee houses, and inns show clothing, celebrations, and customs changing.

267. Goodall, John S. **Story of an English Village, The.** Illus.: Goodall, John S. Atheneum, 1978.
ISBN: 0-689-50125-0; LC: 78-56242. Wordless - signs, Format - half pages.

The same geographic location is shown over a period of 500 years as it changes from a 14th-century village to a congested city of the late 20th century. The market cross, church, and castle serve as markers through the changes. An interaction at a doorway on the right leads to interior scenes in each time period.

268. Goodall, John S. **Story of the Seashore, The.** Illus.: Goodall, John S. Margaret K. McElderry Books, 1990.
ISBN: 0-689-50491-8; LC: 89-8328. Wordless - signs, Format - half pages.

The development of a seaside town from the early 1800s to the present is shown in lively watercolors. The impressionist style conveys a feeling for costumes and customs as the holiday by the sea becomes popular. A more serious note is struck with a rescue during a winter storm and the coastal defenses during war years.

269. Goodall, John S. **Surprise Picnic, The.** Illus.: Goodall, John S. Atheneum, 1977.
ISBN: 0-689-50074-2; LC: 76-28455. Wordless - signs, Format - half pages.

A pleasant picnic turns into a series of surprising events when a mother cat and her two kittens pack a basket, row out to a rocky beach, and lay the picnic out on what appears to be a rock. After the food disappears and the boat floats away, a storm arises and blows them back to land and a friendly tea with neighbors.

270. Goodall, John S. **Victorians Abroad.** Illus.: Goodall, John S. Atheneum, 1980.
ISBN: 0-689-50191-9; LC: 80-67431. Wordless - signs.

English travelers are shown abroad during the period between 1840 and 1890, in detailed watercolors. The "Grand Tour" of Europe and voyages to Egypt, Africa, and India are depicted. Details of dress and manners, landmarks, and modes of transportation are all based on historical research.

271. Goshorn, Elizabeth. **Shoestrings.** Illus.: Goshorn, Elizabeth. Carolrhoda Books, 1975.
ISBN: 0-87614-052-5; LC: 75-14624. Wordless - no print.

A jeans-clad girl whose shoelaces won't tie finds them suddenly transforming into vines, flowers, seaweed, and a variety of other stringy things until finally, amid a terrible tangle, she emerges with neatly tied shoes.

272. Gray, Nigel. **Country Far Away., A.** Illus.: Dupasquier, Philippe. Orchard Books, 1989.
ISBN: 0-531-05792-5; 0-531-08392-6 (lib.); LC: 88-22360. Almost wordless - sentences.

A single, first-person sentence appears on each page, and on each page the illustration shows that sentence's meaning for a boy in Africa and one in a Western country. Helping parents, going to school, playing with friends, welcoming a new sister—the details shown in each picture contrast daily life in each culture.

273. Greeley, Valerie. **Farm Animals.** Illus.: Greeley, Valerie. Bedrick/Blackie Books (dist. Harper and Row), 1981.
ISBN: 0-911745-22-X (board). Series: Valerie Greeley Animal Books.
Wordless - no print, Format - board pages.

Delicate two-page watercolors portray farm animals in their habitat. Baby chicks are near flowers, a duck family is at the pond, a family of pigs is behind a fence, and sheep and cows are in fields.

274. Greeley, Valerie. **Field Animals.** Illus.: Greeley, Valerie. Bedrick/Blackie Books (dist. Harper and Row), 1981.
ISBN: 0-911745-23-8 (board). Series: Valerie Greeley Animal Books. Wordless - no print, Format - board pages.

Naturalistic paintings in harmonious colors show wildlife often seen in meadows and open woods. Field mice, red squirrels, hedgehogs, rabbits, foxes, and voles are shown in appropriate settings, in which foliage and wildflowers can be identified.

275. Greeley, Valerie. **Pets.** Illus.: Greeley, Valerie. Bedrick/Blackie Books (dist. Harper and Row), 1981.
ISBN: 0-911745-21-1 (board). Series: Valerie Greeley Animal Books. Wordless - no print, Format - board pages.

Although the animals shown are kept as pets, in each delicately colored painting they are shown in a natural habitat. Rabbits pose in a flowery meadow, turtle and spaniel are in a spring garden, finch is on a branch with red berries, tropical fish swim among water plants, and the cats peer out of a flower bed.

276. Greeley, Valerie. **Zoo Animals.** Illus.: Greeley, Valerie. Bedrick/Blackie Books (dist. Harper and Row), 1981.
ISBN: 0-911745-24-6 (board). Series: Valerie Greeley Animal Books. Wordless - no print, Format - board pages.

In beautiful, softly colored, detailed illustrations, families of animals found at the zoo are shown in their natural habitat. Polar bears on an ice floe under a starry sky, elephants in tall grass, a lion family, zebras, and flamingoes are featured.

277. Grillis, Carla. **Flowers of the Seasons.** Illus.: Grillis, Carla. Floris Books, 1989.
ISBN: 0-86315-088-8 (board). Wordless - no print, Format - board pages.

Pastel chalk drawings show plants with their flowers or fruits from late winter snowdrops through summer's poppies and back to pine cones in winter again. Insects fly and crawl around the plants, and a spider spins a web above the fallen chestnuts.

278. Grimm, Jacob, and Wilhelm Grimm; retold by John S. Goodall. **Little Red Riding Hood.** Illus.: Goodall, John S. Macmillan, 1988.
ISBN: 0-689-50457-8. Wordless - exclamations, Format - half pages.

In this version of the traditional tale, Red Riding Hood, her mother and grandmother are all expressively painted mice. The wolf is a dapper gentleman wolf, and the woodcutter is a bear whose ax runs red after disposing of the wolf. The half-pages forward the action by changing the scene in each vivid picture.

279. Grimm, Jacob and Wilhelm Grimm; retold by M. Eulalia Valeri; tr. by Leland Northam. **Hansel and Gretel.** Illus.: Rodriguez, Conxita. Silver-Burdett, 1985.
ISBN: 0-382-09072-1; LC: 84-52783. Series: Tell Me a Story. Wordless - no print.

Pictures with a flavor of southern Germany illustrate the familiar story of a brother and sister who are left alone in the woods and find a house made of cake and candy. The story can be followed in the pictures, which show the major scenes, and will help recall the details as the story is retold.

280.   Grimm, Jacob, and Wilhelm Grimm; retold by M. Eulalia Valeri; tr. by Leland Northam. **Sleeping Beauty.** Illus.: Rifa, Fina. Silver-Burdett, 1982. ISBN: 0-382-09068-3; LC: 84-52780. Series: Tell Me a Story. Wordless - no print.

From the sad king and queen who have no child to the triumphant kiss that awakens Thorn Rose, each major part of the story is illustrated in pleasant pastel paintings. The pictures are not meant to retell the entire story, but to give clues to the reader as the story is related.

281.   Gundersheimer, Karen. **ABC Say with Me.** Illus.: Gundersheimer, Karen. Harper and Row, 1984. ISBN: 0-06-022174-7; 0-022175-5 (lib.); LC: 84-47627. Almost wordless - labels.

In a small format, a teeny tiny girl explores common objects such as an apple, a butterfly, and a cup. Clear whimsical drawings in bright colors show her activity, while the verb for each action appears alphabetically below the illustration.

282.   Gundersheimer, Karen. **Shapes to Show.** Illus.: Gundersheimer, Karen. Harper and Row, 1986. ISBN: 0-694-00067-1; 0-06-022197-6 (lib.); LC: 85-45409. Almost wordless - labels.

Two small mice play in various situations in which different shapes are featured. The word for each shape and an outline appear on the left-hand page so that the reader can easily find each respective shape in the lightly colored scene with the mice.

283.   Hamberger, John. **Lazy Dog, The.** Illus.: Hamberger, John. Four Winds Press, 1971. LC: 79-142531. Wordless - no print.

Early morning mishaps begin when a large shaggy dog accidentally knocks a ball off the bedroom window ledge. As his boy sleeps, the dog chases the ball across the countryside, returning the ball and falling asleep just before his owner wakes and tries to get him up. Expressive, realistic drawings with russet and tan tones.

284.   Hamberger, John. **Sleepless Day, A.** Illus.: Hamberger, John. Four Winds Press, 1973. ISBN: 0-590-09996-5. Wordless - no print.

Yawning, a tired owl wings home to his tree—only to begin a day of frustration as a storm destroys his home and he searches for a new one. After encountering problem after problem, he finally finds a heart-shaped hole and a mate. The sketchy drawings with yellow and blue washes give the owl expression.

285.   Hartelius, Margaret A. **Birthday Trombone, The.** Illus.: Hartelius, Margaret A. Doubleday, 1977. ISBN: 0-385-12292-6; 0-385-12293-4 (lib.); LC: 76-14533. Wordless - no print.

Little monkey receives a trombone as a birthday present and proceeds to disturb other jungle animals with her noise, causing numerous mishaps. The other animals chase her but are trapped by a python. She uses her trombone to charm the snake, who becomes her appreciative audience. Line drawings with pale oranges and browns.

286. Hartelius, Margaret A. **Chicken's Child, The.** Illus.: Hartelius, Margaret A. Doubleday, 1975.
ISBN: 0-385-07363-1; 0-385-07370-4 (lib.); LC: 74-18884. Wordless - no print.

A hen finds an egg by a stream and happily hatches it—producing an alligator child. As the alligator grows, he eats everything in sight, including the tractor, and is ordered to leave by the farmer. When the alligator rescues his adopted mother from a fox, he is welcomed back. Cartoon-like drawings with gray/green shades.

287. Hauptmann, Tatjana. **Day in the Life of Petronella Pig, A.** Illus.: Hauptmann, Tatjana. Sunflower Books, 1978.
ISBN: 0-8317-2150-2; LC: 79-3067. Wordless - signs, Format - die-cut pages.

A large mother pig with a small rambunctious pig child plans a dinner party, makes preparations, and after company leaves, takes a bath and goes to bed. Each die-cut page reveals part of the next, creating a three dimensional effect.

288. Heller, Linda. **Lily at the Table.** Illus.: Heller, Linda. Macmillan, 1979.
ISBN: 0-02-743530-X; LC: 79-11415. Wordless - signs.

Lily's plate looks huge, full of food she doesn't want to eat. As she begins to play with it, she is scolded, then embarks on a fantasy of raiding the refrigerator and making a playground of food: swimming in a glass of milk, sliding down the celery, and so on. In the final black-and-white drawing, she has eaten one bite.

289. Henstra, Friso. **Mighty Mizzling Mouse.** Illus.: Henstra, Friso. J.B. Lippincott, 1983.
ISBN: 0-397-32003-5; 0-397-32004-3 (lib.); LC: 82-48459. Wordless - signs.

In a whimsical, cinematic style, a mouse wearing sneakers meets a cat, and the chase is on. Swiss-cheese holes in the ground provide an escape for mouse as a dog takes up the chase, which then goes on to involve an entire absurd circus of characters. Undaunted, mouse is once again taunting the collapsed cat at the end.

290. Henstra, Friso. **Mighty Mizzling Mouse and the Red Cabbage House.** Illus.: Henstra, Friso. Little Brown, 1984.
ISBN: 0-316-35778-2; 0-316-35779-0 (pbk.); LC: 83-19915. Wordless - no print.

The hero leans casually on his axe while his lady selects a giant red cabbage, which he proceeds to chop down and turn into a neatly constructed house. While he offers flowers to his sweetheart, a spotted rabbit emerges from the garden and demolishes the house and his hopes of happiness. Undaunted, he begins again.

291. Heuninck, Ronald. **New Day, A.** Illus.: Heuninck, Ronald. Floris Books, 1987.
ISBN: 0-86315-052-7 (board). Wordless - no print, Format - board pages.

Warm, comfortable illustrations take one preschool girl and her doll through a day with her family. European details in the home add atmosphere, and the use of light in the paintings gives the day a special feeling even though the activities are everyday experiences.

292. Heuninck, Ronald. **Rain or Shine.** Illus.: Heuninck, Ronald. Floris Books, 1989. ISBN: 0-86315-089-6 (board). Wordless - no print, Format - board pages.

From early spring to winter, two children enjoy a variety of outdoor activities. The older sister and younger brother feed a pair of ducks in the rain, and watch the ducklings swim past a flowery late spring field. They play at the beach, in autumn leaves, and in the snow. Full color.

293. Hill, Eric. **At Home.** Illus.: Hill, Eric. Random House, 1982. ISBN: 0-394-85638-4 (board); LC: 82-60627. Series: Baby Bear Books. Wordless - no print, Format - board pages.

A little bear sits in an overstuffed chair watching television, and on each successive page the objects in the house are shown: chair, rug, table, telephone, window, mirror, lamp, and clock, ending with a towel and small bear sitting on a potty.

294. Hill, Eric. **My Pets.** Illus.: Hill, Eric. Random House, 1982. ISBN: 0-394-85637-6 (board); LC: 82-60625. Series: Baby Bear Books. Wordless - no print, Format - board pages.

A small bear and many pet animals are shown in bright colors and flat forms. Pets pictured are rabbit, guinea pig, fish, various birds, turtle, mouse, kitten, and puppy.

295. Hill, Eric. **Park, The.** Illus.: Hill, Eric. Random House, 1982. ISBN: 0-394-85636-8 (board); LC: 82-60615. Series: Baby Bear Books. Wordless - no print, Format - board pages.

Baby bear feeds pigeons, plays with a ball, swings, and enjoys the park. Flowers, a butterfly, a pond with boat and duck, and a very spotted dog are part of the park environment pictured in very simple colorful forms.

296. Hill, Eric. **Up There.** Illus.: Hill, Eric. Random House, 1982. ISBN: 0-394-85635-X (board); LC: 82-60626. Series: Baby Bear Books. Wordless - no print, Format - board pages.

Simplified forms and clear solid color are used to show the sights a small bear sees "up there." Birds, aircraft, kites, clouds, balloons, and the tops of buildings and trees are among the scenes pictured.

297. Hoban, Russell, and Sylvie Selig. **Crocodile and Pierrot: A See-the-Story Book.** Illus.: Selig, Sylvie. Scribners , 1975. ISBN: 0-684-14901-X; LC: 77-73930. Almost wordless - labels.

Pierrot the clown takes a doll from beside sleeping Crocodile. Crocodile follows Pierrot and the doll through a sequence of colorful and mysterious scenes. They go from park to city to country to beach, ending in the park again, sharing the doll. In each scene, various objects extraneous to the story are labeled.

298. Hoban, Tana. **1,2,3.** Illus.: Hoban, Tana. Greenwillow, 1985.
ISBN: 0-688-02579-X (board); LC: 84-10306. Almost wordless - labels, Format - board pages.

Close-up, color photographs of objects young children are likely to recognize illustrate number concepts from one (candle on a cake) to ten (baby toes). The word and numeral appear on each page, with a corresponding number of red dots.

299. Hoban, Tana. **26 Letters and 99 Cents.** Illus.: Hoban, Tana. Greenwillow, 1987.
ISBN: 0-688-06361-6; 0-688-06362-4 (lib.); LC: 86-11993. Wordless - symbols, Format - back to back.

Each capital and lowercase letter is a picture of a glossy three-dimensional toy letter set. Each is accompanied by a close-up photograph of a representative object. When the book is turned around, numbers and coins are shown. The value of the coins add up to the number shown: a dime and a penny for 11, for example.

300. Hoban, Tana. **A, B, See!** Illus.: Hoban, Tana. Greenwillow, 1982.
ISBN: 0-688-00832-1; 0-688-00833-X (lib.); LC: 81-6890. Wordless - symbols.

Each letter of the alphabet is represented with common objects which begin with that letter. The objects appear as silhouetted photogram images, white on black. The entire alphabet appears in gray on the bottom of each page with the letter for the page enlarged in black.

301. Hoban, Tana. **All about Where.** Illus.: Hoban, Tana. Greenwillow, 1991.
ISBN: 0-688-09697-2; 0-688-09698-0 (lib.); LC: 90-30849. Wordless - frame.

Overlapping cut pages of full color photographs are framed by lists of descriptive words on the outside, full size front and back pages. In each photograph, scenes can be used to demonstrate and discuss concepts such as against, over, on, behind.

302. Hoban, Tana. **Big Ones, Little Ones.** Illus.: Hoban, Tana. Greenwillow, 1976.
ISBN: 0-688-80040-8; 0-688-84040-X (lib.); LC: 75-34440. Wordless - no print.

Adult and baby animals from farm and zoo are shown in close-up black-and-white photographs. Two pictures of each type of animal show different actions. The young of each of the animals chosen resembles its parent, leaving the size as the major point of comparison. A page in back identifies all the animals.

303. Hoban, Tana. **Circles, Triangles and Squares.** Illus.: Hoban, Tana. Macmillan, 1974.
ISBN: 0-02-744830-4; LC: 72-93305. Wordless - signs.

Geometric shapes can be found in each black-and-white photograph of common objects and scenes. Photographs are placed so that each shape is reflected from one to the next: the triangular structure of a bridge on one page and that of a swing set on the next, for example.

304. Hoban, Tana. **Count and See.** Illus.: Hoban, Tana. Macmillan, 1972. ISBN: 0-02-744800-2; LC: 72-175597. Almost wordless - labels.

Full page black-and-white photographs show common scenes with objects arranged from one fire hydrant to fifteen cookies. The numbers 20, 30, 40, 50 and 100 are also pictured. Each number is reinforced as a word, numeral, and model set.

305. Hoban, Tana. **Dig, Drill, Dump, Fill.** Illus.: Hoban, Tana. Greenwillow, 1975. ISBN: 0-688-80016-5; 0-688-84016-7 (lib.); LC: 75-11987. Wordless - no print.

Large, black and white photographs show such machines as loaders, cranes, and backhoes in brief sequences showing function and use. Small photographs in the back accompany brief descriptions of each piece of equipment.

306. Hoban, Tana. **Dots, Spots, Speckles, and Stripes.** Illus.: Hoban, Tana. Greenwillow, 1987.
ISBN: 0-688-06862-6; 0-688-06863-4 (lib.); LC: 86-22919. Wordless - no print.

Color photographs of animals, clothing, natural and found objects show a richness of pattern in dots, spots, speckles, and stripes. Freckles on a girl's face are echoed in a speckled lobster; the patterns of light and shadow give texture as they overlay pattern in clothing.

307. Hoban, Tana. **Exactly the Opposite.** Illus.: Hoban, Tana. Greenwillow, 1990. ISBN: 0-688-08861-9; 0-688-08862-7 (lib.); LC: 89-27227. Wordless - signs.

Pairs of color photographs illustrate antonyms in an open-ended way. More than one concept can be read into each pair. For example, the sheep is seen front and back, but it is also lying down and standing up.

308. Hoban, Tana. **I read Signs.** Illus.: Hoban, Tana. Greenwillow, 1983. ISBN: 0-688-02317-7; 0-688-02318-5 (lib.); LC: 83-1482. Almost wordless - labels.

Beginning with "Come in we're open" and ending with "Sorry we're closed," close-up color photographs show common street and store signs. Careful placement makes this more than just a collection of signs; for example, the X of "Railroad Crossing" reflects the x in "Taxi" opposite.

309. Hoban, Tana. **I Read Symbols.** Illus.: Hoban, Tana. Greenwillow, 1983. ISBN: 0-688-02331-2; 0-688-02332-0 (lib.); LC: 83-1481. Wordless - symbols.

Full-color, close-up photographs show signs in which symbols rather than words are read. Beginning with a crossing light showing a man walking, and ending with the red upraised hand which means "Do not walk," signs are carefully chosen to provide comparison and contrast as the pages are turned.

310. Hoban, Tana. **I Walk and Read.** Illus.: Hoban, Tana. Greenwillow, 1984. ISBN: 0-688-02575-7; 0-688-02576-5 (lib.); LC: 83-14215. Almost wordless - labels.

The opening photograph invites the reader "in" and subsequent photographs show the rich variety of environmental print which can be seen along city streets, until the final page and the "End" sign.

311. Hoban, Tana. **Is It Larger? Is It Smaller?** Illus.: Hoban, Tana. Greenwillow, 1985. ISBN: 0-688-04027-6; 0-688-04028-4 (lib.); LC: 84-13719. Wordless - no print.

Within each close-up color photograph are grouped animals or common objects in several sizes for comparison. Each pair of photographs contains other concepts for comparison or contrast, besides larger and smaller.

312. Hoban, Tana. **Is It Red? Is It Yellow? Is It Blue? An Adventure in Color.** Illus.: Hoban, Tana. Mulberry Books, 1978. ISBN: 0-688-07034-5; LC: 78-2549. Wordless - signs.

Color photographs emphasize clear primary colors found in everyday scenes and objects. Under each photograph, solid color dots give clues for colors to find in that picture. Photographs are paired to compare and contrast for shapes, uses of objects, and quantities.

313. Hoban, Tana. **Is It Rough? Is It Smooth? Is It Shiny?** Illus.: Hoban, Tana. Greenwillow, 1984. ISBN: 0-688-03823-9; 0-688-03824-7 (lib.); LC: 83-25460. Wordless - signs.

Color photographs show a variety of textures from the stickiness of taffy apples and roasted marshmallows to the roughness of an elephant's wrinkled skin. In addition to the contrasts in surfaces, photographs are paired for comparison of their content.

314. Hoban, Tana. **Look Again!** Illus.: Hoban, Tana. Macmillan, 1971. ISBN: 0-02-744050-8; LC: 72-127469. Wordless - no print, Format - die-cut windows.

A small, square, die-cut window visually isolates a portion of a close-up, black-and-white photograph. As the page is turned the entire picture is revealed, and on the next page the animal or object is seen as part of a larger picture. The isolated portions are chosen to emphasize texture and pattern.

315. Hoban, Tana. **Look! Look! Look!** Illus.: Hoban, Tana. Greenwillow, 1988. ISBN: 0-688-07239-9; 0-688-07240-2 (lib.); LC: 87-25655. Wordless - no print, Format - die-cut windows.

Small, square, die-cut windows in a black page frame a part of a larger color photograph on the following page. The isolated bit of the picture emphasizes pattern or texture. The concept of part to whole is furthered on the following page, which shows each object in a larger context— the dog with its master, for example.

316. Hoban, Tana. **Of Colors and Things.** Illus.: Hoban, Tana. Greenwillow, 1989. ISBN: 0-688-07534-7; 0-688-07535-5 (lib.); LC: 88-11101. Wordless - no print.

Each page is divided into four boxes by a colored line. Each box frames a clear, close-up photograph of a common object, three of which are primarily the dominant color of the frame. The fourth object includes the primary color along with other colors. For example, with three yellow things are buttons in four colors.

317. Hoban, Tana. **Over, Under & Through: And Other Spatial Concepts.** Illus.: Hoban, Tana. Macmillan, 1973.
ISBN: 0-02-744820-7; LC: 72-81055. Almost wordless - labels.

Sets of positional words *(over, under, through)* begin each section, with the following black and white photographs illustrating spatial concepts. Scenes from a city perspective use traffic and trash cans as well as children and animals in demonstrating relationships.

318. Hoban, Tana. **Push-Pull Empty-Full.** Illus.: Hoban, Tana. Macmillan, 1972.
ISBN: 0-02-744810-X; LC: 72-90410. Almost wordless - labels.

Large black-and-white photographs are paired to illustrate opposites such as up-down, thick-thin, and in-out. From children pushing and pulling a wagon, to a city skyline showing day and night, each concept is clearly shown. The word for each concept appears in large print on the page.

319. Hoban, Tana. **Red, Blue, Yellow Shoe.** Illus.: Hoban, Tana. Greenwillow, 1986.
ISBN: 0-688-06563-5 (board); LC: 86-3095. Almost wordless - labels, Format - board pages.

Close-up, color photographs of simple, common objects and animals illustrate colors. The word for each color is printed in that color with a color dot beside it. The objects are shown in unusual clarity with a plain background.

320. Hoban, Tana. **Round and Round and Round.** Illus.: Hoban, Tana. Greenwillow, 1983.
ISBN: 0-688-01813-0; 0-688-01814-9 (lib.); LC: 82-11984. Wordless - no print.

Wheels and drains, balls and bubbles, balloons and hoops, and many other round things both natural and man-made, are captured in full-color photographs.

321. Hoban, Tana. **Shadows and Reflections.** Illus.: Hoban, Tana. Greenwillow, 1990.
ISBN: 0-688-07089-2; 0-688-07090-6 (lib.); LC: 89-30461. Wordless - signs.

Windows reflecting the sky, a puddle reflecting a street sweeper, patterns created by the shadows of flowers—this collection of color photographs is carefully arranged to do more than simply show images. Each pair reflects a color or pattern or idea that enhances response to the individual picture.

322. Hoban, Tana. **Shapes and Things.** Illus.: Hoban, Tana. Macmillan, 1970.
LC: 70-102965. Wordless - no print.

On each black page are found the white shapes of items that might be recognized from home, school or office. Relationships can be seen between items grouped on each page.

323. Hoban, Tana. **Shapes, Shapes, Shapes.** Illus.: Hoban, Tana. Greenwillow, 1986.
ISBN: 0-688-05832-9; 0-688-05833-7 (lib.); LC: 85-17569. Wordless - signs.

On the first page, shapes are given to look for in the following photographs. Unusual ones such as arcs, parallelograms and trapezoids are included with the more commonly pictured circle, triangle and square. The clear color photographs show scenes and common objects, revealing a plethora of shapes in everyday life.

324. Hoban, Tana. **Take Another Look.** Illus.: Hoban, Tana. Greenwillow, 1981.
     ISBN: 0-688-80298-2; 0-688-84298-4 (lib.); LC: 80-21342. Wordless - no
     print, Format - die-cut windows.

     A die-cut circle on a white page reveals part of a textured object, and when
turned, a close-up view of the object is seen. On the reverse page is a view of the object
in context. Black-and-white photographs with a grainy, dark look.

325. Hoban, Tana. **What Is It?** Illus.: Hoban, Tana. Greenwillow, 1985.
     ISBN: 0-688-02577-3 (board); LC: 84-13483. Wordless - no print, Format -
     board pages.

     Common objects that small children will recognize are shown in simple, close-
up, color photographs. Each pair of objects has a clear relationship; sock is paired with
shoe and spoon with bowl of soup, for example.

326. Hodgson, Jim. **Pointers 1.** Illus.: Hodgson, Jim. The Wright Group, 1987.
     ISBN: 1-55624-450-9 (pbk.); 1-55624-250-6 (set). Series: Pointers. Wordless -
     no print.

     A series of unrelated pictures are presented for a question and answer session
with a child, in each of the books in this series. In this first book, there are cats, fish,
and other objects to count, hidden things in one picture and "wrong" things in another,
as well as pictures featuring attributes such as size and color.

327. Hodgson, Jim. **Pointers 2.** Illus.: Hodgson, Jim. The Wright Group, 1987.
     ISBN: 1-55624-451-7 (pbk.); 1-55624-250-6 (set). Series: Pointers. Wordless - signs.

     In this series of pictures, there are jungle animals to count, a fishing contest to
discuss, hidden pictures in a jungle scene, a show featuring three trained cats, and a
page with misplaced objects to discover.

328. Hodgson, Jim. **Pointers 3.** Illus.: Hodgson, Jim. The Wright Group, 1987.
     ISBN: 1-55624-452-5 (pbk.); 1-55624-250-6 (set). Series: Pointers. Wordless - signs.

     Dark line outline and bright colors, sometimes with a black background, are
used in these humorous cartoons. Sizes, colors, hidden objects, and misplaced things
can be found in these unrelated pictures.

329. Hodgson, Jim. **Pointers 4.** Illus.: Hodgson, Jim. The Wright Group, 1987.
     ISBN: 1-55624-453-3 (pbk.); 1-55624-250-6 (set). Series: Pointers. Wordless - signs.

     From a tree full of owls and socks to the candy store where a bald shopkeeper feeds ice
cream to a cat, each of these colorful pictures offers attributes for discussion: shapes, sizes,
colors, numbers of objects, things misplaced or hidden, and various humorous activities.

330. Hodgson, Jim. **Pointers 5.** Illus.: Hodgson, Jim. The Wright Group, 1987.
     ISBN: 1-55624-454-1 (pbk.); 1-55624-250-6 (set). Series: Pointers. Wordless - signs.

     Six bright pictures offer conversational opportunities. Hidden objects can be
found in a picture of an elephant getting a bath. A jungle scene and an underwater
scene contain animals to compare and count. Details of color, number, and size can be
seen in a chicken yard and a formal garden.

331. Hodgson, Jim. **Pointers 6.** Illus.: Hodgson, Jim. The Wright Group, 1987.
ISBN: 1-55624-455-X (pbk.); 1-55624-250-6 (set). Series: Pointers. Wordless - signs.

A bright cartoon style gives a humorous cast to these colorful pictures which offer a variety of counting, sorting, and comparing opportunities. Birds in an aviary, animals in a pet store, people at a flower show, and toys in a factory can be used for discussing various concepts. A Halloween scene contains objects out of place.

332. Hoest, Bill. **Taste of Carrot, A.** Illus.: Hoest, Bill. Atheneum, 1967.
LC: 67-28287. Wordless - no print.

A simply drawn rabbit is happy eating greens until a large orange carrot appears. Once he has caught and eaten the carrot, he is dissatisfied with the greenery he once enjoyed. When another carrot appears, he chases it into the distance, until both are merely dots on the page. Charcoal outline, minimal color.

333. Hogrogian, Nonny. **Apples.** Illus.: Hogrogian, Nonny. Macmillan, 1972.
LC: 71-146626. Wordless - signs.

Children and animals drop their apple cores in a field near a small country village. Soon an orchard grows with ripe red apples. A peddler picks them and fills his pushcart full of the apples, then leaves. Cheerful, two-page, colored pencil illustrations.

334. Hom, Jesper, and Sven Gronlykke. **For Kids Only.** Illus.: Hom, Jesper and Sven Gronlykke. Delacorte, 1975.
ISBN: 0-440-02690-3 (pbk.); 0-440-02738-1; LC: 76-28183. Wordless - no print.

Black-and-white photographs are carefully arranged to create small sequences, some with a joke, some with a tiny plot, some with concepts such as numbers, size, and shape, others which show relationships and associations. European and African images are predominate.

335. Honda, Nobuo. **Kitten Dreams.** Illus.: Honda, Nobuo. Heian, 1985.
ISBN: 0-89346-253-5 (pbk.). Series: Cat Album. Wordless - no print.

Full-color photographs show appealing kittens yawning, stretching, and sleeping in various poses. Occasionally a pair of pictures shows the same kittens awake and asleep. The sleeping cats and kittens have been caught in unusual positions as well as comfortably curled up.

336. Hoquet, Susan Ramsay. **Solomon Grundy.** Illus.: Hoquet, Susan Ramsay. Dutton, 1986.
ISBN: 0-525-44239-1; LC: 85-20453. Almost wordless - sentences.

In vibrant watercolors this Americanized version of a nursery rhyme spans Solomon's life from his birth to English immigrants to his death as an old man, successfully retired from business. Illustrations were carefully researched and show 19th century New England life. Lines from the rhyme occur every few pages.

337. Howe, Caroline Walton. **Counting Penguins.** Illus.: Howe, Caroline Walton. Harper and Row, 1983.
ISBN: 0-06022618-8; 0-06022619-6 (lib.); LC: 82-48860. Wordless - symbols.

In an Antarctic setting, penguins gather to play and sport on the ice and in the snow. The numbers from zero to nine appear as the penguins ice skate, fish, and ski.

338. Hubbard, Woodleigh. **C is for Curious: An ABC of Feelings.** Illus.: Hubbard, Woodleigh. Chronicle Books, 1990.
ISBN: 0-87701-679-8. Almost wordless - labels.

Bold colors and stylized graphics show imaginative animals demonstrating a feeling for each letter of the alphabet. One word for each picture tells the emotion being shown.

339. Hughes, Shirley. **Up and Up.** Illus.: Hughes, Shirley. Lothrop Lee and Shepard, 1979. ISBN: 0-688-06261-X; LC: 85-24166. Wordless - no print.

A young girl watches birds and tries to fly. She makes wings and blows up balloons with no success. When a large mysterious egg is delivered, she eats part of it and starts flying. Adults try to catch her as she flies around the town and taunts students at school. Black line drawings on multi-paneled tan background.

340. Hurlimann, Ruth. **Hare, The.** Illus.: Hurlimann, Ruth. The Wright Group, 1989.
ISBN: 1-55624-000-7 (set, pbk.). Series: First Nature Watch. Wordless - no print.

The European hare is shown in several settings: feeding, fleeing a fox, sleeping, and with its young. Mating is indicated by one hare giving another a four-leaf clover. A restricted range of color is used in the semi-naturalistic prints.

341. Hurlimann, Ruth. **Squirrel, The.** Illus.: Hurlimann, Ruth. The Wright Group, 1986.
ISBN: 1-55624-000-7 (set, pbk.). Series: First Nature Watch. Wordless - no print.

A red squirrel is seen in her pine needle nest, feeding and gathering stores for winter. A snowy picture shows her search for her hidden stores. In spring, she eyes a mate, then nurses and raises young.

342. Hutchins, Pat. **1 Hunter.** Illus.: Hutchins, Pat. Greenwillow, 1982.
ISBN: 0-688-00614-0; 0-688-00615-9 (lib.); LC: 81-6352. Almost wordless - labels.

As one hunter walks through the jungle with a gun, he is unaware that he is being observed by a numerical progression of animals: two elephants, three giraffes, four ostriches, etc. Animals are hidden in the picture on the right and revealed as the page turns. When all the animals confront the hunter, he runs for his life!

343. Hutchins, Pat. **Changes, Changes.** Illus.: Hutchins, Pat. Macmillan, 1971.
ISBN: 0-02-745870-9; LC: 70-123133. Wordless - no print.

Two wooden folk dolls, living in a wooden block world, build a house. When it begins to burn, they start a series of transformations in which they make various things out of the blocks to solve each new problem. Simple geometric forms in stiffly composed pictures convey the woodenness of characters and setting.

344. Hyman, Trina Schart. **Enchanted Forest, The.** Illus.: Hyman, Trina Schart.
      G.P. Putnam's Sons, 1984.
      ISBN: 0-399-21057-1. Series: Magic Windows. Wordless - no print, Format -
      accordion fold; die-cut pages.

Peering through a round hole in the front cover, the entire book is seen at once
as the die-cut pages are pulled out to create a three-dimensional scene. The fairytale
castle in the distance is seen through a forest vista filled with magical creatures and
characters from make believe stories.

345. Hyman, Trina Schart. **Little Alphabet, A.** Illus.: Hyman, Trina Schart. Little
      Brown, 1980.
      ISBN: 0-316-38705-3; LC: 80-16520. Wordless - symbols.

In this small alphabet book, each capital letter is centered on a page. The letter
is framed and illuminated in black line drawings which include a child and objects
beginning with that letter. For example, the letter *O* shows a child sitting comfortably
in an oak, holding an orange, an arm on an owl, with an ocean behind.

346. Ichikawa, Satomi. **Let's Play.** Illus.: Ichikawa, Satomi. Philomel Books, 1981.
      ISBN: 0-399-20824-0; 0-399-61186-X (lib.); LC: 81-1730. Almost wordless - labels.

A baby and her two older siblings play with a variety of common toys in each
large, softly colored, watercolor picture. The word for a common toy, such as ball,
doll, crayon, or train, appears with a picture of that toy on one page, while the children
and their friends interact with the toy on the opposite page.

347. Imershein, Betsy. **Finding Red/Finding Yellow.** Illus.: Imershein, Betsy. Har-
      court, Brace, Jovanovich, 1989.
      ISBN: 0-15-200453-X; LC: 88-35808. Wordless - signs, Format - back to back.

Color photographs find red in everyday scenes in the first half of this book, following the title page "Finding Red." From the other side, the title "Finding Yellow"
leads to photographs which concentrate on yellow. The organization and placement of
pictures is carefully done to give almost a poetic flow to each sequence.

348. Isadora, Rachel. **City Seen from A to Z.** Illus.: Isadora, Rachel. Greenwillow, 1983.
      ISBN: 0-688-01802-5; 0-688-01803-3 (lib.); LC: 82-11966. Almost wordless -
      labels.

Realistic, finely-drawn, pencil sketches illustrate the diverse scenes and people
found in large United States cities. One word per page directs the eye to a detail of the
picture, for example, the pigeon flying down by the feet of an oriental child walking
with a grandfather.

349. Ivory, Lesley Anne, and Ron van der Meer. **Kittens.** Illus.: Ivory, Lesley Anne.
      Abbeville Press, 1988.
      ISBN: 0-89659-878-0. Series: Abbeville Pop-up Book. Wordless - hidden
      print, Format - pop-up.

With varying degrees of success, five paper-engineered scenes pop up to ani-
mate the playfulness of kittens. The kittens entangle themselves in string, stalk a mosa-
ic bird, nurse, play around a bed, and jump after butterflies. A poem by Eleanor
Farjeon is hidden under a flap in the daisy field spread.

350. James, Robin. **Baby Horses.** Illus.: James, Robin. Price Stern Sloan, 1986. ISBN: 0-8431-1243-3 (board). Series: Baby Animals. Wordless - no print, Format - board pages.

Each page shows a foal in a different pose. Soft watercolors emphasize the large eyes and long legs of the baby horses as they gently explore butterflies, flowers, and birds; as they nibble grass, take a nap, or lift a hind leg to scratch an ear.

351. James, Robin. **Kittens.** Illus.: James, Robin. Price Stern Sloan, 1986. ISBN: 0-8431-1412-6 (board). Series: Baby Animals. Wordless - no print, Format - board pages.

Kittens from a variety of cat breeds tentatively explore their surroundings, both indoors and out. Simple, uncluttered, watercolor pictures capture their fuzzy charm.

352. James, Robin. **Puppies.** Illus.: James, Robin. Price Stern Sloan, 1986. ISBN: 0-8431-1417-7 (board). Series: Baby Animals. Wordless - no print, Format - board pages.

Eight different breeds of dogs are shown as puppies, posed lying or sitting around the house or yard. Watercolor paintings emphasize the pudgy softness of these unusually quiet puppies.

353. John, Sarah. **In My Pocket.** Illus.: John, Sarah. The Wright Group, 1987. ISBN: 1-55624-494-0 (pbk.); 1-55624-257-3 (set). Series: More and More. Wordless - signs.

Dressed in overalls, a girl empties her bank onto her bed and begins to collect things in her pocket. As she and her mother go on a bus to shop, various pocket-sized things are shown that she might pick up. Only in the shop, when she empties her pocket to buy a book, are the contents discovered.

354. Jucker, Sita. **Mouse, The.** Illus.: Jucker, Sita. The Wright Group, 1986. ISBN: 1-55624-000-7 (set, pbk.). Series: First Nature Watch. Wordless - no print.

A mouse in a shop is caught in a trap and released outside. She joins a field mouse underground, where they nibble seeds while a red cat with human eyes waits by their hole. Babies appear and the mother mouse leads them back to a house.

355. Jucker, Sita. **Starling, The.** Illus.: Jucker, Sita. The Wright Group, 1986. ISBN: 1-55624-000-7 (set, pbk.). Series: First Nature Watch. Wordless - no print.

A pair of European starlings move into a nesting box, raise young, then join a large flock migrating to Egypt. In the spring, they return to the same nesting box. Color is used effectively in the concise illustrations, from the purples and greens of the North to the hot oranges and yellows of the South.

356. Junek, Jaroslav. **Cherry Tree, The.** Illus.: Junek, Jaroslav. The Wright Group, 1986. ISBN: 1-55624-000-7 (set, pbk.). Series: First Nature Watch. Wordless - no print.

A sequence of growth from a cherry picked and dropped by a sparrow to a new tree producing fruit is shown in bright naive illustration.

357. Junek, Jaroslav. **Snail, The.** Illus.: Junek, Jaroslav. The Wright Group, 1986. ISBN: 1-55624-000-7 (set, pbk.). Series: First Nature Watch. Wordless - no print.

In a folk art style, the artist shows various aspects of a snail's life. It retreats into the shell for safety, hibernates in winter, and finds a mate under a starry sky. Eggs hatch into tiny miniature snails, who follow their parent across leaves and flowers.

358. Keats, Ezra Jack. **Clementina's Cactus.** Illus.: Keats, Ezra Jack. Viking, 1982. ISBN: 0-670-22517-7; LC: 82-2630. Wordless - no print.

A small girl in sunbonnet is fascinated by a desert cactus and has to be carried away from watching it when a storm arrives. The next morning she rushes to see the cactus and discovers that it has bloomed. Rich color conveys the majesty and change-ability of desert life.

359. Keats, Ezra Jack. **Kitten for a Day.** Illus.: Keats, Ezra Jack. Four Winds Press, 1982. ISBN: 0-590-07813-5; LC: 81-69518. Almost wordless - dialog.

In large watercolor pictures, a friendly puppy joins four kittens in a bowl. He's not sure, but thinks he might be a kitten too, so goes along with their day although he doesn't sound or act like the others. When his mother comes to take him home, he suggests they all be puppies the next time they play.

360. Keats, Ezra Jack. **Pssst! Doggie.** Illus.: Keats, Ezra Jack. Franklin Watts, 1973. ISBN: 0-531-02598-5; LC: 72-8642. Wordless - frame.

A graceful black cat invites a shaggy dog to dance, and their imaginations take over. In costumes, they dance a sailor's hornpipe, an ethnic mask dance, soft shoe, ballet, a minuet, and others before they stop. The elegant cat and the somewhat stout dog perform to imaginary music that can almost be heard.

361. Keats, Ezra Jack. **Skates!** Illus.: Keats, Ezra Jack. Four Winds Press, 1973. ISBN: 0-590-07812-7; LC: 80-70119. Almost wordless - dialog.

Two city dogs find roller skates in a trash can and try to skate. As they trip and stumble they frighten kittens, injure themselves, and are ready to quit when they hear a tiny cry for help from one kitten clinging to a breaking tree branch. Successful in their rescue, they confidently skate off. Bright colors, some dialog.

362. Kent, Jack. **Egg Book, The.** Illus.: Kent, Jack. Macmillan, 1975. ISBN: 0-02-750200-7; LC: 74-13662. Wordless - no print.

In bright, cartoon-like illustrations, a hen goes in search of an egg to hatch. She hatches a turtle, an alligator, and an ostrich who all find their own mothers. Brooding sadly by the barn, she discovers that she has laid an egg and finally has a chick of her own.

363. Kent, Jack. **Scribble Monster, The.** Illus.: Kent, Jack. Harcourt, Brace, Jovanovich, 1981. ISBN: 0-15-271031-0; LC: 81-47533. Wordless - signs.

Under a "No Graffiti" sign two children begin drawing figures in red. They create a monster which comes to life and chases them. They cannot escape the persistent monster, and the other scribble creatures can't harm it. Finally the boy realizes that he can erase the drawings. Black line cartoons with scribbles in red.

364. Kent, Lorna. **Shopping List, The.** Illus.: Kent, Lorna. The Wright Group, 1987. ISBN: 1-55624-490-8 (pbk.); 1-55624-257-3 (set). Series: More and More. Wordless - signs.

A round-faced, jolly family—dad, baby, and big sister—go to the store for groceries. While dad chats with a friend, sister gets friends to help her fill the cart with "Crispy Pops" cereal.

365. Keussen, Gudrun. **This Is How We Live in the Country.** Illus.: Keussen, Gudrun. ARS, 1983. ISBN: 0-86724-025-3 (board). Wordless - signs, Format - board pages.

Beginning with a cutaway view of the interior of a large farmhouse, each busy spread shows a great variety of rural activities in a Bavarian-style countryside. Horse-drawn farm equipment, the water powered mill, and the manual labor shown give the pictures an old-fashioned air, although a car appears in the Sunday scene.

366. Keussen, Gudrun. **This Is How We Live in the Town.** Illus.: Keussen, Gudrun. ARS, 1983. ISBN: 0-86724-026-1 (board). Wordless - signs, Format - board pages.

Scenes depicting life in a southern German small town show the daily activities and occupations of both children and adults. Busy, detailed double-page spreads include a cutaway interior of a home as well as exterior scenes of schools, shops, the train station, and a carnival.

367. Khalsa, Dayal Kaur. **Bon Voyage, Baabee.** Illus.: Khalsa, Dayal Kaur. Tundra Books, 1984. ISBN: 0-88776-146-1 (board). Series: Baabee Books. Wordless - no print, Format - board pages.

Heavy black line, plain forms, and solid color characterize the art in this simple look at transportation. Baabee sits in a car seat; rides in a car and an airplane; sees trains, aircraft, and traffic; and plays with transportation toys.

368. Khalsa, Dayal Kaur. **Happy Birthday, Baabee.** Illus.: Khalsa, Dayal Kaur. Tundra Books, 1984. ISBN: 0-88776-144-5 (board). Series: Baabee Books. Wordless - no print, Format - board pages.

Bright, contrasting colors and simple outlines show the elements of a birthday for a one-year-old.

369. Khalsa, Dayal Kaur. **Merry Christmas, Baabee.** Illus.: Khalsa, Dayal Kaur. Tundra Books, 1984. ISBN: 0-88776-145-3 (board). Series: Baabee Books. Wordless - no print, Format - board pages.

Dark lines shape commonly seen Christmas symbols and scenes, with solid colors filling in each shape.

370. Kightley, Rosalinda. **Opposites.** Illus.: Kightley, Rosalinda. Little Brown, 1986.
      ISBN: 0-316-49931-5; LC: 86-80449. Almost wordless - labels.

Twelve contrasting pairs of words are illustrated in large bright pages with simple form and design. The frog leaps "up" and dives "down"; the mouse on top of a pile of blocks is "high" and on one block is "low". Each page is labeled with the single word concept to be understood from the picture.

371. Kilbourne, Frances. **Overnight Adventure.** Illus.: Powell, Ann. The Women's Press, 1977.
      ISBN: 0-88961-054-1; 0-88961-047-9 (pbk.). Wordless - exclamations.

Two girls set up a yellow tent in the back yard and prepare to spend the night. In their imagination, sounds and events of the night transform their surroundings to a jungle, an ocean, and other adventurous landscapes. When the mother comes out to check on them, they say "We're fine" and fall asleep.

372. Kitamura, Satoshi. **What's Inside? The Alphabet Book.** Illus.: Kitamura, Satoshi. Farrar, Straus, & Giroux, 1985.
      LC: 84-73117. Almost wordless - labels.

Brightly colored, two-page spreads develop an alphabet guessing game. What's inside two boxes marked *a* and *b* ? The following page shows the boxes open and filled with apples and bananas. Letters, clues, and the answers to the previous puzzle are all cleverly worked into nicely composed, nonsensical pictures.

373. Kitchen, Bert. **Animal Alphabet.** Illus.: Kitchen, Bert. Dial, 1984.
      ISBN: 0-8037-0117-9; LC: 83-23929. Wordless - symbols.

Unusual animals, delicately and realistically drawn, are used to illustrate each letter of the alphabet. Each animal interacts with a large capital letter, from armadillo under the cross bar of *A* to zebra standing on the lower slash of *Z*. A page in back identifies the animals.

374. Kitchen, Bert. **Animal Numbers.** Illus.: Kitchen, Bert. Dial, 1987.
      ISBN: 0-8037-0459-3; LC: 87-5365. Wordless - symbols.

Large calligraphic numerals are centered on each page. Arranged around and on them are animals and their young. From one joey in a kangaroo's pouch to the ten Irish setter puppies, the numbers are in sequence. Larger numbers — 15, 25, 50, 75, and 100 — are represented by animals such as the snake and frog.

375. Knobler, Susan. **Tadpole and the Frog, The.** Illus.: Knobler, Susan. Harvey House, 1975.
      ISBN: 0-8178-5302-2; LC: 74-83422. Wordless - no print.

The life cycle of a pond frog is shown from mating, egg laying, development, tadpole growth, and hibernation to the next season's maturity. Two-page illustrations are close ups with large simple pictures in blue, yellow, green, black, and white.

376. Kojima, Naomi. **Flying Grandmother, The.** Illus.: Kojima, Naomi. Thomas Y. Crowell, 1981.
ISBN: 0-690-04142-X; 0-690-04143-8 (lib.); LC: 81-43030. Wordless - signs.

A girl dreaming of wings suddenly discovers that she has them and begins to learn to fly. She finds that her grandmother also has wings, and together they fly, befriend a flock of birds, foil a robbery, and capture thieves. Each tiny line drawing bears a number to follow the sequence through 132.

377. Koontz, Robin Michal. **Dinosaur Dream.** Illus.: Koontz, Robin Michal. G.P. Putnam's Sons, 1988.
ISBN: 0-399-21669-3; LC: 88-18171. Wordless - no print.

Bright, two-page watercolors tell the story of a young boy whose love for dinosaurs shows in his room filled with their images. As he sleeps, a dinosaur comes in his window and takes him to a prehistoric landscape where he meets over 30 different dinosaurs. A guide page tells names and pronunciations for the dinosaurs.

378. Koren, Edward. **Behind the Wheel.** Illus.: Koren, Edward. Holt, Rinehart and Winston, 1972.
ISBN: 0-03-080233-4 (lib.); 0-03-080232-6 (pbk.); LC: 79-150034. Almost wordless - labels.

A variety of machinery is shown in sketchy line drawings with colored washes. The left page pictures a machine and a labeled view of the controls. The right page has a view from the driver's seat. Friendly snaggle-toothed, monster-like animals are shown in each scene.

379. Krahn, Fernando. **Amanda and the Mysterious Carpet.** Illus.: Krahn, Fernando. Clarion Books, 1985.
ISBN: 0-89919-258-0; LC: 84-14201. Wordless - signs.

Amanda is reading Arabian fairytales when a large package is delivered—unrolled, it is an oriental carpet. The carpet takes flight and leads Amanda on a havoc-creating chase until she finds a way to ride it. Her surprised mother rescues her from the roof. Cross-hatching gives dimension to the black line drawings.

380. Krahn, Fernando. **April Fools.** Illus.: Krahn, Fernando. Dutton, 1974.
ISBN: 0-525-25825-6; LC: 73-16279. Wordless - no print.

As an April Fool's Day prank, two boys make the neck and head of an imaginary monster. They prop it in windows, on roofs, and tow it across the lake to create panic and excite interest in their small town. When they become lost in the woods, they hoist the form above the trees and are rescued. Pen and ink, gold tones.

381. Krahn, Fernando. **Arthur's Adventure in the Abandoned House.** Illus.: Krahn, Fernando. Dutton, 1981.
ISBN: 0-525-25945-7; LC: 80-22249. Wordless - signs.

While exploring an abandoned house, Arthur discovers a man tied to a chair and a group of gun-carrying criminals. Locked in the attic of the house, Arthur's resourcefulness brings the police. The house is bulldozed and the criminals caught. Detailed pencil drawings.

382. Krahn, Fernando. **Biggest Christmas Tree on Earth, The.** Illus.: Krahn, Fernando. Little Brown, 1978.
ISBN: 0-316-50309-6; LC: 78-9824. Wordless - no print.

When a girl follows her bouncing ball into the hollow of a giant pine, she discovers a fantastic tree trimming operation. As an honorary squirrel, she assists other squirrels, birds, and spiders in decorating the tree. She returns home and brings everyone from her village out to enjoy the sight. Red wash highlights sketches.

383. Krahn, Fernando. **Catch That Cat!** Illus.: Krahn, Fernando. Dutton, 1978.
ISBN: 0-525-27555-X; LC: 77-20820. Wordless - signs.

A boy gazes out at the harbor from a balcony on which wash is drying and sees a black cat. He begins to chase the cat through the streets and into a shipping crate on the dock. They are loaded on a cargo ship, where they must rescue each other before they are returned home. Shaded, rounded sketches catch the action.

384. Krahn, Fernando. **Creepy Thing, The.** Illus.: Krahn, Fernando. Clarion Books, 1982. ISBN: 0-89919-099-5; LC: 81-18148. Wordless - signs.

A boy out fishing catches a green thing that looks like weeds, but when he plays his harmonica, the thing dances. It escapes from his room at night and causes commotion in the town, until he shows the frightened people how it likes music. The humorous sketches use only a touch of green for effect.

385. Krahn, Fernando. **Flying Saucer Full of Spaghetti, A.** Illus.: Krahn, Fernando. Dutton, 1970.
ISBN: 0-525-29969-6; 0-525-29970-X (lib.); LC: 75-116883. Wordless - signs.

Seven tiny gnomes look inside a shack and see a girl sitting at a bare table. The gnomes go to a mansion and take a plate of spaghetti from the wealthy girl there. Flying the plate across town attracts a lot of attention, causing accidents. The poor child eats hungrily when they land the plate in front of her.

386. Krahn, Fernando. **Funny Friend from Heaven, A.** Illus.: Krahn, Fernando. J.B. Lippincott, 1977.
ISBN: 0-397-31760-3; LC: 77-3549. Wordless - signs.

An unusual angel wearing a bowler hat and carrying a suitcase befriends a sad and ragged hobo. Dressed as clowns, the two have numerous escapades before the angel leaves his charge at a circus. Line drawings with red and green washes.

387. Krahn, Fernando. **Great Ape: Being the True Version of the Famous Saga..., The.** Illus.: Krahn, Fernando. Viking, 1978.
ISBN: 0-670-34840-6; LC: 78-9053. Wordless - no print.

In this version of the "true story" of King Kong, a little girl goes with her father to the island where natives point them to the habitat of the Great Ape. The ape saves the girl as she falls from a cliff, is lured by a giant banana to the ship, and is glad to get a photograph of her in New York as a keepsake.

388. Krahn, Fernando. **Here Comes Alex Pumpernickel!** Illus.: Krahn, Fernando. Little Brown, 1981.
ISBN: 0-316-50311-8; LC: 80-25531. Wordless - titles.

A small clock with each story title shows a day passing as Alex gets into one predicament after another. In each short vignette, Alex's sincere but inept attempts to be helpful lead to problems. Detailed pencil sketches convey the character of an engaging, active, and independent child. Continued in *Sleep Tight, Alex Pumpernickel.*

389. Krahn, Fernando. **How Santa Claus Had a Long and Difficult Journey Delivering His Presents.** Illus.: Krahn, Fernando. Delacorte, 1970.
ISBN: 0-440-03725-5 (pbk.). Wordless - no print.

A bell-ringing bear wakes Santa and helps him dress and load toys for the annual journey. The reindeer break away upon takeoff, and Santa is left to figure out how to become airborne. The best efforts of the toys fail, until passing angels fly the sleigh to the waiting deer on a rooftop. Black and gray with red Santa suit.

390. Krahn, Fernando. **Journeys of Sebastian.** Illus.: Krahn, Fernando. Delacorte, 1968.
LC: 68-26131. Wordless - titles.

Three stories show Sebastian's fantastic adventures as his imagination allows him to shrink, find a world inside a mirror, and pull a strange animal from a hole in the wall. Wonderful sketches with yellow, blue, or red highlights show the humorous detail of each unusual journey.

391. Krahn, Fernando. **Little Love Story.** Illus.: Krahn, Fernando. J.B. Lippincott, 1976. ISBN: 0-397-31700-X; LC: 76-12427. Wordless - no print.

A little boy and his mother bring a present as they come to visit a little girl and her mother. The present is a large red balloon, too big to blow up. Finally a man with a tire pump inflates the red, heart-shaped balloon, just in time to catch the girl falling from the balcony. Gray sketches, with a red balloon.

392. Krahn, Fernando. **Mystery of the Giant Footprints, The.** Illus.: Krahn, Fernando. Dutton, 1977.
ISBN: 0-525-35595-2; LC: 76-50033. Wordless - no print.

Giant footprints appear in the deep snow around a log cabin. The two children sneak out to follow the footprints, and their alarmed parents rouse all the neighbors to track them to a cave in the mountains. Unharmed, the children cradle the ridiculous single-footed, furry animals. Expressive pencil sketches.

393. Krahn, Fernando. **Robot-bot-bot.** Illus.: Krahn, Fernando. Dutton, 1979.
ISBN: 0-525-38545-2; LC: 78-21959. Wordless - no print.

Dad brings home a robot that does household chores. When the daughter rewires it, the robot wildly shoves the easy chair into the dinner table and flings itself through the window and into the trash can. Dad rescues and restores the robot. Humorous pen and ink drawings with gray wash enliven the expressionless robot.

394.   Krahn, Fernando. **Sebastian and the Mushroom.** Illus.: Krahn, Fernando.
       Delacorte, 1976.
       ISBN: 0-440-07694-3; 0-440-07695-1 (lib.); LC: 75-32918. Wordless - no print.

       An ordinary field with a boy picking mushrooms is transformed as the boy finds
himself under a giant mushroom, climbs a ladder into the mushroom observatory, and
is taken on a ride through space on a shooting star. When he slides down the moon, he
ends up in bed asleep. Scratchy ink sketches show this fantasy trip.

395.   Krahn, Fernando. **Secret in the Dungeon, The.** Illus.: Krahn, Fernando. Clari-
       on Books, 1983.
       ISBN: 0-89919-148-7; LC: 82-9595. Wordless - signs.

       While touring a medieval castle with her parents, a young girl slips away from
the group. Her curiosity leads her to a sleeping dragon in the dungeon and a dangerous
escape from its lair. The adults are amused but unbelieving as she recounts her tale.
Black line drawings with a pink wash and red highlights.

396.   Krahn, Fernando. **Self-Made Snowman, The.** Illus.: Krahn, Fernando. J.B.
       Lippincott, 1974.
       ISBN: 0-397-31472-8; LC: 74-551. Wordless - signs.

       High in the mountains a goat knocks a ball of snow off a ledge. As the snow
rolls downhill it gains size, shape, and the features of a giant snowman. Momentum
propels it onto a wagon that careens into town where it becomes the center of a celebration. Detailed charcoal drawings are bound by a thick green border.

397.   Krahn, Fernando. **Sleep Tight, Alex Pumpernickel.** Illus.: Krahn, Fernando.
       Little Brown, 1982.
       ISBN: 0-316-50312-6; LC: 81-20745. Wordless - titles.

       A series of short vignettes show the nighttime activities of a small boy. As the
clock shows the night progressing, Alex has a late night snack, then bad dreams from
too much cake. He disturbs his parents' sleep, then joins the howling dogs disturbing
his sleep. He finally sleeps as the sun rises. Dark gray sketches.

398.   Krahn, Fernando. **Who's Seen the Scissors?** Illus.: Krahn, Fernando. Dutton,
       1975.
       ISBN: 0-525-42710-4; LC: 74-26857. Wordless - no print.

       The tailor's red scissors mysteriously fly away from his table. They cause mis-
chief as they snip their way around the town. When they return to the tailor, he decides
to keep them in a cage. Soft pencil drawings with the scissors and their path in red.

399.   Kraus, Robert. **Poor Mister Splinterfitz!** Illus.: Byrd, Robert. Springfellow
       Books, 1973.
       ISBN: 0-525-61512-1; LC: 72-94868. Wordless - frame.

       Black line drawings show dapper Mr. Splinterfitz who "gets a splinter whenever
he sits." He searches for a seat, but each time he sits, he leaps back up holding his bottom. Exotic spots such as deserts and ice floes don't help. Home again, he gets the idea
to stand on his head instead of sitting.

400. Lazard, Armhel Mona. **Tree, The.** Illus.: Lazard, Armhel Mona. The Wright
      Group, 1986.
      ISBN: 1-55624-067-8 (set, pbk.). Series: First Nature Watch. Wordless - no print.

      A big round tree shows various arboreal characteristics. In one picture it is sur-
      rounded by brightly colored tropical birds, in another it has big purple flowers. It bears
      apples, attracts butterflies, turns red, loses its leaves, and stands bare in the winter.

401. Lemke, Horst. **Places and Faces.** Illus.: Lemke, Horst. Scroll Press, 1971.
      ISBN: 0-87592-041-1; LC: 78-160446. Wordless - signs.

      Each brightly colored, two-page illustration shows a different scene with many
      activities and details. Scenes include a zoo, a train depot, outdoor market, airport, city
      street, harbor, carnival, beach, the inside of a department store, a playground, and a gas
      station. European origin can be seen in the pictures.

402. Lewis, Stephen. **Zoo City.** Illus.: Lewis, Stephen. Greenwillow, 1976.
      ISBN: 0-688-86000-1; LC: 75-35659. Almost wordless - labels, Format - mix-
      and-match.

      A challenging mix-and-match puzzle puts zoo animals on the bottom right half
      of each split page and an inanimate object on the top. Close-up, black-and-white pho-
      tographs make an uncanny relationship between the shapes of the animals and the
      objects. The word for each pair is graphically presented on the left side of each page.

403. Lindblom, Steven. **Let's Give Kitty a Bath.** Illus.: Kelley, True. Addison-Wes-
      ley, 1982.
      ISBN: 0-201-10712-0; LC: 81-19068. Almost wordless - dialog.

      A boy and girl are enthusiastic about bathing their orange tabby cat just as the
      neighbor washes a poodle. When they are ready, the alarmed cat has hidden and
      doesn't respond to their cries of "here kitty, kitty." Finally, lured by smelly fish, the cat
      is caught, but it is the dirty children who end up in the tub.

404. Lionni, Leo. **Colors to Talk About.** Illus.: Lionni, Leo. Pantheon, 1985.
      ISBN: 0-394-87003-4 (board); LC: 84-10092. Series: Pictures to Talk About.
      Wordless - no print, Format - board pages.

      Three simply shaped mice are shown in various colors: yellow as they look at a
      yellow chick, green as they pluck clover, and so on. They are joined by two other mice
      as they dance in all the colors on the last page.

405. Lionni, Leo. **Who?** Illus.: Lionni, Leo. Pantheon, 1983.
      ISBN: 394-86030-6 (board); LC: 83-4081. Series: Pictures to Talk About.
      Wordless - no print, Format - board pages.

      In simple, torn-paper figures, a small mouse meets various animals. Both solid
      and marbled paper are used to create the squirrel, turtle, rabbit, hen, owl, and porcu-
      pine pictured.

406. Lisker, Sonia O. **Attic Witch, The.** Illus.: Lisker, Sonia O. Four Winds Press, 1973. LC: 73-76453. Wordless - signs.

After being scolded for playing in the rain, a little girl is sent to her room with her cat. They go to the attic, find a magical broom, and enter the land of friendly witches through a mirror. As magical adventures begin, the drawings gain color. When the girl returns to her room, they become black and white.

407. Lisker, Sonia O. **Lost.** Illus.: Lisker, Sonia O. Harcourt Brace Jovanovich, 1975. ISBN: 0-15-249363-8; LC: 74-22281. Wordless - signs.

A family with six children goes to the zoo. One boy has a puppet monkey that he waves at the animals. When he separates from his family, the zoo seems frightening until he befriends a smaller Asian child who is lost. When all are reunited, the families picnic together. Colors in oranges, pinks, and yellows.

408. Lisowski, Gabriel. **Invitation, The.** Illus.: Lisowski, Gabriel. Holt, Rinehart and Winston, 1980. ISBN: 0-03-051016-3; LC: 79-21908. Wordless - signs.

Pig chases butterflies; his friends rabbit and bear get an invitation, which they hide from him. As the other animals plan to go somewhere without him, pig feels left out. He tries to get even, then discovers that they were going to a surprise party for him. Large pictures in brown and olive tones show a happy ending.

409. Lovis-Miler, Katerina. **Hen, The.** Illus.: Lovis-Miler, Katerina. The Wright Group, 1986. ISBN: 1-55624-067-8 (set, pbk.). Series: First Nature Watch. Wordless - no print.

Various views of a chicken yard and hen house show a rooster and several hens as they peck around and roost. One hen broods a clutch of eggs, and yellow chicks hatch and follow her around the yard. The rooster sweet-talking a blushing hen under a starry sky indicates mating.

410. MacDonald, Suse. **Alphabatics.** Illus.: MacDonald, Suse. Bradbury Press, 1986. ISBN: 0-02-761520-0; LC: 85-31429. Almost wordless - labels.

Bold, full-color graphics show the transformation of each letter into an object or animal. *L* in four small yellow boxes becomes the nose of a lion, the magnificent lion and the word *lion* follow on the opposite page.

411. MacDonald, Suse, and Bill Oakes. **Numblers.** Illus.: MacDonald, Suse and Bill Oakes. Dial, 1988. ISBN: 0-8037-0547-6; 0-8037-0548-4 (lib.); LC: 87-32736. Almost wordless - labels.

Each number from one to ten transforms into a portion of a large colorful picture. Each pictured object is composed of the appropriate number of transformed numerals; for example, nine is a squirrel made from nine nines.

412. MacGregor, Marilyn. **Baby Takes a Trip.** Illus.: MacGregor, Marilyn. Four Winds Press, 1985.
ISBN: 0-02-761940-0; LC: 85-4340. Wordless - no print.

After mother puts baby down for a nap, he/she crawls out with a favorite toy and wakes the dog. Together they create a mess in the living room and kitchen before finding mother napping and deciding to sleep with her. Simple, expressive use of black line and wash show this intrepid baby explorer.

413. MacGregor, Marilyn. **On Top.** Illus.: MacGregor, Marilyn. Wm. Morrow and Co., 1988.
ISBN: 0-688-07490-1; 0-688-07491-X (lib.); LC: 87-12481. Wordless - no print.

An independent sheep leaves the flock to climb to the top of a mountain to view the world from above. He returns to the flock and looks until he finds another to join him in looking up the mountain. Simple black line drawings effectively tell this fable.

414. Mari, Iela. **Eat and Be Eaten.** Illus.: Mari, Iela. Barron's, 1980.
ISBN: 0-8120-5396-6. Wordless - no print.

Bold graphics show a chain of predators, each in the act of attacking the one ahead. From the black panther's tail on the title page to the same fierce cat at the end, each predator can be guessed by its tail or foot before the page is turned. The mosquito hunts a man hunting a tiger as part of the chain.

415. Mari, Iela. **L'albero.** Illus.: Mari, Iela. Emme Edizioni, 1975.
Wordless - no print.

A single oak tree and the squirrel that burrows beside it are shown during four seasons. Bold graphic design portrays the tree and its environment from one winter to the next. Natural changes can be observed as grass and weeds grow, flower, and seed; birds nest, raise babies, and migrate; and the tree alters seasonally.

416. Mari, Iela. **Magic Balloon, The.** Illus.: Mari, Iela. S. G. Phillips, 1967.
LC: 69-11041. Wordless - no print.

A boy blows a red bubble, which floats away as a balloon, and gently changes shape to an apple, a butterfly, a flower, and finally an umbrella as the boy walks away in the rain. Simple black outline indicates boy and background, with the balloon and its transformations in solid red shapes.

417. Mari, Iela, and Enzo Mari. **Apple and the Moth, The.** Illus.: Mari, Iela and Enzo Mari. Pantheon, 1969.
LC: 70-101180. Wordless - no print.

In simple, bold graphics, a worm grows as it eats through an apple and then leaves to spin a cocoon. When spring comes, a moth emerges and flies to apple blossoms to lay eggs and start the cycle again.

418. Mari, Iela, and Enzo Mari. **Chicken and the Egg, The.** Illus.: Mari, Iela, and Enzo Mari. Pantheon, 1969.
LC: 74-101181. Wordless - no print.

A realistically drawn hen prepares a nest, lays an egg, and broods it until her chick hatches. The development of the chick is shown from yolk to hatching. The chick learns to eat and sleeps by the hen. Simple illustrations in black, red, and yellow keep sizes in perspective.

419. Mariotti, Mario. **Hanimals.** Illus.: Marchiori, Roberto. Green Tiger Press, 1980.
ISBN: 0-914676-90-3; 0-516-09405-X (lib.); LC: 84-144738. Wordless - no print.

Human hands are painted and arranged imaginatively to represent various animals. Close-up, color photographs and well-contrasted single color backgrounds bring the "hanimals" to life.

420. Mariotti, Mario. **Hanimations.** Illus.: Marchiori, Roberto. Kane/Miller Book Publishers, 1989.
ISBN: 0-916291-22-7; LC: 89-2441. Wordless - no print.

Brightly painted and cleverly posed, the hands of the author and his daughter become lively animals. Some are wonderfully simple, such as the tiger and leopard, while others are elaborate and complicated. X-rays of hands become dinosaur displays, viewed by two tiny finger people.

421. Mariotti, Mario. **Humages.** Illus.: Marchiori, Roberto. Green Tiger Press, 1984.
ISBN: 0-88138-058-X; 0-516-09407-6 (lib.); LC: 85-070420. Wordless - no print.

Illusions and double images are created by body paint on the author's face, hands, and feet. Close-up color photographs are carefully arranged to further the sometimes unsettling effect of the images.

422. Mariotti, Mario. **Humands.** Illus.: Marchiori, Roberto. Green Tiger Press, 1983.
ISBN: 0-88138-019-9; LC: 84-144838. Wordless - no print.

Striking color photographs of hands, painted and posed, represent people, animals, or objects. Harlequin and Pierrot, a full orchestra with singers, an astronaut, a skier, and a rude profile are a few of the imaginative roles taken on by the hands of the author.

423. Maris, Ron. **My Book.** Illus.: Maris, Ron. Julia MacRae Books/Franklin Watts, 1983.
ISBN: 0-531-04610-9; LC: 82-62565. Almost wordless - labels, Format - half pages.

A cat with a strong sense of ownership goes from the outside gate, "My gate," through the house to "My bedroom" where he falls asleep on his owner's bed. Realistic watercolors show details of the yard and house. Half pages show each gate or door opening for the cat.

424. Marol, Jean-Claude. **Vagabul and His Shadow.** Illus.: Marol, Jean-Claude. Creative Education, 1983.
ISBN: 0-87191-889-7; LC: 82-72677. Series: Vagabul. Wordless - no print.

The small white man shape known as Vagabul angrily discovers that his shadow has a life of its own. As he tries to control the shadow, it becomes part of him, and Vagabul slowly darkens while his shadow becomes white. They return to themselves and decide to cooperate. Simple shapes in soft aqua, pink, and blue.

425. Marol, Jean-Claude. **Vagabul Escapes.** Illus.: Marol, Jean-Claude. Creative Education, 1983.
ISBN: 0-87191-888-9; LC: 82-72678. Series: Vagabul. Wordless - no print.

Vagabul, in prison clothes, draws a musical staff on the prison wall, then escapes by pulling part of the wall down with an anchor and line. He continues with the line theme as he cuts down power lines, uses the poles as stilts, and finally unties a boat and sails away, discarding his prison garb.

426. Marol, Jean-Claude. **Vagabul Goes Skiing.** Illus.: Marol, Jean-Claude. Creative Education, 1983.
ISBN: 0-87191-886-2; LC: 82-72680. Series: Vagabul. Wordless - no print.

Vagabul approaches a very small bump in his long red skis, ready to slide downhill. The snow and the skis take on a life of their own, giving him a wild ride as a snowball propels him skyward, and the skis assume unusual shapes. Minimal background and simple forms take the little Vagabul on his winter adventure.

427. Marol, Jean-Claude. **Vagabul in the Clouds.** Illus.: Marol, Jean-Claude. Creative Education, 1981.
ISBN: 0-87191-887-0; LC: 82-72679. Series: Vagabul. Wordless - no print.

When Vagabul's airplane is shot by arrows and loses its wings, he paddles it into a cloud. Pieces of airplane rain out of the cloud, and down they go to the ground. Undismayed, Vagabul ties his plane under the cloud and sails away in the manner of a hot-air balloon. Simply told with soft colors.

428. Martin, Rafe. **Will's Mammoth.** Illus.: Gammell, Stephen. G.P. Putnam's Sons, 1989. ISBN: 0-399-21627-8; LC: 88-11651. Wordless - frame.

Will fills his room with mammoth toys and pictures, convinced they live even when his parents say they're extinct. Out in the snow, Will finds a mammoth and rides through an ice age landscape until called home for dinner. The text framing Will's wordless adventures is part of the colorful paintings.

429. Matthews, Rodney. **On the Planet.** Illus.: Matthews, Rodney. Child's Play, 1975. ISBN: 0-85953-057-4 (board). Series: The Blue Planet. Wordless - no print, Format - board pages.

Sporting purple helmets, two child astronauts land on a strange planet. As they explore the alien landscape, they encounter many fanciful creatures. The inhabitants become threatening, and the two astronauts run for their ship and blast off. Imaginative flora and fauna are shown in colorful, cartoon-like drawings.

430. Mayer, Marianna. **Alley Oop!** Illus.: McDermott, Gerald. Holt, Rinehart and Winston, 1985. ISBN: 0-03-070469-0; LC: 84-15730. Wordless - exclamations.

An animal acrobatic troupe forms a pyramid with a stout mouse as the base. As animals enter they call "alley oop!" and take their places, until the small butterfly, number 10, lands on the elephant's trunk and all collapse..."oops!" Numerals are balanced on the left.

431. Mayer, Mercer. **AH-CHOO.** Illus.: Mayer, Mercer. Dial, 1976. ISBN: 0-8037-4894-9; 0-8037-4895-7 (lib.); LC: 75-9205. Wordless - exclamations.

When mouse offers elephant a bouquet, the flowers make him sneeze and blow down a house. His courtroom sneeze lands him in jail, and his jailhouse sneeze knocks down the jail. A passing lady hippo with equally loud reactions to flowers sneezes and blows away the jailer. Expressive and humorous black line drawings

432. Mayer, Mercer. **Boy, a Dog and a Frog, A.** Illus.: Mayer, Mercer. Dial, 1967. LC: 67-22254. Wordless - no print.

When a boy and dog go to the pond to catch a frog, they end up wet and disgusted after various failed attempts. Frog follows their wet footprints home and joins them in a bath. Brown line drawings convey mishaps, emotions, and camaraderie.

433. Mayer, Mercer. **Bubble Bubble.** Illus.: Mayer, Mercer. Four Winds Press, 1973. ISBN: 0-590-07759-7; LC: 80-16777. Wordless - signs.

After buying magical bubble solution, a boy blows marvelous shapes and animals. When menacing shapes appear, he empties the rest of the liquid on the ground, walking away without noticing the sad bubble monster peering after him. The transparency of bubbles is realized in expressive lines and subtle watercolor.

434. Mayer, Mercer. **Frog Goes to Dinner.** Illus.: Mayer, Mercer. Dial, 1974. ISBN: 0-8037-3386-0; 0-8037-2733-X (lib.); LC: 74-2881. Wordless - signs.

Frog sneaks into the boy's pocket as the family goes out to a "Fancy Restaurant." While the family looks at the menu, frog hops into a saxophone, a salad, and a wine glass, causing commotion throughout the dining room. The boy claims his friend, and they leave in disgrace — to the secret delight of boy and frog.

435. Mayer, Mercer. **Frog on His Own.** Illus.: Mayer, Mercer. Dial, 1973. ISBN: 0-8037-2716-X; LC: 73-6017. Wordless - signs.

Frog has his own adventures when boy takes him along to the park with turtle and dog. In detailed, brown line drawings frog gets stung by a bee, disrupts a picnic, sinks a boat, displaces a baby, and is chased by a cat before boy comes and reunites his pets.

436. Mayer, Mercer. **Frog, Where Are You?** Illus.: Mayer, Mercer. Dial, 1969. LC: 72-85544. Wordless - signs.

In this sequel to *A Boy, a Dog and a Frog,* frog leaves while boy and dog are sleeping. Their search for frog leads to mishaps such as being chased by bees and falling into a pond. Frog is found with a female frog and a family of little frogs, one of whom goes off with the boy and dog. Brown line drawings.

437. Mayer, Mercer. **Great Cat Chase, The.** Illus.: Mayer, Mercer. Four Winds Press, 1974.
ISBN: 0-590-07400-8; LC: 74-13120. Wordless - no print.

A girl dressed in her mother's clothes pushes her cat in a baby buggy. When cat escapes, the girl recruits a boy in policeman outfit and a younger boy to join her in the chase. Their humorous mishaps end with scratches and bruises, and the girl cheerfully changes into her nurse outfit and serves cookies. Line drawings.

438. Mayer, Mercer. **Hiccup.** Illus.: Mayer, Mercer. Dial, 1976.
ISBN: 0-8037-3592-8 (lib.); 0-8037-3590-1 (pbk.); LC: 76-2284. Wordless - exclamations.

Humorous black line drawings show a simpering lady hippopotamus and her gentleman friend going for a boat ride and picnic. When she begins to hiccup, he throws water in her face, beginning a series of disastrous cures. He enjoys himself until, back on land, she returns his cures with glee.

439. Mayer, Mercer. **Oops.** Illus.: Mayer, Mercer. Dial, 1977.
ISBN: 0-8037-6569-X; LC: 76-42934. Wordless - exclamations.

An unperturbed lady hippopotamus enters with a crash as her car strikes a traffic signal. She moves from disaster to disaster as she upsets a fruit stand, shatters china in a shop, wrecks a dinosaur skeleton in a museum, and causes a train wreck. Humorous black line drawings show her mild response ("oops") to each event.

440. Mayer, Mercer. **Two Moral Tales.** Illus.: Mayer, Mercer. Four Winds Press, 1974.
ISBN: 0-590-07366-4; LC: 74-7487. Wordless - no print, Format - back to back.

Two separate stories are bound back-to-back in this tiny book. In "Bear's New Clothes," a bear finds old items of clothing and fancies himself well-dressed in them until a goat laughs at him. In "Bird's New Hat," a top hat that appears funny on a furry bird becomes another bird's nest until it is reclaimed.

441. Mayer, Mercer. **Two More Moral Tales.** Illus.: Mayer, Mercer. Four Winds Press, 1974.
ISBN: 0-590-07367-2; LC: 74-8109. Wordless - signs, Format - back to back.

Detailed line drawings tell two humorous back-to-back stories. "Just a Pig at Heart" shows two young pigs carefully dressing for a romantic evening which ends in a mud puddle. In "Sly Fox's Folly," fox tricks elegant ladies into purchasing discounted furs and hats, which are actually live animals that return to him.

442. Mayer, Mercer, and Marianna Mayer. **Boy, a Dog, a Frog and a Friend, A.** Illus.: Mayer, Mercer. Dial, 1971.
LC: 70-134857. Wordless - no print.

Expressive brown line drawings show the friends from *A Boy, a Dog and a Frog* out fishing. The line is snagged by a mischievous turtle who plays tricks on poor dog. When turtle appears to be dead, the boy prepares to bury him, but dog discovers the pretense and turtle joins the friends as they go home.

443. Mayer, Mercer, and Marianna Mayer. **Mine!** Illus.: Mayer, Mercer, and Marianna Mayer. Simon and Schuster, 1970.
ISBN: 671-65145-5; 671-65146-3 (lib.); LC: 76-123243. Almost wordless - dialog.

Black line drawings show a boy falsely claiming various things which belong to others. In each encounter, he asserts "mine" but is convinced one way or another that it is "yours". When he returns home he confidently claims his messy room, and his mother hands him a broom and agrees "yours."

444. Mayer, Mercer, and Marianna Mayer. **One Frog Too Many.** Illus.: Mayer, Mercer. Dial, 1975.
ISBN: 0-8037-6734-X; LC: 75-6325. Wordless - no print.

Boy, dog, and turtle are pleased when a surprise package contains a new, smaller frog. The old frog is not pleased. The older frog's jealous behavior upsets the others as they go on an outing and results in losing the new frog temporarily. Brown and white drawings give telling expression to the characters.

445. McCully, Emily Arnold. **Christmas Gift, The.** Illus.: McCully, Emily Arnold. Harper and Row, 1988.
ISBN: 0-06-024211-6; 0-06-024212-4 (lib.); LC: 87-45758. Wordless - no print.

The mouse family prepares for Christmas and opens special gifts in the morning. Little mouse has a remote control airplane that is so wonderful that it must go along to grandparents—where it crashes and is broken. Grandfather saves the day with a special toy, a wind-up train, from his childhood. Bright holiday colors.

446. McCully, Emily Arnold. **First Snow.** Illus.: McCully, Emily Arnold. Harper and Row, 1985.
ISBN: 0-06-024128-4; 0-06-024129-2 (lib.); LC: 84-43244. Wordless - no print.

Winter colors make an inviting landscape as the mouse family goes on a sledding trip in the snow. While the older ones eagerly fling themselves down the hill, the littlest mouse is left alone on top. After finally taking the first plunge, the little one enjoys it so much that she doesn't want to quit to go home.

447. McCully, Emily Arnold. **New Baby.** Illus.: McCully, Emily Arnold. Harper and Row, 1988.
ISBN: 0-06-024130-6; 0-06-024131-4 (lib.); LC: 87-45294. Wordless - no print.

A young mouse wakes to find excitement in the house—mother has a new baby. Feeling left out, the little mouse tries to recapture attention in various ways before finally realizing that there is enough love for all. The large and active mouse family is shown in black line drawings and watercolors in spring hues.

448. McCully, Emily Arnold. **Picnic.** Illus.: McCully, Emily Arnold. Harper and Row, 1984.
ISBN: 0-06-024099-7; 0-06-024100-4 (lib.); LC: 83-47913. Wordless - no print.

As the mouse family's truck takes them into the woods for a picnic, the littlest mouse bounces out of the back. Unaware, the family continues, leaving little mouse and a special toy mouse behind. Bright paintings with green, summery hues show the feelings, activities, and eventual reunion of the large family.

449. McCully, Emily Arnold. **School.** Illus.: McCully, Emily Arnold. Harper and Row, 1987.
ISBN: 0-06-024132-2; 0-06-024133-0 (lib.); LC: 87-156. Wordless - no print.

As the older mice children leave for school, the youngest decides to follow, slipping out while mother reads. At school, the little mouse tries to fit in amid the laughter of the others. Teacher treats the little one kindly and lets mother know where her stray has gone. Fine line drawings with bright watercolors.

450. McMillan, Bruce. **Alphabet Symphony, The.** Illus.: McMillan, Bruce. Greenwillow, 1977.
ISBN: 0-688-80112-9; 0-688-84112-0 (lib.); LC: 77-5491. Wordless - symbols.

Unusual black-and-white photographs of a symphony orchestra show each letter of the alphabet formed by parts of instruments. Below each photograph, a white silhouette provides a guide to finding the form of the letter in the picture. A guide page in back identifies all of the instruments.

451. McMillan, Bruce. **Becca Backward, Becca Frontward: A Book of Concept Pairs.** Illus.: McMillan, Bruce. Lothrop Lee and Shepard, 1986.
ISBN: 0-688-06282-2; 0-688-06283-0 (lib.);86-7221. Almost wordless - labels.

Clear color photographs portray a young girl illustrating contrasting concepts such as bottom and top, same and different. Becca jumps above her bed and crawls below it, pours a full glass of milk and drains an empty one, and rides her tricycle backward and "frontward." Single word per page.

452. McMillan, Bruce. **Counting Wildflowers.** Illus.: McMillan, Bruce. Lothrop Lee and Shepard, 1986.
ISBN: 0-688-02859-4; 0-688-02860-8 (lib.); LC: 85-16607. Almost wordless - labels.

Close-up, color photographs show wildflowers in groups from one to twenty, with the last picture "too many to count!" Under each large picture are dots, with the number of colored circles corresponding to the number and color of flowers on the page.

453. McMillan, Bruce. **Dry or Wet?** Illus.: McMillan, Bruce. Lothrop Lee and Shepard, 1988.
ISBN: 0-688-07100-7; 0-688-07101-5 (lib.); LC: 86-27345. Wordless - no print.

Full- page, color photographs contrast children in wet and dry situations; for example, the girl is dry as she jumps from a diving board and wet as she splashes into the pool in the next picture.

454.   McMillan, Bruce. **Fire Engine Shapes.** Illus.: McMillan, Bruce. Lothrop Lee and Shepard, 1988.
       ISBN: 0-688-07842-7; 0-688-07843-5 (lib.); LC: 87-38145. Wordless - signs.

Close- up, color photographs show a young girl exploring a fire engine and the geometric shapes found there. Information in the back of the book identifies the type of engine and the various shapes to locate on each page. Each pair of photographs echoes the same shape.

455.   McMillan, Bruce. **Growing Colors.** Illus.: McMillan, Bruce. Lothrop Lee and Shepard, 1988.
       ISBN: 0-688-07844-3; 0-688-07845-1 (lib.); LC: 88-2767. Almost wordless - labels.

As they grow, fruits and vegetables are shown in a small picture, then in a close view revealing their natural color in this photographic color book. The word for the color being shown is printed in that color. The fruits and vegetables are identified in a guide page at the back of the book.

456.   McMillan, Bruce. **One, Two, One Pair!** Illus.: McMillan, Bruce. Scholastic, 1991.
       ISBN: 0-590-43767-4; LC: 90-37410. Almost wordless - labels.

As the steps in getting dressed to go ice skating are shown in large full-color photographs, the words of the title are repeated to accompany hands, eyes, feet, and other paired things. The pair of ice skaters provide a surprise—twins.

457.   McMillan, Bruce, and Brett McMillan. **Puniddles.** Illus.: McMillan, Bruce. Houghton Mifflin, 1982.
       ISBN: 0-395-32082-8; 0-395-32076-3 (pbk.); LC: 81-20130. Wordless - titles.

Two black-and-white photographs on each page create a visual pun. For example, a bear cub stands above a photo of two feet to show "bare feet" and pictures of a chicken and a baseball form "foul ball." Answers are printed upside down on the bottom of each page.

458.   McPhail, David. **David McPhail's Animals A to Z.** Illus.: McPhail, David. Scholastic, 1988.
       ISBN: 0-590-40715-5; LC: 87-4955. Wordless - signs.

Each letter of the alphabet is represented by an animal shown in a frame with objects beginning with the letter. Whimsical bright watercolors show such animals as a porcupine painting a picture of a pumpkin for *P.* The animals are identified in the back.

459.   McPhail, David. **Oh, No, Go (a Play).** Illus.: McPhail, David. Little Brown, 1973.
       LC: 73-8144. Almost wordless - dialog.

A hot-air balloon lands, becomes a tent, and the basket becomes a ticket booth. Animals buy tickets and become the audience for an imaginative play of few words. As the actor fishes, water flows off the stage and floods the audience. He hooks a mermaid, and the detailed drawings elaborate the fantastic happenings.

460. McTrusty, Ron. **Dandelion Year.** Illus.: McTrusty, Ron. Harvey House, 1975. ISBN: 0-8178-5292-1; LC: 74-83424. Wordless - no print.

Large block prints in browns, greens, and golds show the life cycle of a dandelion from bloom to seed, to a new plant and a new bloom the next year. Seeds, blown by a child and carried by wind, land near woods. Various animals are seen as winter passes, the roots begin to grow, and the new plant develops.

461. Mendoza, George. **Inspector, The.** Illus.: Parnall, Peter. Doubleday, 1970. LC: 79-97672. Wordless - no print.

The inspector, shortsighted in more ways than one, follows giant footprints with his large magnifying glass. Behind him, his dog devours the many monsters along the way, growing larger and more like the monsters with each one. Line drawings with only a touch of bloody red detail the trek and the dog's transformation.

462. Meyer, Renate. **Hide-and-Seek.** Illus.: Meyer, Renate. Bradbury Press, 1972. ISBN: 0-87888-039-9; LC: 70-174350. Wordless - no print.

In full-color reproductions of oil paintings, a young girl in reds and pinks seeks a smaller child in blues. The game starts outside and moves to the barn, the house, and back outside as a parent watches out a window. Fluid, with expressive flow of shape and color, the paintings conceal as much as they reveal.

463. Meyer, Renate. **Vicki.** Illus.: Meyer, Renate. Atheneum, 1969. LC: 69-11859. Wordless - no print.

A young girl is left out as her friend joins other children, who play and ignore her. She makes a playmate from materials found in the lush garden. As she plays with this imaginary friend, the others come to watch and invite the two to join their circle. Introspective artwork in rich color and texture reveals her moods.

464. Mill, Eleanor. **My Schoolbook of Picture Stories.** Illus.: Mill, Eleanor. Holt, Rinehart and Winston, 1967. LC: 66-10186. Wordless - signs.

Large, colorful, realistic pictures show children in a preschool or kindergarten classroom engaged in typical activities. The multicultural group plays, has a snack, goes outside, demonstrates the activity areas in the class, and interacts with each other. After cleaning up, they have a birthday party with cupcakes.

465. Miller, Barry. **Alphabet World.** Illus.: Miller, Barry. Macmillan, 1971. LC: 77-127470. Wordless - symbols.

Black-and-white photographs of everyday scenes contain the forms of letters of the alphabet in this unusual alphabet book. The shapes of letters are outlined on thin pages overlaying the photographs to help identify each one. In this way, Q is seen in a roll of tape and L in the handle of a pencil sharpener.

466. Mitchelhill, Barbara. **Birthday.** Illus.: Chesterman, Jo. The Wright Group, 1986.
      ISBN: 1-55624-059-7 (set, pbk.). Series: White Level Little Books, Set 1.
      Wordless - signs.

Preparations and party exhaust the parents of a girl turning five years old. From the mailman bringing cards and presents to the final mess after guests leave, each step of the day's activities is shown in colored drawings.

467. Mitchelhill, Barbara. **Dora the Dragon.** Illus.: Bottomley, Jane. The Wright
      Group, 1986.
      ISBN: 1-55624-060-0 (set, pbk.). Series: White Level Little Books, Set 2.
      Wordless - signs.

The dragon's tail is hidden in the corner of the opening picture of a knight, a charger, and a castle. In each picture, as the knight delivers large envelopes to wood-cutter and giant, the dragon can be seen hiding and watching—and finally, a delighted baby dragon is invited to the prince's birthday party too.

468. Mitchelhill, Barbara. **Going to School.** Illus.: Chesterman, Jo. The Wright
      Group, 1986.
      ISBN: 1-55624-059-7 (set, pbk.). Series: White Level Little Books, Set 1.
      Wordless - no print.

An Indian or Pakistani mother fixes breakfast, then takes her little girl to school. Tearful and clinging at first, the little girl becomes comfortable playing at the sand table and has a painting to share when her mother returns to pick her up.

469. Mitchelhill, Barbara. **Home from School.** Illus.: Smith, Lesley. The Wright
      Group, 1986.
      ISBN: 1-55624-060-0 (set, pbk.). Series: White Level Little Books, Set 2.
      Wordless - signs.

A little girl meets her grandmother after school. As they slowly make their way home, there are many people and shops to see, and stops to make as Grandmother fills her bag with purchases. The french fries and fish they bring home to eat are appreciated by the girl's pregnant mother.

470. Mitchelhill, Barbara. **Seaside.** Illus.: Sleight, Katy. The Wright Group, 1986.
      ISBN: 1-55624-059-7 (set, pbk.). Series: White Level Little Books, Set 1.
      Wordless - signs.

Packing and preparing for a day at the beach occupy a family of four and their dog. They enjoy a sunny day swimming and eating, but as the children pack their father in sand, dark clouds come up. He awakes immobilized as raindrops hit and the others run to the car.

471. Mitchelhill, Barbara. **Shoes.** Illus.: Bottomley, Jane. The Wright Group, 1986.
      ISBN: 1-55624-059-7 (set, pbk.). Series: White Level Little Books, Set 1.
      Wordless - signs.

A black mother and her small son are going downtown on the bus. They join crowds on the street, and the little boy falls and skins his knee. A lollipop makes him feel better. When they find a shoe store, he picks out new bright red sneakers.

472. Mitchelhill, Barbara. **Star, The.** Illus.: Biro, Val. The Wright Group, 1986.
ISBN: 1-55624-060-0 (set, pbk.). Series: White Level Little Books, Set 2.
Wordless - no print.

Unhappy at first, a little boy becomes excited about his role as an angel holding a star in the nativity play at school. Practice and preparation for the play lead to a costumed performance in the multicultural classroom.

473. Mitchelhill, Barbara. **Supermarket, The.** Illus.: Sleight, Katy. The Wright
Group, 1986.
ISBN: 1-55624-060-0 (set, pbk.). Series: White Level Little Books, Set 2.
Wordless - signs.

Father and three children go to the supermarket to do the grocery shopping. They select and pay for food, then go home to help cook and eat dinner. Bright colors, in pictures busy with details. Books in this series are also available as "big books" for group sharing.

474. Mitchelhill, Barbara. **Wedding, The.** Illus.: Smith, Robina. The Wright Group, 1986.
ISBN: 1-55624-060-0 (set, pbk.). Series: White Level Little Books, Set 2. Wordless
- no print.

A mischievous-looking, black-haired girl dresses to be a flower girl in a wedding and tucks her pet rat into her flower basket. When the rat escapes, the wedding party collapses. Drawn with doll-like people and flat colors.

475. Mitchelhill, Barbara. **What Shall We Wear?** Illus.: Biro, Val. The Wright
Group, 1986.
ISBN: 1-55624-060-0 (set, pbk.). Series: White Level Little Books, Set 2.
Wordless - signs.

A brother and sister demonstrate various types of outdoor wear as they put on raincoats to go shopping with their mother on a rainy day, winter coats to play outside in the snow with their father, and bathing suits to play in a pool in the backyard. Finally, they don pajamas for bedtime.

476. Moak, Allan. **Big City ABC, A.** Illus.: Moak, Allan. Tundra Books, 1984.
ISBN: 0-88776-161-5. Almost wordless - sentences.

The city of Toronto, Canada is shown from a child's perspective in colorful, busy paintings. Each scene is briefly identified in a simple sentence: "O is for October" for example, accompanies an autumn leaf-raking scene with Canadian geese flying in a wedge. The guide in back gives more detail; the house pictured is the artist's.

477. Mogensen, Jan. **46 Little Men, The.** Illus.: Mogensen, Jan. Greenwillow
Books, 1990.
ISBN: 0-688-09283-7; 0-688-09284-5; LC: 90-36470. Wordless - frame.

Forty-six little men live in a picture on the nursery wall. Finding a map and rope ladder, they leave to begin a journey to the Island of the Elves, stopping to play in the nursery on the way. When their adventure ends they return to the picture through a tunnel. Soft watercolors with busy detail.

478.   Montresor, Beni. **A for Angel: Beni Montresor's ABC Picture-Stories.** Illus.: Montresor, Beni. Alfred A. Knopf, 1969.
LC: 68-15320. Wordless - symbols.

Each page has numerous objects representing a letter. A guide in the beginning of the book suggests a title for each story told by the objects. The titles are intriguing: "Mister Monster and the Moon-Mermaid," for example. On the page, mysterious relationships between the darkly printed objects are implied.

479.   Moodie, Fiona. **Penguin, The.** Illus.: Moodie, Fiona. The Wright Group, 1986.
ISBN: 1-55624-000-7 (set, pbk.). Series: First Nature Watch. Wordless - no print.

A pair of penguins separate from the flock to feed and cuddle together. They produce an egg, welcome and feed a chick, then lead the new one back to the flock. Prints in limited colors reflect their stark and watery environment.

480.   Mordillo, Guillermo. **Crazy Cowboy.** Illus.: Mordillo, Guillermo. Harlin Quist, 1972.
ISBN: 0-8252-0087-3; 0-8252-0088-1 (lib.); LC: 72-78356. Wordless - signs.

The zany cowboy has escaped from the front papers to take a madcap trip through a wild western landscape, exchanging one form of transportation for another. Finally, from his campfire from atop a skyscraper, he sails off into the night in a hot air balloon, returning to his place in the endpapers. Bright, cartoon-like drawings.

481.   Mordillo, Guillermo. **Damp and Daffy Doings of a Daring Pirate Ship, The.** Illus.: Mordillo, Guillermo. Harlin Quist, 1971.
ISBN: 8252-0071-7; 8252-0072-5 (lib.); LC: 72-146838. Wordless - no print.

Bold colors and imaginative drawing tell the adventures of an unlikely crew of pirates as they trot through a city carrying their ship, launch it, battle on the high seas, defeat a monster, and hide their treasure before becoming shipwrecked. Humor and action abound.

482.   Morris, Terry Nell. **Goodnight, Dear Monster!** Illus.: Morris, Terry Nell. Alfred A. Knopf, 1980.
ISBN: 0-394-84221-9; 0-394-94221-3 (lib.); LC: 79-26904. Wordless - no print.

A pajama-clad girl and her special teddy bear are preparing for bed when a monster appears. Told firmly to go away, the monster begins crying and the girl finally decides there is room for all three to sleep in her bed. Simple drawings give character to the worried bear, the anxious monster, and the confident little girl.

483.   Morris, Terry Nell. **Lucky Puppy! Lucky Boy!** Illus.: Morris, Terry Nell. Alfred A. Knopf, 1980.
ISBN: 0-394-94220-5 (lib.); LC: 79-27024. Wordless - signs.

A boy longs for the puppy in the pet shop window, ignoring an eager stray puppy trying to get his attention. The brown and white spotted pup does all he can, even standing on his head, to make the boy notice him. Finally, as the puppy walks away, the boy calls him back for a happy ending.

484. Muller, Jorg. **Changing City, The.** Illus.: Muller, Jorg. Atheneum, 1977.
ISBN: 0-689-10782-X; LC: 76-46646. Wordless - signs, Format - portfolio.

A portfolio of eight full-color, foldout pictures shows the same urban scene from 1953 to 1976. A gradual process of decay and change is seen. This is shown as much by the people at work and play as by the changing architecture. The city is based on studies of large Swiss and German cities.

485. Muller, Jorg. **Changing Countryside, The.** Illus.: Muller, Jorg. Atheneum, 1973.
ISBN: 0-689-50085-8. Wordless - signs, Format - portfolio.

Eight full-color, foldout pictures show the same European countryside from 1953 to 1972. A farm, with a small village in the back- ground, a dirt road, and a rail-road, gradually changes with the years and the seasons to a four lane super-highway passing giant discount stores and suburbs.

486. Munro, Roxie. **Christmastime in New York City.** Illus.: Munro, Roxie. Dodd, Mead , 1987.
ISBN: 0-396-08909-7; LC: 86-32914. Almost wordless - labels.

Beginning with Macy's Thanksgiving Day parade and ending with New Year's Eve at Times Square, the city's holiday traditions are shown in richly detailed, realistic watercolors. Labels identify the New York City landmarks, and a page in back gives information about each special part of the season's celebration pictured.

487. Munro, Roxie. **Inside-Outside Book of London, The.** Illus.: Munro, Roxie. Dutton, 1989.
ISBN: 0-525-44522-6; LC: 89-12023. Almost wordless - labels.

Bright, detailed paintings show noted sights in London with two-page spreads of exterior, then interior views. For example, the front of the British Museum as seen from Great Russell Street is followed by a view of decorated mummy cases on display inside. Titles identify each scene. An information page comes at the end.

488. Munro, Roxie. **Inside-Outside Book of New York City, The.** Illus.: Munro, Roxie. G.P. Putnam's Sons, 1985.
ISBN: 0-399-22034-8; LC: 89-3699. Almost wordless - labels.

Detailed illustrations show exterior and interior views of street scenes and famous landmarks in New York City. The beauty of city architecture and the vitality of city activities are displayed in such varied scenes as the Museum of Natural History, the subway, the Stock Exchange, and the Statue of Liberty.

489. Munro, Roxie. **Inside-Outside Book of Washington, D.C., The.** Illus.: Munro, Roxie. Dutton, 1987.
ISBN: 0-525-44298-7; LC: 86-24267. Almost wordless - labels.

Famous landmarks in the nation's capital are shown with two-page exterior views, followed by interior views. This process is interestingly reversed when the Washington Post is first seen as it is being printed, then as a rolled-up newspaper delivered on a townhouse doorstep. Labels identify each scene.

490. Neumeier, Marty, and Byron Glaser. **Action Alphabet.** Illus.: Neumeier, Marty, and Byron Glaser. Greenwillow, 1985.
ISBN: 0-688-05703-9; 0-688-05704-7 (lib.); LC: 84-25322. Almost wordless - labels.

In bold black and white graphics the letters of the alphabet become part of the illustration. *O* is an orbit around the earth while *U* is simply "up" at the top of the page. *V* becomes the fangs of a vampire and the rain comes down in *R*s. A completely blank page illustrates "Gg : gone."

491. Nolan, Dennis. **Alphabrutes.** Illus.: Nolan, Dennis. Prentice-Hall, 1977.
ISBN: 0-13-022822-2 (lib.); LC: 76-45439. Almost wordless - sounds.

Comical green monsters in a wild variety of shapes and sizes join a monster protecting a mysterious basket. Each monster enters wearing a letter of the alphabet and making a sound which begins with that letter. When all are gathered, the tiny baby in the basket is revealed, wearing *Z* and sleeping—"zzzzzzz."

492. Nolan, Dennis. **Monster Bubbles.** Illus.: Nolan, Dennis. Prentice-Hall, 1976.
ISBN: 0-13-600635-3; LC: 76-10167. Wordless - no print.

In softly shaded pencil sketches, a monster blowing one bubble is joined by other comical and expressive creatures who take turns blowing bubbles at one another until the bubble mixture is spilled. The number of pink and blue bubbles progresses from one to twenty.

493. Noll, Sally. **Off and Counting.** Illus.: Noll, Sally. Greenwillow, 1984.
ISBN: 0-688-02795-4; 0-688-02796-2 (lib.); LC: 83-16366. Almost wordless - labels.

A wind-up frog jumps over toys arranged numerically from one castle to ten blocks. The numerals appear on the page, and the word for each number is repeated in a band along the bottom. Geometric shapes in bold solid colors make striking graphic designs of each page.

494. Nygren, Tord. **Red Thread, The.** Illus.: Nygren, Tord. R&S Books, 1987.
ISBN: 91-29-59005-1; LC: 87-32204. Wordless - no print.

A group of children follow a red thread as it winds around and through fantastic scenes filled with characters from literature and art and with unusual details. Each elaborate and imaginative painting contains allusions to other parts of the book, with the red thread leading the eye from detail to detail.

495. Oakley, Graham. **Graham Oakley's Magical Changes.** Illus.: Oakley, Graham. Atheneum, 1979.
ISBN: 0-689-30732-2; LC: 79-2784. Wordless - signs, Format - mix-and-match.

Split pages allow Graham Oakley's paintings to mix-and-match, the five central columns serving to unify each resultant picture. The scenes combine in surrealistic ways—the trunks of trees connect to the strands of spaghetti, for example—producing an imaginative work filled with symbolism and British history and humor.

496. Oechsli, Kelly. **It's Schooltime.** Illus.: Oechsli, Kelly. Holt, Rinehart and Winston, 1967.
ISBN: 03-059315-8; LC: 66-10708. Almost wordless - dialog.

A cheerful black city boy leaves home in the morning and happily runs to school through his integrated neighborhood. The boy says "hello" arriving at school on one page and "goodbye" as he leaves on the next. He plays on the way home. All of the workers shown are male, all the teachers female. Pastel color and line drawing.

497. Olschewski, Alfred. **Winterbird.** Illus.: Olschewski, Alfred. Houghton Mifflin, 1969. LC: 70-82481. Wordless - exclamations.

A small bird walks through the snow, unaware that a cat is trailing him. The cat is unaware that they are followed by a dog. Cat leaps at bird, dog leaps at cat, and bird calls for help. Flocks of birds hear the call and scare away the dog and cat. Simple, effective black lines, cross-hatching, and print.

498. Ormerod, Jan. **Moonlight.** Illus.: Ormerod, Jan. Lothrop Lee and Shepard, 1982.
ISBN: 0-688-00846-1; 0-688-00847-X (lib.); LC: 81-8290. Wordless - no print.

After dinner, a young girl prepares for bed. Her familiar bedtime rituals include a bath and a bedtime book but do not put her to sleep. Alternating from the dark bedroom to the lighted living room, panels show the parents trying various ploys to get her to sleep—and falling asleep themselves.

499. Ormerod, Jan. **Sunshine.** Illus.: Ormerod, Jan. Lothrop Lee and Shepard, 1981.
ISBN: 0-688-00552-7; 0-688-00553-5 (lib.); LC: 80-84971. Wordless - no print.

The earliest riser in the family is the little girl, who quietly reads to herself before waking her father, helping fix breakfast, and getting herself ready for the day. Soft colors and multiple panels show a warm and loving family life. The same family is pictured in a companion volume, *Moonlight.*

500. Oxenbury, Helen. **Beach Day.** Illus.: Oxenbury, Helen. Dial, 1982.
ISBN: 0-8037-0439-9 (board); LC: 81-69273. Series: Very First Books. Wordless - no print, Format - board pages.

The various activities of a little boy at a sandy beach are shown in two-page vignettes. He plays with sand, water, and a ball and interacts with his parents in simply drawn and softly colored illustrations.

501. Oxenbury, Helen. **Dressing.** Illus.: Oxenbury, Helen. Wanderer Books, 1981.
ISBN: 0-671-42113-1 (board); LC: 80-52220. Series: Baby Board Books. Almost wordless - labels, Format - board pages.

Each piece of clothing is shown with a word identifying it, then a bald, round-headed toddler is shown wearing it. Simple drawings with plain backgrounds.

502. Oxenbury, Helen. **Family.** Illus.: Oxenbury, Helen. Wanderer Books, 1981.
ISBN: 0-671-42110-7 (board); LC: 80-52218. Series: Baby Board Books.
Almost wordless - labels, Format - board pages.

Each member of the family is shown alone, and then holding baby. The word for each family member appears on one page. Simple, round-faced characters are sketched in uncluttered pictures.

503. Oxenbury, Helen. **Friends.** Illus.: Oxenbury, Helen. Wanderer Books, 1981.
ISBN: 0-671-42111-5 (board); LC: 80-52216. Series: Baby Board Books.
Almost wordless - labels, Format - board pages.

A toddler meets a variety of animals in this simple book. Each animal is first pictured alone with its name printed on the page. Then the toddler is shown interacting with the animal.

504. Oxenbury, Helen. **Good Night, Good Morning.** Illus.: Oxenbury, Helen. Dial, 1982.
ISBN: 0-8037-2980-4 (board); LC: 81-69272. Series: Very First Books. Wordless - no print, Format - board pages.

A father and child have an enjoyable evening routine with bath, playtime, and a story. In the morning, the toddler watches dad shave, tries the shaving lotion, and complicates attempts to make the bed. White backgrounds with subdued colors show the pajama-clad child with minimal detail.

505. Oxenbury, Helen. **Monkey See, Monkey Do.** Illus.: Oxenbury, Helen. Dial, 1982.
ISBN: 0-8037-5436-1 (board); LC: 81-69271. Series: Very First Books. Wordless - no print, Format - board pages.

A boy, wrapped up for outdoor play, engages in a variety of physical activities. Each of his actions is paired with a zoo animal engaging in a similar action; for example, when the boy swings on a pole, a monkey swings in a tree.

506. Oxenbury, Helen. **Mother's Helper.** Illus.: Oxenbury, Helen. Dial, 1982.
ISBN: 0-8037-5425-6 (board); LC: 81-68773. Series: Very First Books. Wordless - no print, Format - board pages.

An engaging toddler watches and "helps" in various typical ways, such as sitting on the vacuum, then pushing the nozzle; watching mother cook and then licking the spoon; or welcoming company and then offering a younger baby a drink.

507. Oxenbury, Helen. **Playing.** Illus.: Oxenbury, Helen. Wanderer Books, 1981.
ISBN: 0-671-42109-3 (board); LC: 80-52217. Series: Baby Board Books.
Almost wordless - labels, Format - board pages.

A picture of something to play with appears with its name, then a bald toddler in red rompers plays with it. Some traditional toys—blocks, wagon, bear, ball—and some non-toy playthings—pot, box—are included.

508. Oxenbury, Helen. **Shopping Trip.** Illus.: Oxenbury, Helen. Dial, 1982.
ISBN: 0-8037-7939-9 (board); LC: 81-69274. Series: Very First Books. Wordless - no print, Format - board pages.

A toddler goes shopping with his mother and engages in typical behavior: being lifted to push the elevator button, trying on large shoes, getting into his mother's purse, spinning a display, and so forth.

509. Oxenbury, Helen. **Working.** Illus.: Oxenbury, Helen. Wanderer Books, 1981.
ISBN: 0-671-42112-3 (board); LC: 80-52219. Series: Baby Board Books.
Almost wordless - labels, Format - board pages.

Objects that are part of baby's world are shown, then baby using the object. The round-headed hairless baby in yellow rompers eats in a high chair, sits on a potty, rides in a carriage, takes a bath, and sleeps in a crib.

510. Page, Robin. **Count One to Ten.** Illus.: Page, Robin. WJ Fantasy, Inc., 1990.
ISBN: 1-56021-017-6 (board). Almost wordless - labels, Format - board pages; accordion.

Color photographs of fruit accompany the numeral and the word for each number in this accordion-folded board book.

511. Palmer, Kim. **Dream, The.** Illus.: Palmer, Kim. Salem House, 1988.
ISBN: 0-88162-311-3; LC: 87-13039. Wordless - symbols.

This elaborate rebus puzzle uses illustration to represent the sound, rather than the meaning, of words. The black-and-white drawings resemble old-fashioned etchings. Those who solve the puzzle and read this "modern moral tale" are invited to send their solution to the publishers for a prize.

512. Panek, Dennis. **Catastrophe Cat.** Illus.: Panek, Dennis. Bradbury Press, 1978.
ISBN: 0-87888-130-1; LC: 77-90951. Wordless sequence in book.

The introduction explains the quiet life of a family cat and the origin of his name, followed by the wordless sequence of a disastrous day out when the cat encounters traffic, dogs, the subway, and a parade. The hapless misadventures of the round-eyed orange cat are detailed in ink, chalk, and wash paintings.

513. Panek, Dennis. **Catastrophe Cat at the Zoo.** Illus.: Panek, Dennis. Bradbury Press, 1979.
ISBN: 0-87888-147-6; LC: 78-26369. Wordless - frame.

Large colorful two-page illustrations show Catastrophe Cat on a bus ride to the zoo and a somersaulting trip through it. He has a close, if quick, look at each of the zoo animals as he leaps and is tossed from enclosure to enclosure. The giraffe lifts him from the panda's head and places him on the bus home.

514. Park, William B. **Charlie-Bob's Fan.** Illus.: Park, William B. Harcourt Brace Jovanovich, 1981. ISBN: 0-15-216221-6; LC: 80-25166. Wordless - no print.

On an extremely hot day, Charlie-Bob drags himself into the house to cool off in front of a fan. It's hard for a dog to turn on the fan, and he tries begging, offering it a bone, barking at it—but only when he chases the teasing cat is the fan accidentally turned on. Humorous ink drawings delineate mood and action.

515. Parkin, Geo. **Monsters Came to Stay, The.** Illus.: Parkin, Geo. The Wright Group, 1987. ISBN: 1-55624-458-4 (pbk.); 1-55624-251-4 (set). Series: This Weekend. Wordless - signs.

In a style straight out of *Mad Magazine,* a boy and his family prepare for weekend guests who are literally monsters. The blue blobby father smokes heavily, the baby is only a giant yelling mouth, the purple and green children break toys and smash windows, and the warty mother cuts prize flowers.

516. Parkin, Geo. **We Took the Robots to the Zoo.** Illus.: Parkin, Geo. The Wright Group, 1987. ISBN: 1-55624-459-2 (pbk.); 1-55624-251-4 (set). Series: This Weekend. Wordless - signs.

A zany pink and yellow robot and a green frog-headed robot are taken to a zoo by two girls. The robots cause trouble with their pranks until they are lost and the zoo closes. When the children return to the zoo, they find the robots happily caged. The use of comic book drawings and clashing colors creates a madcap mood.

517. Patri, Giacomo. **White Collar: A Novel in Linocuts.** Illus.: Patri, Giacomo. Celestial Arts, 1975.
ISBN: 0-89087-180-9; 0-89087-101-9 (pbk.); LC: 75-9440. Wordless - signs.

Originally published in 1940 for the U.S. labor movement, this adult wordless novel is a moving documentary of the Great Depression and its effects on one young man struggling against sudden poverty, a broken life, and hopelessness. Dramatic linoleum prints use both realistic and symbolic elements.

518. Peppe, Rodney. **Circus Numbers.** Illus.: Peppe, Rodney. Delacorte, 1969. ISBN: 0-385-29424-7; LC: 75-86381. Almost wordless - labels.

Colorful illustrations use simple shapes to show a circus ring in which the performers increase from one ringmaster to ten clowns. The numeral, name of the number, and word for the performers are printed on each page. Blue stars accumulate sequentially up to 10 and, after 20 doves and 100 elephants, are swept up with trash.

519. Perkins, Diana. **Have You Seen My Shoe?** Illus.: Bottomley, Jane. The Wright Group, 1986. ISBN: 1-55624-059-7 (set, pbk.). Series: White Level Little Books, Set 1. Wordless - no print.

A perplexed giant examines his toes sticking out of his sock and goes in search of his mysteriously missing shoe. He shows foot and problem to a sequence of fairy-tale characters including pirates, witches, and unicorns, before finding that an old woman is raising lots of children in his shoe.

520. Perrault, Charles; retold by M. Eulalia Valeri; tr. by Leland Northam. **Cinderella.**
Illus.: Rodriguez, Conxita. Silver-Burdett, 1985.
ISBN: 0-382-09067-5; LC: 84-52781. Series: Tell Me a Story. Wordless - no print.

The scenes from the classic French fairytale "Cinderella" are arranged to remind the storyteller of the highpoints of the tale. The illustrations follow a traditional version, with a very young Cinderella who forgives her mean stepsisters in the end.

521. Perrault, Charles; retold by John S. Goodall. **Puss in Boots.** Illus.: Goodall, John S. Margaret K. McElderry Books, 1990.
ISBN: 0-689-50521-3. Wordless - no print, Format - half pages.

The well-known tale of a clever cat who takes his young master from rags to riches is told in lush watercolor illustration. Half pages between each two-page spread change the scene, showing the action. The confident puss here is a large ginger cat clad in red boots and with a long feather in his hat.

522. Perrault, Charles; retold by M. Eulalia Valeri; tr. by Leland Northam. **Puss in Boots.** Illus.: Rodriguez, Conxita. Silver-Burdett, 1982.
ISBN: 0-382-09069-1; LC: 84-52784. Series: Tell Me a Story. Wordless - no print.

The highlights of the classic fairytale are given here in richly colored paintings. The clever cat who helps his poor master acquire riches is shown as an orange tabby in soft red boots. The back of the book summarizes the story to help make connections between the pictures.

523. Pierce, Robert. **Look and Laugh.** Illus.: Pierce, Robert. Golden Press, 1974.
LC: 73-86477. Wordless - titles.

Twelve humorous short stories are told in colorful cartoons, four panels to a page in a comic book format. A red-headed boy and his spotted hound dog are featured as the boy tries to play the violin, cook a cake, learn self-defense, join a football team, and challenge a girl to water sports.

524. Piers, Helen. **Puppy's ABC.** Illus.: Piers, Helen. Oxford, 1987.
ISBN: 0-19-520606-1. Almost wordless - labels.

Color photographs pose a brown and white puppy with objects for each letter of the alphabet. The letter and a word for the object appear on the page. The engaging puppy obligingly is interested in ice cream, sits on stairs, wades in water, and performs admirably in each situation.

525. Ponti, Claude. **Adele's Album.** Illus.: Ponti, Claude. Dutton, 1988.
ISBN: 0-525-44412-2; LC: 88-11106. Wordless - signs.

Oversized pages are filled with an array of images of both common and uncommon objects. As the objects and animals appear and reappear, they combine, interact, and change size. The effect is both humorous and mysterious. Set on a white background, the tiny drawings resemble old-fashioned, hand-colored prints.

526. Poulet, Virginia. **Blue Bug and the Bullies.** Illus.: Charles, Donald. Children's Press, 1971.
LC: 79-159789. Almost wordless - labels.

An expressive blue bug is bullied by numerous other insects. He demonstrates various verbs as he escapes from them, until he finally decides to stand and chases them all away with a "boo!" Single words label each action pictured in dull colors with large, simple objects.

527. Pragoff, Fiona. **Alphabet: From A-Apple to Z-Zipper.** Illus.: Pragoff, Fiona. Doubleday, 1985.
ISBN: 0-385-24171-2 (board). Series: Fiona Pragoff's Photo Board Books.
Almost wordless - labels, Format - board pages.

In bright color and clear photographs, representative objects are shown for each letter of the alphabet. One word appears with each upper- and lowercase letter of the alphabet for each picture; however, hidden links between pictures and clues to other alphabetical words for each letter may also be found.

528. Pragoff, Fiona. **Clothes.** Illus.: Pragoff, Fiona. Doubleday, 1989.
ISBN: 0-385-26388-0 (board). Series: Fiona Pragoff's Photo Board Books.
Almost wordless - labels, Format - board pages.

Brightly colored photographs show a child getting dressed on a winter morning. Each item he is going to wear is hidden on the page before he puts it on; each page offers opportunities for counting both clothing and items in the room.

529. Pragoff, Fiona. **Growing: From First Cry to First Step.** Illus.: Pragoff, Fiona. Doubleday, 1987.
ISBN: 0-385-24174-7 (board). Series: Fiona Pragoff's Photo Board Books.
Almost wordless - labels, Format - board pages.

Clear, uncluttered photographs show babies from birth "crying" to toddlerhood "walking." Each page shows a developmental activity as performed by a wonderful variety of babies. A word on each page labels the baby's activities.

530. Pragoff, Fiona. **How Many? From 0 to 20.** Illus.: Pragoff, Fiona. Doubleday, 1986.
ISBN: 0-385-24172-0 (board). Series: Fiona Pragoff's Photo Board Books.
Wordless - symbols, Format - board pages.

Carefully arranged objects are shown in close-up, color photographs. From one key to twenty toes, each spread has a sequential number of objects. The numeral and dice with a corresponding number of spots appear with the photograph.

531. Pragoff, Fiona. **Odd One Out.** Illus.: Pragoff, Fiona. Doubleday, 1989.
ISBN: 0-385-26410-0 (board). Series: Fiona Pragoff's Photo Board Books.
Almost wordless - labels, Format - board pages.

From the time a young girl wakens to find her giant blue toothbrush on the windowsill until she goes back to bed at night, she finds objects out of place and returns each one to its proper location. Clear, well-posed photographs show a house filled with bright primary colors.

532. Pragoff, Fiona. **Opposites.** Illus.: Pragoff, Fiona. Doubleday, 1989.
ISBN: 0-385-26409-7 (board). Series: Fiona Pragoff's Photo Board Books.
Almost wordless - labels, Format - board pages.

A boy and his teddy bear begin the day inside a bright yellow make-believe house, and go outside to enjoy a day playing and demonstrating concepts. Each pretend scene is enhanced with props in bright primary colors and the boy and bear enjoy a variety of activities which show opposites.

533. Pragoff, Fiona. **Shapes.** Illus.: Pragoff, Fiona. Doubleday, 1989.
ISBN: 0-385-26408-9 (board). Series: Fiona Pragoff's Photo Board Books.
Almost wordless - labels, Format - board pages.

A girl with long red hair and her plush toy pig are posed in a variety of play situations, each illustrating one of eight shapes. Her play gives clues to the featured shape, and the photographs give color and design clues as well. The opening page indicates both color and shape for each shape.

534. Pragoff, Fiona. **What Color? A Rainbow Zoo.** Illus.: Pragoff, Fiona. Doubleday, 1987.
ISBN: 0-385-24173-9 (board). Series: Fiona Pragoff's Photo Board Books.
Almost wordless - labels, Format - board pages.

Colorful animals seem to embody their color in each clear photograph. The flat yellow background makes the yellow chicks seem even fluffier; the gray background brings out the subtle details of the gray mouse. Unusual colors, such as gold or silver in fish, and unusual page design, such as a page of pink pigs, are used.

535. Prater, John. **Gift, The.** Illus.: Prater, John. Viking, 1985.
ISBN: 0-670-80952-7; 0-14-050589-X (pbk.); LC: 85-40589. Wordless - no print.

The gift arrives in a large cardboard box, which delights the two children much more than the chairs inside it. Seated in the box, they take a fantasy flight through town, to the beach, and on underwater and jungle adventures before returning home. Multiple panels in various sizes; rich colors.

536. Ramage, Corinne S. **Joneses, The.** Illus.: Ramage, Corinne S. J.B. Lippincott, 1975.
ISBN: 0-397-31644-5; LC: 75-2491. Almost wordless - dialog.

In an outlined house, 23 children sleep while their mother leaves for work, and their aproned father waves goodbye. In tiny line drawings the children and father appear on the left side of the page, while mother's underwater job is shown on the right. Shows certain strangeness of scene and action and a most unusual family.

537. Rappus, Gerhard. **When the Sun Was Shining.** Illus.: Rappus, Gerhard. Altberliner Verlag, 1981. ISBN: 89175207. Wordless - frame.

The sun is just rising as a barefoot country boy pulls a stubborn goat across a bridge and tethers him in a meadow. City people arrive by bicycle to picnic, play, and fish. An almost overhead perspective shows the activities of the elongated people and simplified animals, while shadows indicate the sun's movement.

538. Raynor, Dorka. **My Friends Live in Many Places.** Illus.: Raynor, Dorka.
     Albert Whitman and Co., 1980.
     ISBN: 0-8075-5353-0; LC: 79-27655. Almost wordless - labels.

     Engaging black-and-white photographs show children in 23 countries. Costumes
     and customs differ, but common childhood pastimes, attitudes, and emotions are seen
     worldwide.

539. Reese, Bob. **Going Bananas.** Illus.: Reese, Bob. Aro Publishing, 1983.
     ISBN: 0-89868-143-X (lib.). Series: Going Ape Books. Wordless - no print.

     A small ape peels and eats bananas until he discovers how to shoot them out of
     their skins. He and his ape friends bombard a sleeping crocodile, then hide as the irri-
     tated crocodile tries to discover the source of the annoyance. "Apricot Ape" appears in
     all 6 books of the series, drawn in lively, unrefined style.

540. Reese, Bob. **Jungle Train, The.** Illus.: Reese, Bob. Aro Publishing, 1983.
     ISBN: 0-89868-151-0 (lib.). Series: Going Ape Books. Wordless - signs.

     Apricot Ape awakens high in a tree and carries his bright blue lunch box off to
     gather bananas. His transportation across the jungle is a complicated arrangement rem-
     iniscent of a Rube Goldberg device. Each of the various animals who form part of the
     "train" are rewarded with one of his bananas on the way home.

541. Reich, Hanns. **Animals of Many Lands.** Illus.: International photographers.
     Hill and Wang, 1966.
     LC: 67-25685. Wordless - no print.

     Striking black and white photographs capture the character of animals around
     the globe, both on land and in the oceans. Both wild and domestic creatures appear in a
     variety of habitats and activities, some natural and some showing man's control.

542. Reich, Hanns. **Children of Many Lands.** Illus.: Over 100 international pho-
     tographers. Hill and Wang, 1958.
     ISBN: 0-8090-2034-3; 0-8090-1515-3 (pbk.); LC: 60-105 10. Almost wordless -
     labels.

     This collection of black-and-white photographs is a powerful portrayal of chil-
     dren of all ages from around the world. Sometimes joyful, sometimes painful, these
     portraits show both cultural diversity and childhood's universality. Housing, health,
     clothing, school activities, and types of play are pictured.

543. Reich, Hanns, editor. **Human Condition, The.** Illus.: International photogra-
     phers. Hill and Wang, 1973.
     ISBN: 0-8090-2088-2; LC: 73-81581. Wordless - no print.

     Black-and-white photographs from around the world show people of all ages
     engaged in various activities. Designed to emphasize the essential commonality of the
     human experience, the pictures range from a new baby to prisoners of war, from prayer
     to pain, from labor of all sorts to play and celebration.

544.   Reich, Hanns, editor; Heinz Held, text. **Laughing Camera.** Illus.: International
       photographers. Hill and Wang, 1965.
       LC: 67-14654. Wordless - no print.

The universal nature of humor is explored in black-and-white photographs
showing funny situations around the world. Some are incongruous situations, others
make wry comments on the human character. A smoke ring halos a priest, and a bird
sits on the helmet of a trombone player in a military band, for example.

545.   Reich, Hanns; text by Eugen Roth. **Children and Their Fathers.** Illus.: Over
       50 international photographers. Hill and Wang, 1960.
       ISBN: 0-8090-2030-0; LC: 62-12002. Wordless - no print.

Reaching around the world for images of fathers and children, this collection of
black-and-white photographs develops a theme of caring and love that transcends cul-
tural diversity. The universality of the theme serves as a background to the rich display
of variety in human cultures and customs.

546.   Reiss, John J. **Shapes.** Illus.: Reiss, John J. Bradbury Press, 1974.
       ISBN: 0-02-776190-8; LC: 73-76545. Almost wordless - labels.

In vibrant glossy pictures a fox and a mole introduce shapes and show common
objects utilizing that shape— for example, buttons and thumb tacks for circles. The
word for each shape and for each object appears in large print.

547.   Remington, Barbara. **Boat.** Illus.: Remington, Barbara. Doubleday, 1975.
       ISBN: 0-385-02676-5; 0-385-02686-2 (lib.); LC: 70-180101. Wordless - signs.

Unusual creatures watch as two bearded men with umbrellas draw plans on the
sand of a bay and begin to build a boat. They pull tools from inside their umbrellas and
work quickly as the water evaporates, leaving the boat high and dry when finished.
Many subplots appear in the complicated black ink drawings.

548.   Rice, Brian, and Tony Evans. **English Sunrise, The.** Illus.: Evans, Tony. Flash
       Books, 1973.
       Wordless - signs.

The motif of the rising sun with its spreading beams has been found by the
authors on signs, architecture, labels, carpets, and other common and uncommon
objects all over England. Each one appears in a small color photograph within a large
white border. Pairs of photographs reinforce texture and variations of design.

549.   Richter, Mischa. **Quack?** Illus.: Richter, Mischa. Harper and Row, 1978.
       ISBN: 0-06-025020-8; 0-06-025021-6 (lib.); LC: 77-11828. Almost wordless -
       sounds.

Lonely duck looks for a friend, first in his reflection in the pond, then searching
on land. As he meets each animal he quacks and each animal responds with its own
sound. All animal noises appear in voice balloons. At last a flock of ducks land and
quack to him. Simple black outlines with yellow and gray highlights.

550. Richter, Mischa. **To Bed, to Bed!** Illus.: Richter, Mischa. Prentice-Hall, 1981.
ISBN: 0-13-922922-1; LC: 81-2250. Wordless - frame.

The parents of a young prince send him off to bed while the sun is still up. The red-clad prince takes a long and dawdling way to bed, pausing to pick apples, play in the fountain, climb the flagpole, and in general poke around and play until it is dark. Black line sketches with red highlights.

551. Riggio, Anita. **Wake up, William!** Illus.: Riggio, Anita. Atheneum, 1987.
ISBN: 0-689-31344-6; LC: 86-25866. Almost wordless - dialog.

William pretends to be asleep, standing by the parrot. His little brother with an ice cream cone, the dog with a slurpy tongue, the ballerina sister, and the cat with a smelly fish can't get him to budge. Discouraged, having created a mess, they turn to leave, and William wakes and startles them all. Simple, expressive drawing.

552. Ringi, Kjell. **Magic Stick, The.** Illus.: Ringi, Kjell. Harper and Row, 1968.
LC: 68-21259. Wordless - no print.

A stick lying on the ground is discovered by a boy, who picks it up and uses his imagination to transform the stick and himself. Simple black line drawings show the boy on one page, while the opposite page shows his fantasies in elaborate colored pictures. When other children come, the boy drops the stick.

553. Ringi, Kjell. **Winner, The.** Illus.: Ringi, Kjell. Harper and Row, 1969.
LC: 69-18191. Wordless - no print.

Two simply clad, look-alike neighbors stare at each other. One at a time they leave to acquire a bit of fancier finery. As the competition escalates, the images get larger. When one rides in on a big horse, the other enters on a dragon, which devours them both. Simple shapes in garish color with lots of white space.

554. Rispin, Colin. **Off on Holiday.** Illus.: Rispin, Colin. The Wright Group, 1987.
ISBN: 1-55624-493-2 (pbk.); 1-55624-257-3 (set). Series: More and More.
Wordless - signs.

A black family prepares for a trip to Spain, but as the adults pack, the little girl takes out what they have packed and hides each object. She puts her toys, dolls, and books in the bags instead.

555. Roberts, Thom. **Barn, The.** Illus.: Fiammenghi, Gioia. McGraw-Hill, 1975.
ISBN: 0-07-053130-7 (lib.); LC: 74-23499. Wordless - signs.

A neglected barn is worthless to the farm family and becomes more weathered with every season. A city couple is delighted to find and buy it, carefully dismantling and transporting it to a building site where it is reconstructed as a cozy home. Sketches with red and green washes show the details of the process.

556. Rockwell, Anne. **Albert B. Cub and Zebra: An Alphabet Storybook.** Illus.: Rockwell, Anne. Thomas Y. Crowell, 1977.
ISBN: 0-690-01350-7; 0-690-01351-5 (lib.); LC: 76-54224. Wordless - signs.

When zebra is abducted (in *A*), Albert B. Cub, a plump bear, searches for him throughout the alphabet. In each busy scene, objects and activities for each letter are incorporated into the ongoing search. Below each picture, the upper and lower case letter is printed, and the entire story in words is in the back.

557. Roennfeldt, Robert. **Day on the Avenue, A.** Illus.: Roennfeldt, Robert. Viking Kestrel, 1984.
ISBN: 0-7226-5865-6. Wordless - signs.

In large full-color paintings two houses on "The Avenue" are pictured from morning to night. Everyday activities such as people going to work and school, deliveries of milk and bread, and garbage pick-up are interspersed with a painter's mishaps on a roof, the arrival of company, and a dog's active day.

558. Rojankovsky, Feodor. **Animals on the Farm.** Illus.: Rojankovsky, Feodor. Alfred A. Knopf, 1967.
LC: 67-18586. Almost wordless - labels.

A variety of farm animals are drawn in softly shaded, detailed pencil illustrations. Each large picture shows animals in natural poses, with a large print word naming the animal. Backgrounds include other animals and parts of the farm and countryside.

559. Root, Betty. **Slapstick.** Illus.: Round, Graham. The Wright Group, 1986.
ISBN: 1-55624-059-7 (set, pbk.). Series: White Level Little Books, Set 1. Wordless - signs.

A clown intends his pie for a friend, but when the other clown bends down just as the pie is thrown, a sequence of mishaps is begun. Each pratfall or spill leads to another, leaving the two friends shaking with laughter. Bright circus colors decorate the comical figures.

560. Ross, Pat. **Hi Fly.** Illus.: Wallner, John C. Crown, 1974.
ISBN: 0-517-514257; LC: 73-89362. Wordless - frame.

A young girl, seeing a fly on the kitchen ceiling, imagines herself his size. She pictures the house as seen from the eyes of a tiny creature, in which the cat, a spider, and even her own father are giant dangers. The adventures of the girl and the fly are shown in unusual perspective in black-and-white line drawings.

561. Sacre, Marie-Jose. **Cat, The.** Illus.: Sacre, Marie-Jose. The Wright Group, 1986.
ISBN: 1-55624-000-7 (set, pbk.). Series: First Nature Watch, Set 1. Wordless - no print.

One tiger kitten stands out in a litter of white kittens. Adopted by a little girl, he grows up, mates, and watches over his own kittens.

562. Sacre, Marie-Jose. **Dandelion, The.** Illus.: Sacre, Marie-Jose. The Wright Group, 1986.
ISBN: 1-55624-000-7 (set, pbk.). Series: First Nature Watch. Wordless - no print.

In rounded, soft paintings, a European-looking countryside is shown through the seasons. A single dandelion blooms, surrounded by tiny insects with smiling faces. Its seeds are blown by a little girl, and the following spring the entire field is covered with dandelions.

563. Sagara, Shinjiro. **Kittens on Vacation.** Illus.: Sagara, Shinjiro. Kodansha International, 1990.
ISBN: 0-87011-696-7 (pbk.); LC: 90-4635. Almost wordless - labels.

Color photographs of kittens as they peek, sniff, and play through various countries of the world. They sit by a koala bear in Sydney and romp in the Swiss Alps.

564. Salsberg, Barbara. **Your Own Story.** Illus.: Salsberg, Barbara. Annick Press, 1977.
ISBN: 0-920236-01-4 (pbk.). Wordless - no print.

Four color lithographs use three differently shaped and colored characters to symbolize the problems and benefits of communication and cooperation, both on a personal and on a global level.

565. Saltzberg, Barney. **Yawn, The.** Illus.: Saltzberg, Barney. Atheneum, 1985.
ISBN: 0-689-31073-0; LC: 85-7950. Wordless - no print.

In simple black line drawings a boy's morning yawn is humorously passed on throughout the day. Beginning with a large shaggy dog, it is passed to progressively outrageous characters, from unusual animals to space beings. In the evening, the yawn is returned to the boy by the moon.

566. Sara. **Across Town.** Illus.: Sara. Orchard Books, 1991.
ISBN: 0-531-05932-4; 0-531-08532-5 (lib.); LC: 90-7982. Wordless - no print.

Torn tan paper on a glossy black background creates a simple and very effective story. The lonely man walking in a city at night encounters two glowing eyes in the shadows under a bridge. The man and cat approach each other in a sequence of carefully composed pages, and disappear into the dark together.

567. Sasaki, Isao. **Snow.** Illus.: Sasaki, Isao. Viking, 1982.
ISBN: 0-670-65364-0; LC: 82-2659. Wordless - no print.

In the morning, large flakes of snow fill the sky above a tiny railway station. Throughout the day, snow continues to fall, while trains come and go, passengers and packages wait on trains, and the stationmaster shovels the walks. A quiet exploration of a snowy day from a single perspective, in evocative paintings.

568. Schaaf, Peter. **Apartment House Close Up, An.** Illus.: Schaaf, Peter. Four Winds Press, 1980. ISBN: 0-590-07670-1; LC: 80-11301. Almost wordless - labels.

Small, black-and-white photographs take a tour of an apartment building showing general and specific examples for each word shown. For example, the front doorway of the building and a hall door to an apartment illustrate *doors,* and meter boxes and an electric outlet illustrate *electricity.*

569. Schick, Eleanor. **Making Friends.** Illus.: Schick, Eleanor. Macmillan, 1969.
LC: 75-78077. Wordless - signs.

As mother and young son go about the city on errands, the boy finds a variety of animals and insects. At the park, he runs to greet a little girl, and the children play while the mothers talk. Realistic pencil drawings with touches of yellow.

570. Schories, Pat. **Mouse Around.** Illus.: Schories, Pat. Farrar Straus, & Giroux, 1991.
ISBN: 0-374-35080-9; LC: 90-56156. Wordless - no print.

A drip from a leaky faucet interests a baby mouse, who falls into the plumber's pocket investigating it. The mouse's curiosity continues to lead it into adventure and exploration throughout the city until coincidence takes it home again. Large full-color pictures have small insets showing the places that mouse hides.

571. Schubert, Dieter. **Where's My Monkey?** Illus.: Schubert, Dieter. Dial, 1987.
ISBN: 0-8037-0069-5; LC: 86-16578. Wordless - no print.

A small child takes a beloved stuffed animal monkey on a bicycle outing with his mother. When a storm comes up, monkey falls and is lost. Monkey's adventures—with a family of mice, prickly hedgehog children, a thieving magpie, and underwater until hooked by a fisherman—eventually bring him back to his owner. Warm watercolors.

572. Schweninger, Ann. **Dance for Three.** Illus.: Schweninger, Ann. Dial, 1979.
ISBN: 0-8037-1629-X; 0-8037-1630-3 (lib.); LC: 78-72197. Wordless - titles.

Three magical short stories are told with softly drawn characters and simple backgrounds. In "A Dance for Three" the musician blows a horn and slowly becomes an elephant. The couple out rowing in "Don't Rock the Boat" are joined by many make-believe creatures. The animal musicians in "Moon Makers" play to create a full moon.

573. Selig, Sylvie. **Kangaroo.** Illus.: Selig, Sylvie. Jonathan Cape, 1980.
ISBN: 0-224-01746-2. Wordless - no print, Format - half pages.

A young kangaroo is carried away by an eagle while on an outing with his family. A hunter fires at the eagle, the kangaroo drops and is rescued by the hunter's family. The two families picnic together after the little one is reunited with his parents. The exotic setting is shown in color with half pages changing action.

574. Sewell, Helen. **Head for Happy, A.** Illus.: Sewell, Helen. Macmillan, 1931.
LC: 31-23356. Wordless sequence in book.

The oldest of three girls, tired of her toys, creates a life-size doll from a pillow. It needs a head, but an apple is too small and a pumpkin too big. They take a trip all the way around the world to find a coconut head at last. Stylized lithographs in black and white with minimal text between wordless sequences.

575. Shimin, Symeon. **Special Birthday, A.** Illus.: Shimin, Symeon. McGraw-Hill, 1976. ISBN: 0-07-056901-0; 0-07-056902-9 (lib.); LC: 76-14777. Wordless - no print.

While kitten watches, a father places one end of a roll of ribbon by a sleeping girl, then creates a tangle unwinding it throughout the house. When the girl wakes on her birthday, she follows the ribbon, finding her presents hidden along its path, ending in the loving arms of her father. Warm colors, realistic drawing.

576. Shore, Stephen. **Uncommon Places.** Illus.: Shore, Stephen. Aperture, 1982. ISBN: 0-89381-101-7; LC: 82-70770. Wordless - no print.

Almost all of these color photographs of very common scenes could have been taken from a car window. They dwell on the everyday and the ordinary as a passer-by might view them. The pictures view the plainness of places that will never be pictured on postcards, but which are instantly recognizable.

577. Simmons, Ellie. **Dog: A Book You Can Read Before You Know How.** Illus.: Simmons, Ellie. David McKay, 1967.
LC: 67-19908. Series: Books You Can Read before You Know How. Wordless - signs.

A child in a large hat looks at various dogs for sale before taking home a tiny, fluffy lamb-like puppy. Small detailed black line drawings show the child making the puppy at home, taking care of the puppy, worrying while the puppy goes to the vet, and taking the puppy to bed.

578. Simmons, Ellie. **Family.** Illus.: Simmons, Ellie. David McKay, 1970.
LC: 79-97806. Series: Books You Can Read before You Know How. Wordless - signs.

A family's routine through a day is shown as father goes to work while mother and daughter clean and cook. When mother goes into labor and leaves for five days, grandmother stays with the little girl. They play and prepare for the new baby. Line drawings on pink paper show a warm family with very traditional roles.

579. Simmons, Ellie. **Wheels.** Illus.: Simmons, Ellie. David McKay, 1969.
LC: 69-13785. Series: Books You Can Read before You Know How. Wordless - signs.

A boy and his father attend a fair at which they ride on a train and view many wheeled vehicles. At home the boy wants his own transportation and tries to make one in various ways. A sulky trip to the grocery store includes a surprise visit to a bike shop and a tricycle. Warm drawings in brown line on tan paper.

580. Simpson, Kate. **All Dressed Up.** Illus.: Simpson, Kate. The Wright Group, 1987. ISBN: 1-55624-495-9 (pbk.); 1-55624-257-3 (set). Series: More and More. Wordless - no print.

While a father dresses one twin, the big sister dresses the other. Her twin ends up with plastic pants on his head and clothing all awry. A very pink and strawberry blonde family, drawn with exaggeration against a plain white background.

581. Sis, Peter. **Beach Ball.** Illus.: Sis, Peter. Greenwillow, 1990.
ISBN: 0-688-09181-4; 0-688-09182-2 (lib.); LC: 89-2076. Almost wordless -
labels.

The beach is crowded with details for the reader to observe as Mary chases her wind-blown ball from page to page. Counting, finding shapes and opposites, naming animals, hunting objects from A to Z, and finding a way through a maze provide the pretext for the minutely fashioned full-color drawings.

582. Smith, Buckley. **Moonsailors.** Illus.: Smith, Buckley. Green Tiger Press, 1985.
ISBN: 0-88138-039-3 (pbk.); LC: 85-70301. Wordless - no print.

Charcoal sketches on gray background with pale blue chalk touches create a mysterious nighttime world. An old sailor is seen with his pipe. As he puffs, a small sailing ship floats off on the smoke and into the night sky, tacking around the moon, and casting a fishing net which becomes a quilt on a child's bed.

583. Snyder, Agnes. **Old Man on Our Block, The.** Illus.: Lynch, Donald. Holt,
Rinehart and Winston, 1964.
LC: 64-12022. Wordless - no print.

A serene old man befriends neighborhood children, telling them stories and accompanying them on various trips to the docks, the park, and the museum. A mutually satisfying relationship is shown in full-color paintings.

584. Spier, Peter. **Crash! Bang! Boom! A Book of Sounds.** Illus.: Spier, Peter.
Doubleday, 1972.
ISBN: 0-385-26569-7 (board). Almost wordless - sounds, Format - board
pages.

Each page is crowded with related noisemakers to identify. In the kitchen, sounds of kettles whistling and eggs cooking mingle with a dish breaking and water gurgling out the drain. School and play scenes, traffic and construction scenes, even the instruments of the orchestra and a marching band fill the busy pages.

585. Spier, Peter. **Dreams.** Illus.: Spier, Peter. Doubleday, 1986.
ISBN: 0-385-19336-X; 0-385-19337-8 (lib.); LC: 85-13130. Wordless - frame.

A boy and girl lie back on a grassy meadow watching the sky. Vague cloud masses on one page become elaborate cloud pictures on the next as the children transform the sky with their imagination. Birds, insects, aircraft, and hot-air balloons can be seen in the airy sky. Softly colored illustrations invite day-dreaming.

586. Spier, Peter. **Fast-Slow High-Low.** Illus.: Spier, Peter. Doubleday, 1972.
ISBN: 0-385-06781-X; 0-385-02876-8 (lib.); LC: 72-76207. Almost wordless -
labels.

A pair of words in a box with an illustration showing the meaning of the pair appears on pages busy with various ways in which those opposites might be used. For example, *on - off* includes the ideas of clothes on and off, a light turned on or off, a bird on and off a nest and so on, in small but detailed color sketches.

587. Spier, Peter. **Gobble Growl Grunt: A Book of Animal Sounds.** Illus.: Spier, Peter. Doubleday, 1988.
   ISBN: 0-385-24094-5 (board). Almost wordless - sounds, Format - board pages.
   Animals of all types are drawn in fine line and realistically watercolored. Each double page spread is crowded with animals grouped by type or habitat, with humorous surprises to find on each page. The noises made by each animal are represented in print.

588. Spier, Peter. **Noah's Ark.** Illus.: Spier, Peter. Doubleday, 1977.
   ISBN: 0-385-09473-6; 0-035-12730-8 (lib.); LC: 76-43630. Wordless - frame.
   This richly detailed pen and watercolor portrayal of the biblical story of Noah's ark includes a one-page translation of a Dutch poem, "The Flood," by Jacobus Revius. The traditional story of the great flood is enriched with humor and insight.

589. Spier, Peter. **Peter Spier's Christmas.** Illus.: Spier, Peter. Doubleday, 1983.
   ISBN: 0-385-13183-6; 0-385-13184-4 (lib.); LC: 80-2875. Wordless - signs.
   Colorful, realistic watercolor drawings illustrate a family's Christmas preparations. Each step is detailed, from the withdrawal of savings club money, through shopping, decorating, and Christmas dinner. The aftermath, returning presents and starting a new Christmas club account, completes the season's activities.

590. Spier, Peter. **Peter Spier's Rain.** Illus.: Spier, Peter. Doubleday, 1982.
   ISBN: 0-385-15484-4; 0-385-15485-2 (lib.); 0-385-24105-4 (pbk.); LC: 81-43056. Wordless - no print.
   As storm clouds gather, a brother and sister play outside, then explore the myriad aspects of a rainy day. Wet weather activities outside, followed by a warm bath and cozy indoor activities are shown in detailed watercolor drawings. The passage of the storm during the night is especially effective.

591. Steiner, Charlotte. **I Am Andy: You-Tell-a-Story Book.** Illus.: Steiner, Charlotte. Alfred A. Knopf, 1960.
   LC: 61-6055. Wordless - titles.
   Thirteen short stories presented in numbered frames tell simple adventures of a young boy. Included are episodes about Easter, Washington's Birthday, Halloween, Thanksgiving and Christmas, some of which appeared earlier in *Humpty-Dumpty Magazine.* Black line cartoons with yellow or blue color.

592. Stevenson, James. **Grandpa's Great City Tour.** Illus.: Stevenson, James. Greenwillow, 1983.
   ISBN: 0-688-02323-1; 0-688-02324-X (lib.); LC: 83-1459. Wordless - signs.
   Grandpa takes his two grandchildren on a tour of a city in which they explore some extremely odd scenes. Two-page watercolor illustrations create an alphabetically arranged story sequence crowded with unusual animals and objects starting with each letter.

593. Stobbs, Joanna, and William Stobbs. **One Sun, Two Eyes, and a Million Stars.** Illus.: Stobbs, Joanna, and William Stobbs. Oxford, 1981. ISBN: 0-19-279747-6; LC: 80-41872. Almost wordless - labels.

A farm child plays all day in orchard and pasture, until the one sun sets and she runs home to bed with a million stars outside her window. Each scene includes groups of objects to count from one to twenty. Full-color illustration is textured, as if seen through a screen.

594. Stobbs, William. **Animal Pictures.** Illus.: Stobbs, William. The Bodley Head, 1981. ISBN: 0-370-30341-5. Wordless - no print.

Two page spreads of animals in a naturalistic habitat are shown in soft colors. Both common and uncommon animals are included: zebras as well as rabbits, elephants as well as ponies. Predators (including man) are shown in some of the realistic drawings.

595. Stoddard, Darrell. **Hero, The.** Illus.: Reese, Bob. Aro Publishing, 1974. Series: I Can Read Underwater. Wordless - signs.

Searching for success, a small boy seeks to become a hero at various sports. Saddened by his continued failure, he is walking past a river when he sees someone drowning. His rescue attempt makes him a real hero. Blocky black line drawings show his efforts.

596. Sugano, Yoshikatsu. **Kitten's Adventure, The.** Illus.: Sugano, Yoshikatsu. McGraw-Hill, 1971. LC: 78-99205. Wordless - no print.

Clear, uncluttered color photographs show a silvery white Persian kitten investigating a large red cylinder of paper. After turning over the tube of paper, the kitten crawls inside, then stands on the unrolled sheets. The plain background enhances the deep red color and contrasts with the kitten's fluffiness.

597. Sugita, Yutaka. **My Friend Little John and Me.** Illus.: Sugita, Yutaka. McGraw-Hill, 1973. ISBN: 0-07-062458-5; LC: 72-8799. Wordless - no print.

A huge dog patiently puts up with the activities of his small master. As the small child plays, the dog becomes part of each pretend situation. The two eat, bathe, and sleep together, and the child even has a pull-toy that is the image of the giant dog. The gentle dog and cheerful child are shown in double-page watercolors.

598. Tafuri, Nancy. **All Year Long.** Illus.: Tafuri, Nancy. Greenwillow, 1983. ISBN: 0-688-01414-3; 0-688-01416-X (lib.); LC: 82-9275. Almost wordless - labels.

Combining the days of the week with the months of the year, each picture shows a child engaged in an appropriate activity for a "Sunday in January" through "Saturday in December." The use of space and foreground make the simple outline pictures visually challenging. Each conceals objects to count from one to twelve.

599. Tafuri, Nancy. **Do Not Disturb.** Illus.: Tafuri, Nancy. Greenwillow, 1987.
ISBN: 0-688-06541-4; 0-688-06542-2 (lib.); LC: 86-357. Almost wordless - sounds.

"It was the first day of summer..." as a family backpacks into a wooded area and sets up camp. The inhabitants of the woods and pond are disturbed by the activities of the people and their dog, but when night falls, the animals create so much noise that the family cannot sleep. Dramatically designed pictures in full color.

600. Tafuri, Nancy. **Early Morning in the Barn.** Illus.: Tafuri, Nancy. Greenwillow, 1983.
ISBN: 0-688-02328-2; 0-688-02329-0 (lib.); LC: 83-1436. Almost wordless - sounds.

Large, bright, two-page pictures illustrate an early morning farm yard from a chick's eye perspective. Rooster crows as the sun rises, and each waking animal makes its own sound as the chicks scurry past. The words for each sound are printed by the animal making the sound.

601. Tafuri, Nancy. **Follow Me!** Illus.: Tafuri, Nancy. Greenwillow, 1990.
ISBN: 0-688-08773-6; 0-688-08774-4 (lib.); LC: 89-23259. Wordless - no print.

A wakeful baby sea lion sees a red crab scuttling past and begins to follow it. Over rocks and past the flora and fauna of the coast, the curious baby follows until the bright red crab is lost in a whole colony of crabs. The watchful mother urges baby back to rejoin other young sea lions.

602. Tafuri, Nancy. **Have You Seen My Duckling?** Illus.: Tafuri, Nancy. Greenwillow, 1984.
ISBN: 0-688-02797-0; 0-688-02798-9 (lib.); LC: 83-17196. Almost wordless - dialog.

"Early one morning..." one duckling chases a butterfly and leaves the nest. When mother returns to find one missing, she takes the rest of the brood around the pond to query each of the animals "Have you seen my duckling?" The missing duckling can be seen in each picture concealed in the background.

603. Tafuri, Nancy. **Junglewalk.** Illus.: Tafuri, Nancy. Greenwillow, 1988.
ISBN: 0-688-07182-1; 0-688-07183-X (Lib.); LC: 87-8558. Wordless - no print.

After reading a book on jungles, a boy falls asleep and his dream self follows his cat out the window and into a jungle. The cat is transformed into a tiger and prowls a colorful, animal-filled world until morning. Brilliant color and bold design bring the nighttime world to life.

604. Tafuri, Nancy. **Rabbit's Morning.** Illus.: Tafuri, Nancy. Greenwillow, 1985.
ISBN: 0-688-04063-2; 0-688-04064-0 (lib.); LC: 84-10229. Wordless - frame.

A small rabbit explores a springtime meadow, seeing a variety of animals and their young before returning home. Illustration uses black outline filled with watercolor to delineate the habitat and inhabitants.

605. Tafuri, Nancy. **Who's Counting?** Illus.: Tafuri, Nancy. Greenwillow, 1986. ISBN: 0-688-06130-3; 0-688-06131-1 (lib.); LC: 85-17702. Almost wordless - labels.

The pudgy brown puppy is only partially seen in each picture, while the animal or thing being counted is in the foreground. For example, six pink piglets sleep in the mud, while puppy hangs over the fence in the background watching them. When ten puppies race to be fed, the counting puppy carries a flower in his mouth.

606. Tanaka, Hideyuki. **Happy Dog, The.** Illus.: Tanaka, Hideyuki. Atheneum, 1983. ISBN: 0-689-50259-1; LC: 82-72248. Wordless - titles.

A shaggy white dog stars in three stories. While playing baseball, the ball dirties laundry hung out to dry, and the little dog only makes matters worse trying to clean the spot. On a rainy day, the dog cheerfully splashes in puddles. In the final story, he plays with a large red balloon. Drawings with color follow the action.

607. Tharlet, Eve. **Crocodile, The.** Illus.: Tharlet, Eve. The Wright Group, 1986. ISBN: 1-55624-000-7 (set, pbk.). Series: First Nature Watch, Set 1. Wordless - no print.

Slightly whimsical, stylized illustrations show crocodiles eying each other, holding paws, and the female laying eggs. The hatchlings are greeted by both parents as the young ones join them in the water.

608. Tolstoy, A., adaptor; tr. by Zheleznova, Irina. **Emelya and the Pike.** Illus.: Barsukov, A. Malysh Publishers, 1985. Wordless - no print, Format - pop-up.

A lively pop-up version of a traditional Russian folktale which is similar to the Grimms' "Fisherman and His Wife." A retelling of the tale is followed by the wordless pop-up sequence showing Emelya's rise in fortune after tossing the talking pike back into the ice-covered river.

609. Turk, Hanne. **Bon Appetit Max.** Illus.: Turk, Hanne. Neugebauer Press, 1986. ISBN: 0-907234-88-7 (pbk.). Series: Max the Mouse, #18. Wordless - no print.

Max is cooking a soup in a small blue pot, chopping vegetables, tasting, adding seasoning—but he adds too much seasoning. Amusing watercolors illustrate the dilemma of the cook trying to make things come out right by adding more of this and more of that. Max ends up making a huge amount of tasty soup.

610. Turk, Hanne. **Butterfly Max.** Illus.: Turk, Hanne. Neugebauer Press, 1984. ISBN: 0-907234-63-1. Series: Max the Mouse. Wordless - no print.

Max makes a butterfly net and goes out to catch butterflies. Each swipe brings disaster—a rip in the net, a bent rim, a broken handle—and no butterflies. When he abandons the net and lies down in the grass, brightly colored butterflies come to float around him, and one lands on his nose.

611. Turk, Hanne. **Chocolate Max.** Illus.: Turk, Hanne. Neugebauer Press, 1985. ISBN: 0-907234-86-0. Series: Max the Mouse. Wordless - signs.

Max buys and eats a whole bag of chocolate, which results in a terrible toothache. He tries to cope in various ways, but at last he must go to the dentist. On his way home, Max buys cheese and passes up the candy store. Gentle watercolors with minimal background show the plight of the little mouse.

612. Turk, Hanne. **Friendship Max.** Illus.: Turk, Hanne. Neugebauer Press, 1985. ISBN: 0-907234-65-8. Series: Max the Mouse. Wordless - no print.

Max works hard building a boat to make his dreams of an island adventure come true. When the boat is finished, Max launches off to sea, but his sad tiger cat toy is left behind on the beach. Max returns for the cat, while his brand new boat sails off without him.

613. Turk, Hanne. **Fright for Max, A.** Illus.: Turk, Hanne. Neugebauer Press, 1986. ISBN: 0-887080-35-9. Series: Max the Mouse. Wordless - no print.

The dark is scary for Max, and he can't sleep—especially when he sees a monstrous shadow on the wall. Shades of blue and gray in soft washes establish the mood of nighttime fear. Max's fears are finally banished when the light comes on and shows him what was making the shadow.

614. Turk, Hanne. **Good Sport Max.** Illus.: Turk, Hanne. Neugebauer Press, 1984. ISBN: 0-907234-64-1. Series: Max the Mouse. Wordless - no print.

Max finds an ad in the newspaper about muscle building and visits a gym to try it out. His feet won't reach the pedals on the bike, and he isn't big or strong enough for any of the other things he tries. When he leaves, tossing the newspaper in the trash, he turns somersaults in the grass.

615. Turk, Hanne. **Goodnight Max.** Illus.: Turk, Hanne. Neugebauer Press, 1983. ISBN: 090723439-9. Series: Max the Mouse. Wordless - no print.

Max carefully checks the time, then goes to watch television, plumping up his pillows for comfort. He laughs and responds as he watches, but when he walks up to the set, he finds that his special cat pull-toy has been sitting in an empty television case entertaining him and he carries the toy off to bed.

616. Turk, Hanne. **Happy Birthday, Max.** Illus.: Turk, Hanne. Neugebauer Press, 1984. ISBN: 0-907234-42-2. Series: Max the Mouse. Wordless - symbols.

After anticipating his birthday, Max is disappointed when the day arrives and it seems no one has remembered him. Max brings home a cake and celebrates by himself. His eating is happily interrupted when the phone rings and flowers arrive at the door, showing that he has not been forgotten. Subtle watercolors.

617. Turk, Hanne. **Lesson for Max, A.** Illus.: Turk, Hanne. Neugebauer Press, 1983.
      ISBN: 090723423-2. Series: Max the Mouse. Wordless - no print.

Max the mouse sneaks to the cigarette machine to buy a pack of cigarettes. At home he lights one, posing in front of a mirror, but rapidly becomes nauseated. He tries to rest, and finally feels better after eating all the carrots in the refrigerator.

618. Turk, Hanne. **Max Packs.** Illus.: Turk, Hanne. Neugebauer Press, 1984.
      ISBN: 0-907234-40-2 (pbk.). Series: Max the Mouse. Wordless - no print.

A mouse tail trails out of a suitcase on the title page, and Max the mouse climbs out and begins to pack. He tosses all manner of summer vacation paraphernalia in and ties onto the crammed case pillows and pails that wouldn't fit in. However, when it's time to go, Max runs happily off with only his hat and toy cat.

619. Turk, Hanne. **Max the Artlover.** Illus.: Turk, Hanne. Neugebauer Press, 1983.
      ISBN: 0-907234-25-9 (pbk.). Series: Max the Mouse. Wordless - signs.

Max the mouse rests in the middle of his living room, which is decorated with various modern art pieces. In search of a new item for his collection, he examines all the works in a gallery until he finds the perfect painting—a realistic portrait of cheeses. Light watercolors convey the humor of Max's reaction to art.

620. Turk, Hanne. **Max Versus the Cube.** Illus.: Turk, Hanne. Neugebauer Press, 1982.
      ISBN: 0-907234-19-4 (pbk.). Series: Max the Mouse. Wordless - no print.

Max has a puzzle cube and begins to turn the sides. He works and works, but cannot get the colors to line up again on each side. Throwing and pounding the cube produce no results, so inventive Max gets out paint and colors the sides of the cube. Max and the cube appear in watercolor against a white background.

621. Turk, Hanne. **Merry Christmas, Max.** Illus.: Turk, Hanne. Neugebauer Press, 1983.
      ISBN: 090723437-2. Series: Max the Mouse. Wordless - no print.

Max the mouse gathers utensils and ingredients, mixing up a bowl of batter and rolling out star-shaped cookies. He falls asleep while they cook and awakes to a smoky room and burnt cookies. Tearfully he answers the doorbell—and finds a surprise package full of Christmas cookies. Minimal watercolor on white background.

622. Turk, Hanne. **Rainy Day Max.** Illus.: Turk, Hanne. Neugebauer Press, 1983.
      ISBN: 0-907234-24-0 (pbk.). Series: Max the Mouse. Wordless - no print.

Max and his little cat pull-toy walk in and out of showers on a spring day. Although Max has his large blue umbrella along, each time it rains, something prevents his umbrella from keeping him dry. When the umbrella is finally carried away by the wind, Max and the cat enjoy jumping into puddles.

623. Turk, Hanne. **Raking Leaves with Max.** Illus.: Turk, Hanne. Neugebauer Press, 1983. ISBN: 0-907234-8-0. Series: Max the Mouse. Wordless - no print.

Max the mouse takes a basket to rake autumn leaves, assisted by his cat pull-toy. When he bends over to pick up the last leaf, all the leaves spill, and he tosses them around before packing up his basket again. Simple watercolor illustrations with white backgrounds and fall hues.

624. Turk, Hanne. **Robinson Max.** Illus.: Turk, Hanne. Neugebauer Press, 1985. ISBN: 0-907234-87-9. Series: Max the Mouse. Wordless - signs.

As Max the mouse reads *Robinson Crusoe,* he imagines himself in the story with his faithful toy cat. Max is pictured as a reader cuddled on his pillow and emotionally responding to the story; the shipwreck adventure is shown as his thoughts. Eloquent watercolors with a minimum of detail carry the double story.

625. Turk, Hanne. **Rope Skips Max, The.** Illus.: Turk, Hanne. Neugebauer Press, 1982. ISBN: 0-907234-20-8 (pbk.). Series: Max the Mouse. Wordless - no print.

Max has a jumping rope with red handles but he cannot master skipping. The rope catches on his feet, breaks in two, and snaps against his chin. Max finally goes off hopping and twirling the rope by one handle at his side. Simple but expressive watercolor pictures with white background.

626. Turk, Hanne. **Snapshot Max.** Illus.: Turk, Hanne. Neugebauer Press, 1984. ISBN: 0-907234-41-2 (pbk.). Series: Max the Mouse. Wordless - no print.

Max prepares to take his own picture at the beach, posing in front of the camera in his big hat, with his toy cat, with a starfish on his chest, in sunglasses, and with his inflated tube. The camera has only caught a small part of each picture, and the final page shows the funny results.

627. Turk, Hanne. **Surprise for Max, A.** Illus.: Turk, Hanne. Neugebauer Press, 1982. ISBN: 0-907234-18-6. Series: Max the Mouse. Wordless - no print.

Max, a plump gray mouse, is surprised to see a large present for him. Simple watercolors show his problems in unwrapping the gift and his joy at finding a cat pull-toy inside.

628. Turkle, Brinton. **Deep in the Forest.** Illus.: Turkle, Brinton. Dutton, 1976. ISBN: 0-525-28617-9; LC: 76-21691. Wordless - signs.

In this reversal of the story of the three bears, a curious bear cub explores a cabin belonging to a frontier family. His destruction of the baby's bowl and chair, then hiding under the baby's quilt parallel Goldilocks' adventures. Charcoal sketches with gray and tan washes create a realistic deep woods setting.

629. Ueno, Noriko. **Elephant Buttons.** Illus.: Ueno, Noriko. Harper and Row, 1973. ISBN: 06-026160-9; 06-026161-7 (lib.); LC: 72-10264. Wordless - no print.

Whimsical, shaded sketches show a sequence of unbuttonings. The elephant has four buttons on its belly. On the next page, the buttons have been undone, and a horse climbs out—also equipped with buttons. Each animal in turn reveals a smaller animal inside, until a mouse unbuttons and the original elephant climbs out.

630. Ungerer, Tomi. **One, Two, Where's My Shoe?** Illus.: Ungerer, Tomi. Harper and Row, 1964. LC: 64-12811. Wordless - frame.

A boy pointing at his shoeless foot recites "one, two, where's my shoe?" while the shoe has become part of the form of the head of his dog. In each picture, shoes and boots are hidden in the shapes of each object, until on the last page the boy finds his shoe "three, four, on the floor."

631. Ungerer, Tomi. **Snail, Where Are You?** Illus.: Ungerer, Tomi. Harper and Row, 1962. LC: 62-7946. Wordless - frame.

The shape of a snail's shell is found as part of each picture: in the curled body of a horn, in the repeated curls of waves, and in the curled tail of a pig. Finally the curves are seen in the *S* of "Snail, where are you?," and the snail appears, saying "Here I am." Blocky forms with bold black line and dark colors.

632. Valeri, M. Eulalia, reteller; tr. by Leland Northam. **Pied Piper of Hamelin, The.** Illus.: Rius, Maria. Silver-Burdett, 1985.
ISBN: 0-382-09070-5; LC: 84-52785. Series: Tell Me a Story. Wordless - no print.

This German folktale tells of the magical piper who rid the town of Hamelin of a plague of rats. When the ungrateful townspeople refused the promised payment, he piped to enchant the children and led them away. The warm watercolors place the town and the burghers in the Middle Ages.

633. Van Allsburg, Chris. **Ben's Dream.** Illus.: Van Allsburg, Chris. Houghton Mifflin, 1982.
ISBN: 0-395-32084-4; LC: 81-20029. Wordless sequence in book.

While studying for a geography test, Ben falls asleep listening to the rain. In a wordless sequence he dreams of traveling among the landmarks of the world, all submerged in the flood carrying him along. When he wakes, his friend has had the same dream. The intricate black-and-white prints present unusual views of scenes.

634. Van den Berghe, Chantal. **Hamster, The.** Illus.: Van den Berghe, Chantal. The Wright Group, 1986.
ISBN: 1-55624-067-8 (set, pbk.). Series: First Nature Watch. Wordless - no print.

The European hamster emerges from an underground burrow in early spring, and is seen through summer and fall raising young and collecting food. When winter comes, the hamsters retreat to their well-stocked underground home. The solemn colors of the painting echo the nocturnal life of the hamster.

635. van der Meer, Ron, and Atie van der Meer. **What's Missing?** Illus.: van der Meer, Ron, and Atie van der Meer. Franklin Watts, 1983.
ISBN: 531-03583-2 (board). Series: Surprise Series. Wordless - no print, Format - accordion fold; board pages.

The simple object shown on the first side of each page is missing a part. The object lifts up to show the whole object underneath. The reverse of the page shows the object in use with a little girl.

636. Van Soelen, Philip. **Cricket in the Grass and Other Stories.** Illus.: Van Soelen, Philip. Sierra Club Books, 1979.
ISBN: 0-684-16110-9; LC: 79-4108. Wordless - titles.

The five wordless sections of the book present natural stories based on close observation of relationships between plants and animals in a watershed. The title story begins with a tiny animal in the grass which is eaten by a larger one, who is in turn eaten. Black line sketches. Informational notes in back.

637.   Venus, Pamela. **I Had Measles.** Illus.: Venus, Pamela. The Wright Group, 1987.
        ISBN: 1-55624-456-8 (pbk.); 1-55624-251-4 (set). Series: This Weekend.
        Wordless - no print.

A sick child's weekend begins when she wakes up crying and her mother discovers red splotches all over her. Soft colors show the family from *We Got a Puppy* coping with illness.

638.   Venus, Pamela. **We Got a Puppy.** Illus.: Venus, Pamela. The Wright Group, 1987.
        ISBN: 1-55624-457-6 (pbk.); 1-55624-251-4 (set). Series: This Weekend.
        Wordless - signs.

Two children and their mother go to pick out a new puppy from a litter of dachshunds. The soft colors and details of pencil illustrations show their selection of a new pet and the puppy eating, sleeping, and playing in its new home.

639.   Vincent, Gabrielle. **Breakfast Time, Ernest and Celestine.** Illus.: Vincent,
        Gabrielle. Greenwillow, 1985.
        ISBN: 0-688-04555-3; LC: 84-25899. Wordless - no print.

Ernest the bear wakes the little mouse Celestine for breakfast. She doesn't want any, pushes it away, and breaks her bowl. She is sorry and insists on cleaning up the mess by herself before accepting another bowl. Soft watercolors show a respectful relationship between characters.

640.   Vincent, Gabrielle. **Ernest and Celestine's Patchwork Quilt.** Illus.: Vincent,
        Gabrielle. Greenwillow, 1985.
        ISBN: 0-688-04557-X; LC: 84-25891. Wordless - no print.

Ernest, a large bear, and Celestine, a small mouse, make a quilt for his bed from fabric samples. But one quilt is not enough — Celestine looks at her plain bed and wants one too. The two make another quilt, and the little mouse falls asleep cuddled under it. Delicate watercolors show the caring of each for the other.

641.   von Fischer, Sibylle. **Wild Duck, The.** Illus.: von Fischer, Sibylle. The Wright
        Group, 1986.
        ISBN: 1-55624-000-7 (set, pbk.). Series: First Nature Watch. Wordless - no print.

Soft pencil illustration shows a pond and children around it throughout the seasons. Close-up pictures show the life of the ducks on the pond: nesting, raising young, leaving the pond in winter, and returning to it in the spring.

642.   Vreuls, Diane. **Sums: A Looking Game.** Illus.: Vreuls, Diane. Viking, 1977.
        ISBN: 0-670-68325-6 (lib.); LC: 76-58012. Wordless - no print.

In these visual puzzles, parts of common objects are shown as addition problems. When the page is turned the whole object is shown as the "sum" or answer to the problem. For example, circle plus hand plus circle plus hand plus circle equals two hands juggling.

643. Ward, Lynd. **God's Man: A Novel in Woodcuts.** Illus.: Ward, Lynd. Jonathan Cape and Harrison Smith, 1929. Wordless - titles.

An adult novel in five parts told entirely in dramatic woodcuts contains the story of an impoverished artist who gives way to temptation. His bargain with a dark stranger gains him money, fame, and a mistress. When he finally finds happiness, however, a harsh payment is due. 409 copies were originally printed.

644. Ward, Lynd. **Madman's Drum: A Novel in Woodcuts.** Illus.: Ward, Lynd. Jonathan Cape and Harrison Smith, 1930. Wordless - no print.

In a distant time and place, the protagonist is involved in the slave trade and kills for a native drum which influences him throughout the book. As the story unfolds, universal themes become apparent along with the broad implications of social systems and individual behavior. Dramatic woodblock prints.

645. Ward, Lynd. **Silver Pony, The.** Illus.: Ward, Lynd. Houghton Mifflin, 1973. ISBN: 0-395-14753-0; LC: 72-5402. Wordless - no print.

A lonely Midwestern farm boy unexpectedly meets a winged horse. On its back, he explores the world beyond his farm, seeing lifestyles across the United States. He rescues flood victims and a lost lamb. Eighty realistic gray and white illustrations are divided into chapters showing fantasy adventures and farm reality.

646. Ward, Lynd. **Wild Pilgrimage.** Illus.: Ward, Lynd. Harrison Smith and Robert Haas, 1932. Wordless - no print.

The protagonist attempts to escape ills of an industrial environment by going to the country where he witnesses racial injustice and encounters hard work, hunger, and loneliness. Returning to the factory town, he becomes involved in a riot and meets his death. External and internal worlds are shown with alternating black and red block prints.

647. Ward, Nick. **Bag of Tricks, A.** Illus.: Ward, Nick. Oxford, 1984. ISBN: 0-19-272143-7 (pbk.). Series: Cat on the Mat Books. Wordless - signs.

A mysterious handbag marked 'do not touch' has been left on a bench in the park. A schoolboy in shorts and tie pulls out a toy bear, a birthday cake, and a banana, followed by a fierce gorilla that pulls the boy into the satchel. A small final picture shows a hand picking up the closed bag.

648. Ward, Nick. **Surprise Present, The.** Illus.: Ward, Nick. Oxford, 1984. ISBN: 0-19-272142-9. (pbk.). Series: Cat on the Mat Books. Wordless - no print.

When an older brother finds a real magic wand in a surprise package, he uses it to turn the baby into a giant, then into a great pink elephant baby. When he changes baby to a dragon, baby grabs the wand and restores himself, making the older brother disappear.

649. Ward, Sally G. **Charlie and Grandma.** Illus.: Ward, Sally G. Scholastic, 1986. ISBN: 0-590-33954-0. Wordless sequence in book.

While grandma hangs up clothes, hungry Charlie goes inside. He piles objects on a chair to reach the fruit basket and loses his balance. Grandma rushes in, trips, and falls on the mess inside. Happily no one is hurt, and they share the bright red apple. Outline drawings show a loving relationship.

650. Ward, Sally G. **Molly and Grandpa.** Illus.: Ward, Sally G. Scholastic, 1986. ISBN: 0-590-33955-9. Wordless sequence in book.

Molly wants to bake and helps grandpa get the cookbooks. While he finds a recipe, she starts adding ingredients to a bowl of blueberries. Her muffins are ready to bake when grandpa wakes from his nap over the cookbooks and the kitchen is ready to be cleaned. Humorous line drawings with blue color for the berries.

651. Watson, Aldren A. **River, The.** Illus.: Watson, Aldren A. Holt, Rinehart and Winston, 1963. LC: 63-9572. Wordless - no print.

From its beginning in snow-covered mountains, a river flows gently to the sea. It provides a home for wildlife, recreation for children, water for farm animals, industrial energy, and is finally a busy waterway crowded with barges and ships. Black line and watercolor show the changes man creates in the river's peace.

652. Watson, Aldren A. **Town Mouse Country Mouse: A Book of Story Pictures.** Illus.: Watson, Aldren A. Holt, Rinehart and Winston, 1966. ISBN: 03-085811-9; LC: 66-28668. Wordless - titles.

Mice engaged in many activities are featured in scenes of country and city life. Shopping at the supermarket or at the country store, playing on a city street or down a country lane, each busy scene features multiple activities and mini stories. Outline and watercolor pictures in subdued colors have an old-fashioned air.

653. Wattenberg, Jane. **Mrs. Mustard's Baby Faces.** Illus.: Wattenberg, Jane. Chronicle Books, 1990. ISBN: 0-87701-659-3 (board). Wordless - no print, Format - board pages; accordion fold.

Each of the baby faces in this accordion-fold baby book is shown twice—once happy and smiling and once sad and crying. Color photographs show a multi-ethnic group of babies.

654. Wattenberg, Jane. **Mrs. Mustard's Beastly Babies.** Illus.: Wattenberg, Jane. Chronicle Books, 1990. ISBN: 0-87701-683-6; board pages. Wordless - no print, Format - accordion fold; board pages.

Babies from a variety of ethnic groups are making faces in each color photograph. Paired with the baby's face is a photograph of an animal making a similar face. For example, the tiger is shown with its tongue out next to a picture of a boy with his tongue out.

655. Webber, Helen. **What Is Sour? What Is Sweet?** Illus.: Webber, Helen. Holt, Rinehart and Winston, 1967.
ISBN: 03-085778-3; LC: 66-10192. Wordless - no print.

Large full-page prints in dull colors illustrate opposite concepts. Fast and slow, winter and summer, quiet and active, and inside and outside are examples of the attributes pictured. In addition to antonyms, other commonly paired words such as *cat* and *dog* are illustrated.

656. Wegen, Ron. **Balloon Trip.** Illus.: Wegen, Ron. Clarion Books, 1981.
ISBN: 0-395-30370-2; LC: 80-25902. Wordless - signs.

A father and two children lift off in a hot-air balloon. As the balloon ascends, a dizzying perspective shows other balloons following. They travel over New York City, viewing the harbor and Statue of Liberty, then cross an early autumn countryside before landing just ahead of a storm. Pictures look like colored photos.

657. Weiss, Nicki. **Dog Boy Cap Skate.** Illus.: Weiss, Nicki. Greenwillow, 1989.
ISBN: 0-688-08275-0; 0-688-08276-9 (lib.); LC: 88-16390. Almost wordless - labels.

A boy takes his dog to a frozen pond in the park to meet friends and try ice skating. Four words per page identify objects or actions and provide a rhyming chant to accompany the pictured story. Full-color gouache paintings illustrate the challenges of the sport.

658. Weiss, Nicki. **Sun Sand Sea Sail.** Illus.: Weiss, Nicki. Greenwillow, 1989.
ISBN: 0-688-08270-X; 0-688-0271-8 (lib.); LC: 88-16391. Almost wordless - labels.

Pastel colors set the tone for a warm and loving family outing as two children and their parents prepare for a day at the beach. While the illustrations tell the story of their day, single words appear on each page labeling objects which can be found in the picture (*Crab Gull Ant Fish*).

659. Wetherbee, Holden. **Wonder Ring, The.** Illus.: Wetherbee, Holden. Doubleday, 1978.
ISBN: 0-385-13262-X (pbk.); 0-385-13263-8 (lib.); LC: 77-16955. Wordless - no print.

Intricate hand-cut silhouettes tell a fairytale-like story. The poor lad is scolded for not chopping enough wood, his faithful dog is put outside, and he is sent to bed. There he dreams of leaving home, slaying a giant, and wedding a princess, all with the help of a magic ring.

660. Wezel, Peter. **Good Bird, The.** Illus.: Wezel, Peter. Harper and Row, 1964.
LC: 66-1491. Wordless - no print.

A bird flying by a house sees a fish inside in a bowl. The fish is fearful when the bird sits near the bowl, but the bird flies out to get a worm to share with the fish. The two unlikely companions fall asleep happily facing each other. Simple forms and large areas of color are used in the crayon drawings.

661.   Wezel, Peter. **Naughty Bird, The.** Illus.: Wezel, Peter. Follett, 1967.
       LC: 67-17801. Wordless - no print.

Large crayon illustrations use simple outlines to show the story of a white bird that disrupts a peaceful afternoon. The bird escapes from its cage, teases the family, lures the cat into rousing the dog, and enjoys the resultant chase. The cat ends up in the cage while the naughty bird stands on top of it.

662.   Wiesner, David. **Free Fall.** Illus.: Wiesner, David. Lothrop Lee and Shepard, 1988.
       ISBN: 0-688-05583-4; 0-688-05584-2 (lib.); LC: 87-22834. Wordless - no print.

A boy falls asleep holding a book, and as he dreams, the images from his room flow into a surrealistic sequence of adventure and imagination. A map and quilt transform throughout as characters from literature and folklore move in and out of the dream. The elaborate full-color paintings are appropriately dream-like.

663.   Wiesner, David. **Tuesday.** Illus.: Wiesner, David. Clarion Books, 1991.
       ISBN: 0-395-55113-7; LC: 90-39358. Wordless - titles.

As the full moon rises above a bog on a Tuesday evening around 8:00, the pond's frogs take off on their lily pads, zooming above the town, astonishing birds and a dog and enjoying the freedom of flight. The mysterious fantasy ends with dawn, but one is left anticipating "next Tuesday." Whimsical watercolors.

664.   Wijngaard, Juan. **Bear.** Illus.: Wijngaard, Juan. Crown, 1990.
       ISBN: 0-517-58201-5 (board); LC: 90-81897. Series: Baby Animal Board
       Books. Almost wordless - labels, Format - board pages.

Each two-page spread tells a simple cause-and-effect story which features a bear cub. One word per page identifies an element of the sequence; for example, the word *water* appears with bear looking at a ball floating in a tub, then in the tub splashing both ball and water. Color drawings with white background.

665.   Wijngaard, Juan. **Cat.** Illus.: Wijngaard, Juan. Crown, 1990.
       ISBN: 0-517-58202-3 (board); LC: 90-81860. Series: Baby Animal Board
       Books. Almost wordless - labels, Format - board pages.

Kitten explores and finds surprises in each tiny two-page episode of this book. The carefully drawn kitten looks in a mirror, accidentally triggers a jack-in-the-box, and makes a bed in a drawer, among other short sequences.

666.   Wijngaard, Juan. **Dog.** Illus.: Wijngaard, Juan. Crown, 1990.
       ISBN: 0-517-58203-1 (board); LC: 90-81895. Series: Baby Animal Board
       Books. Almost wordless - labels, Format - board pages.

An appealing puppy appears in a series of active scenes before collapsing on a bed. White space and minimal background focus attention on the puppy's playful explorations of a sandbox, the telephone, a ball, and several pigeons.

667. Wijngaard, Juan. **Duck.** Illus.: Wijngaard, Juan. Crown, 1990.
     ISBN: 0-517-58204-X (board); LC: 90-81896. Series: Baby Animal Board
     Books. Almost wordless - labels, Format - board pages.

A realistically drawn duckling is perched on a toy dump truck on the cover of
this board book, and on the back the truck has dumped the duckling. Each two-page
spread shows the duckling in a simple sequence.

668. Wildsmith, Brian. **Animal Shapes.** Illus.: Wildsmith, Brian. Oxford, 1980.
     ISBN: 0-19-279733-6. Almost wordless - labels.

Brightly colored, two-page spreads show two pictures of the same wild animal:
one with textured detail in a more realistic style and the other in flat, smooth, geometric shapes. The name of each animal is printed on the page.

669. Wildsmith, Brian. **Apple Bird, The.** Illus.: Wildsmith, Brian. Oxford, 1983.
     ISBN: 0-19-272136-4 (pbk.). Series: Cat on the Mat Books. Wordless - no print.

A skinny bird watches an apple fall from a tree, then looks at it carefully before
beginning to eat. As the apple grows smaller, the bird grows larger, until a slender
apple core remains beside a round apple-shaped bird. Large uncluttered shapes with
blended bright colors and pastel backgrounds tell the simple story.

670. Wildsmith, Brian. **Brian Wildsmith's ABC.** Illus.: Wildsmith, Brian. Franklin
     Watts, 1962.
     ISBN: 531-01525-4; LC: 63-7131. Almost wordless - labels.

Dynamic paintings in vibrant colors show a single thing for each letter of the
alphabet. The use of color in background and in the lettering adds to the impact of the
illustration. The gold and orange of the lion are intensified by a deep blue background,
for example. Words are repeated in lower- and uppercase letters.

671. Wildsmith, Brian. **Brian Wildsmith's Circus.** Illus.: Wildsmith, Brian.
     Franklin Watts, 1970.
     ISBN: 531-01541-6; LC: 71-102917. Wordless - frame.

Bright colors, geometric forms, and bold patterns show lots of energy as "the
circus comes to town." Clowns, bears, acrobats, a horseback rider, wild animals, and
trained pets all enter center ring before "the circus goes on to the next town."

672. Wildsmith, Brian. **Nest, The.** Illus.: Wildsmith, Brian. Oxford, 1983.
     ISBN: 0-19-272134-8 (pbk.). Series: Cat on the Mat Books. Wordless - no
     print.

A bird perches on bare, pointed branches and proceeds to court a mate, build a
nest, incubate and hatch three eggs, then feed the nestlings. Only when the babies are
ready to fly is the full scene shown and the nest is seen on the antlers of a deer. Bright
backgrounds and simply shaped forms with complex shading.

673. Wildsmith, Brian. **Trunk, The.** Illus.: Wildsmith, Brian. Oxford, 1982.
ISBN: 0-19-272124-0 (pbk.). Series: Cat on the Mat Books. Wordless - no print.

A squirrel, cat, and monkey follow each other up what appears to be a tree trunk. When all are up, the tree turns out to be an elephant and the three animals slide down the elephant's trunk. Colorful backgrounds add to the effect.

674. Wildsmith, Brian. **Whose Shoes?** Illus.: Wildsmith, Brian. Oxford, 1984.
ISBN: 0-19-272145-3 (pbk.). Series: Cat on the Mat Books. Wordless - no print.

Bright colors show a variety of footwear from tennis shoes and ice skates to clown shoes and ballet slippers. The final page shows the single creature wearing all these shoes and more—a many-legged centipede.

675. Wilks, Mike. **Annotated Ultimate Alphabet, The.** Illus.: Wilks, Mike. Henry Holt, 1988.
ISBN: 0-8050-0918-3; LC: 88-81517. Almost wordless - labels.

Elaborate paintings illustrate between 30 and 1,229 words which might be discovered for each letter of the alphabet. Some are easily seen, others concealed in the surrealistic juxtaposition of each composition. A dictionary is keyed to an outline drawing for each picture in which the terms are numbered.

676. Willey, Lynne. **Up in the Big Tree.** Illus.: Willey, Lynne. The Wright Group, 1987.
ISBN: 1-55624-492-4 (pbk.); 1-55624-257-3 (set). Series: More and More. Wordless - no print.

Full-color paintings move from a close-up view of a blackbird at the beginning to a distant view of the whole tree at the end. One illustration hints at the next; for example, the shoelace hanging beside the magpie gives a clue to the following picture of a girl climbing up the tree. A lost kite provides a slight story.

677. Wilson, April; with nature notes by A.J. Wood. **LOOK! The Ultimate Spot-the-Difference Book.** Illus.: Wilson, April. Dial, 1990.
ISBN: 0-8037-0925-0. Wordless - titles.

Pairs of exquisitely detailed paintings at first look identical. Close observation reveals twelve differences between each pair: the mating animals have produced young, the predator has taken the prey, the young animal has matured. Diverse exotic habitats around the world, with extensive informational notes at the end.

678. Winter, Paula. **Bear & the Fly, The.** Illus.: Winter, Paula. Crown, 1976.
ISBN: 0-517-52605-0; 0-517-56552-8 (pbk.); LC: 76-2479. Wordless - no print.

As the bear family sits down to a civilized dinner, a pesky fly comes through the window. The father bear tries to swat the fly, knocking his family and pet unconscious, wrecking the room, and finally collapsing himself. The unconcerned fly proceeds out the window. Line drawing with red and yellow wash depicts the humor.

679. Winter, Paula. **Sir Andrew.** Illus.: Winter, Paula. Crown, 1980.
ISBN: 0-517-53911-X; 80-14069. Wordless - signs.

A dapper donkey is oblivious to everything but himself and his looks. Admiring his reflection as he strolls down the street, he falls into an open hole and ends up with a broken leg. Once in a cast and on the street again, he chases his hat without noticing the accidents he has caused. Line drawings with limited color.

680. Wondriska, William. **Long Piece of String, A.** Illus.: Wondriska, William.
Holt, Rinehart and Winston, 1963.
LC: 63-10790. Wordless - no print.

This unusual alphabet book contains no letters or words, only a long black string going from page to page and tying together an alphabetical sequence of objects. Simple red block prints provide a challenge for the reader to identify each item.

681. Wood, Leslie. **Dig Dig.** Illus.: Wood, Leslie. Oxford, 1988.
ISBN: 0-19-272185-2 (pbk.). Series: Cat on the Mat Books. Almost wordless - labels.

Simple, colorful paintings show various ways to "dig dig" from a child with a sand shovel and a gardener with a spade to backhoes and steam shovels.

682. Wright, Cliff. **When the World Sleeps.** Illus.: Wright, Cliff. Ideals, 1989.
ISBN: 0-8249-8443-9. Wordless - frame.

One moonlit night, a small boy awakes to see the moon fall out of the sky. The boy and his dog hasten out and find the moon, with a droll, mustached face, in a tangle of broken branches. The boy finds unexpected help in returning the moon to the sky. Watercolor illustrations create a dream-like atmosphere.

683. Young, Ed. **Other Bone, The.** Illus.: Young, Ed. Harper and Row, 1984.
ISBN: 0-06-026870-0; 0-06-026871-9 (lib.); LC: 83-47706. Wordless - no print.

Soft charcoal sketches retell the Aesop fable of a greedy dog who isn't content with just one bone. After dreaming of a bone, the dog finds one in a trash can only to lose it in a pond when he tries to take the bone away from his reflection.

684. Young, Ed. **Up a Tree.** Illus.: Young, Ed. Harper and Row, 1983.
ISBN: 0-06-026813-1; 0-06-026814-X (lib.); LC: 82-47733. Wordless - no print.

A kitten chasing a butterfly finds itself caught in a tree, where a dog responds to its yells by chasing it higher. Turbaned villagers try a rescue with a ladder, only to find a furious cat too hard to bring down. Hunger and the smell of fish finally lure the cat down. Minimal soft sketches set the story in India.

685. Zacrel, Stepan. **Butterfly, The.** Illus.: Zacrel, Stepan. The Wright Group, 1986.
ISBN: 1-55624-067-8 (set, pbk.). Series: First Nature Watch. Wordless - no print.

A folk art style is used in the watercolor paintings in this brief nature book. Two children chase blue butterflies, and the butterfly is shown laying eggs, the caterpillars eating leaves, the chrysalis hanging from a plant, the new butterfly emerging, and once again the two children running after butterflies.

Title Index

Format Index

Die-cut pages

Die-cut windows

Index to Use of Print

Almost wordless — sentences

Almost wordless — sounds

Wordless — exclamations

Mayer, Mercer. AH-CHOO, 431
_____. Hiccup, 438
_____. Oops, 439
Olschewski, Alfred. Winterbird, 497

Wordless — frame
Anno, Mitsumasa. Dr. Anno's Magical
  Midnight Circus, 33
Aruego, Jose. Look What I Can Do, 40
Carle, Eric. Do You Want to Be My
  Friend?, 108
_____. I See a Song, 109
Day, Alexandra. Carl Goes Shopping, 150
_____. Good Dog, Carl, 152
Emberley, Edward R. Butterfly/The
  Dandelion, The, 189
_____. Chicken/The Chameleon, The, 190
_____. Frog/The Hare, The, 191
Hoban, Tana. All about Where, 301
Keats, Ezra Jack. Pssst! Doggie, 360
Kraus, Robert. Poor Mister Splinterfitz!,
  399
Martin, Rafe. Will's Mammoth, 428
Mogensen, Jan. 46 Little Men, The, 477
Panek, Dennis. Catastrophe Cat at the
  Zoo, 513
Rappus, Gerhard. When the Sun Was
  Shining, 537
Richter, Mischa. To Bed, to Bed!, 550
Ross, Pat. Hi Fly, 560
Spier, Peter. Dreams, 585
_____. Noah's Ark, 588
Tafuri, Nancy. Rabbit's Morning, 604
Ungerer, Tomi. One, Two, Where's My
  Shoe?, 630
_____. Snail, Where Are You?, 631
Wildsmith, Brian. Brian Wildsmith's
  Circus, 671
Wright, Cliff. When the World Sleeps, 682

Wordless — hidden print
Gibson, Barbara Leonard. Who's There?,
  235
Ivory, Lesley Anne, and Ron van der Meer.
  Kittens, 349

Wordless — no print
Adams, Pam. Angels, 1
_____. Zoo, The, 2
Alexander, Martha. Magic Box, The, 5
_____. Magic Hat, The, 6
_____. Magic Picture, The, 7
_____. Out! Out! Out!, 8

Amery, Heather. Farm Picture Book, The,
  10
_____. Seaside Picture Book, The, 11
_____. Zoo Picture Book, The, 12
Amoss, Berthe. By the Sea, 13
Andersen, Hans Christian; retold by M.
  Eulalia Valeri; tr. by Leland
  Northam. Ugly Duckling, The, 15
Anderson, Lena. Bunny Bath, 16
_____. Bunny Box, 17
_____. Bunny Fun, 18
_____. Bunny Party, 19
_____. Bunny Surprise, 21
Anno, Mitsumasa. Anno's Animals, 23
_____. Anno's Britain, 24
_____. Anno's Counting House, 26
_____. Anno's Flea Market, 28
_____. Anno's Journey, 30
_____. Anno's Peekaboo, 31
Ardizzone, Edward. Wrong Side of the
  Bed, The, 35
Asch, Frank. In the Eye of the Teddy, 43
Bakken, Harald. Special String, The, 48
Ball, Sara. Animals in Africa, 49
_____. Farmyard Families, 50
_____. Somewhere in Canada, 51
_____. Teddy, 52
Bang, Molly. Grey Lady and the Straw-
  berry Snatcher, The, 54
Barner, Bob. Elephant's Visit, The, 55
Baum, Willi. Birds of a Feather, 59
Blades, Ann. Fall, 62
_____. Spring, 63
_____. Summer, 64
_____. Winter, 65
Blanco, Josette. On the Farm, 66
_____. Playtime, 67
_____. Sport, 68
_____. Weather, The, 69
Bonners, Susan. Just in Passing, 70
Briggs, Raymond. Snowman, The, 74
_____. Snowman: Building the Snowman,
  The, 72
_____. Snowman: Dressing Up, The, 73
_____. Snowman: The Party, The, 75
_____. Snowman: Walking in the Air,
  The, 76
Brinckloe, Julie. Spider Web, The, 77
Brown, Craig. Patchwork Farmer, The, 78
Bruna, Dick. Another Story to Tell, 80
_____. Miffy's Dream, 81
_____. Story to Tell, A, 82
Burgin, Norma. Just Out for a Walk, 84

Wordless — symbols

Anno, Mitsumasa. Anno's Alphabet: An Adventure in Imagination, 22

_____. Anno's Counting Book, 25

Arnosky, Jim. Mouse Numbers and Letters, 36

_____. Mouse Writing, 37

Burningham, John. Count Up: Learning Sets, 88

_____. Five Down: Numbers as Signs, 89

_____. Just Cats: Learning Groups, 93

_____. Pigs Plus: Learning Addition, 94

_____. Ride Off: Learning Subtraction, 96

Carle, Eric. My Very First Book of Numbers, 111

Craig, Helen. Mouse House 1,2,3, The, 136

_____. Mouse House ABC, The, 137

Feldman, Judy. Alphabet in Nature, The, 214

Floyd, Lucy, and Kathryn Lasky. Agatha's Alphabet: With Her Very Own Dictionary, 225

Hoban, Tana. 26 Letters and 99 Cents, 299

_____. A, B, See!, 300

_____. I Read Symbols, 309

Howe, Caroline Walton. Counting Penguins, 337

Hyman, Trina Schart. Little Alphabet, A, 345

Kitchen, Bert. Animal Alphabet, 373

_____. Animal Numbers, 374

McMillan, Bruce. Alphabet Symphony, The, 450

Miller, Barry. Alphabet World, 465

Montresor, Beni. A for Angel: Beni Montresor's ABC Picture-Stories, 478

Palmer, Kim. Dream, The, 511

Pragoff, Fiona. How Many? From 0 to 20, 530

Turk, Hanne. Happy Birthday, Max, 616

Wordless — titles

Arnosky, Jim. Mud Time and More: Nathaniel Stories, 38

Burton, Marilee Robin. Elephant's Nest: Four Wordless Stories, The, 98

dePaola, Tomie. Flicks, 159

Feldman, Judy. Shapes in Nature, 215

Florian, Douglas. Airplane Ride, 218

Fromm, Lilo. Muffel and Plums, 227

Krahn, Fernando. Here Comes Alex Pumpernickel!, 388

_____. Journeys of Sebastian, 390

_____. Sleep Tight, Alex Pumpernickel, 397

McMillan, Bruce, and Brett McMillan. Puniddles, 457

Pierce, Robert. Look and Laugh, 523

Schweninger, Ann. Dance for Three, 572

Steiner, Charlotte. I Am Andy: You-Tell-a-Story Book, 591

Tanaka, Hideyuki. Happy Dog, The, 606

Van Soelen, Philip. Cricket in the Grass and Other Stories, 636

Ward, Lynd. God's Man: A Novel in Woodcuts, 643

Watson, Aldren A. Town Mouse Country Mouse: A Book of Story Pictures, 652

Wiesner, David. Tuesday, 663

Wilson, April; with nature notes by A. J. Wood. LOOK! The Ultimate Spot-the-Difference Book, 677

Series Index

Illustrator Index

This index lists only those illustrators who are not also the author of the title. Numbers cited in this index are entry numbers.

Subject Index

Cherries

Chickens

Childcare

Chimpanzees. *See* Monkeys/apes

Chores

Christmas

Krahn, Fernando. Biggest Christmas
 Tree on Earth, The, 382
_____. How Santa Claus Had a Long
 and Difficult Journey Delivering
 His Presents, 389
McCully, Emily Arnold. Christmas Gift,
 The, 445
Mitchelhill, Barbara. Star, The, 472
Munro, Roxie. Christmastime in New
 York City, 486
Spier, Peter. Peter Spier's Christmas, 589
Turk, Hanne. Merry Christmas, Max,
 621

Cigarettes
Parkin, Geo. Monsters Came to Stay,
 The, 515
Turk, Hanne. Lesson for Max, A, 617

Circular stories
Cannon, Beth. Cat Had a Fish about a
 Dream, A, 100
Carroll, Ruth. Rolling Downhill, 117
Charlip, Remy, and Jerry Joyner.
 Thirteen, 124
Elzbieta. Little Mops and the Butterfly,
 183
Henstra, Friso. Mighty Mizzling Mouse,
 289
Hoban, Russell, and Sylvie Selig. Croco-
 dile and Pierrot: A See-the-Story
 Book, 297
Hogrogian, Nonny. Apples, 333
Mari, Iela. Eat and Be Eaten, 414
Mordillo, Guillermo. Crazy Cowboy, 480
Ueno, Noriko. Elephant Buttons, 629

Circuses/carnivals
Anno, Mitsumasa. Dr. Anno's Magical
 Midnight Circus, 33
Carroll, Ruth. Chimp and the Clown,
 The, 115
Demi. Where Is It? A Hide-and-Seek
 Puzzle Book, 158
Dinardo, Jeffrey. Day at the Circus, A,
 164
Dupasquier, Philippe. Great Escape,
 The, 174
Goodall, John S. Adventures of Paddy
 Pork, The, 239
_____. Edwardian Entertainments, 244
_____. Midnight Adventures of Kelly,
 Dot, and Esmeralda, The, 251

Henstra, Friso. Mighty Mizzling Mouse,
 289
Krahn, Fernando. Funny Friend from
 Heaven, A, 386
Lemke, Horst. Places and Faces, 401
Peppe, Rodney. Circus Numbers, 518
Root, Betty. Slapstick, 559
Wildsmith, Brian. Brian Wildsmith's
 Circus, 671

Cities/city life. *See also* **Everyday life**
Barton, Byron. Applebet Story, 56
_____. Where's Al?, 58
Bradman, Tony. Sandal, The, 71
Capdevila, Roser. City, The, 102
_____. Our House, 103
_____. Shopping, 104
Donnelly, Liza. Dinosaur Day, 168
Dupasquier, Philippe. Great Escape,
 The, 174
Emberley, Rebecca. City Sounds, 192
Florian, Douglas. City, The, 220
Goodall, John S. Story of a Main
 Street, The, 266
_____. Story of an English Village,
 The, 267
Hoban, Tana. I Read Signs, 308
_____. I Read Symbols, 309
_____. I Walk and Read, 310
_____. Over, Under & Through: And
 Other Spatial Concepts, 317
_____. Shapes, Shapes, Shapes, 323
Isadora, Rachel. City Seen from A to
 Z, 348
Keussen, Gudrun. This Is How We Live
 in the Town, 366
Lemke, Horst. Places and Faces, 401
Lewis, Stephen. Zoo City, 402
Moak, Allan. Big City ABC, A, 476
Muller, Jorg. Changing City, The, 484
Munro, Roxie. Christmastime in New
 York City, 486
_____. Inside-Outside Book of London,
 The, 487
_____. Inside-Outside Book of New
 York City, The, 488
_____. Inside-Outside Book of
 Washington, D.C., The, 489
Oechsli, Kelly. It's Schooltime, 496
Panek, Dennis. Catastrophe Cat, 512
Prater, John. Gift, The, 535
Sara. Across Town, 566

Remington, Barbara. Boat, 547
Salsberg, Barbara. Your Own Story, 564

Costumes
Alexander, Martha. Magic Box, The, 5
Degen, Bruce. Aunt Possum and the
    Pumpkin Man, 154
Dinardo, Jeffrey. Day in Space, A, 165
Grimm, Jacob, and Wilhelm Grimm;
    retold by John S. Goodall. Little
    Red Riding Hood, 278
Keats, Ezra Jack. Pssst! Doggie, 360
Mitchelhill, Barbara. Star, The, 472
Pierce, Robert. Look and Laugh, 523
Ueno, Noriko. Elephant Buttons, 629

Counting books
Anno, Mitsumasa. Anno's Counting
    Book, 25
_____. Anno's Counting House, 26
Arnosky, Jim. Mouse Numbers and
    Letters, 36
Ball, Sara. Teddy, 52
Burningham, John. Count Up: Learning
    Sets, 88
_____. Five Down: Numbers as Signs,
    89
_____. John Burningham's 1 2 3, 90
_____. Just Cats: Learning Groups, 93
_____. Pigs Plus: Learning Addition,
    94
_____. Read One: Numbers as Words,
    95
Carle, Eric. 1,2,3 to the Zoo, 107
_____. My Very First Book of Numbers,
    111
Chwast, Seymour, and Martin Stephen
    Moskof. Still Another Number
    Book, 129
Craig, Helen. Mouse House 1,2,3, The,
    136
Ernst, Lisa Campbell. Up to Ten and
    Down Again, 212
Generowicz, Witold. Train, The, 232
Gibson, Barbara Leonard. Pile of
    Puppies, 233
Hoban, Tana. 1,2,3, 298
_____. 26 Letters and 99 Cents, 299
_____. Count and See, 304
Howe, Caroline Walton. Counting
    Penguins, 337
Hutchins, Pat. 1 Hunter, 342
Kitchen, Bert. Animal Numbers, 374

MacDonald, Suse, and Bill Oakes.
    Numblers, 411
Mayer, Marianna. Alley Oop!, 430
McMillan, Bruce. Counting Wildflowers,
    452
Nolan, Dennis. Monster Bubbles, 492
Noll, Sally. Off and Counting, 493
Page, Robin. Count One to Ten, 510
Peppe, Rodney. Circus Numbers, 518
Perkins, Diana. Have You Seen My
    Shoe?, 519
Pragoff, Fiona. Clothes, 528
_____. How Many? From 0 to 20, 530
Sis, Peter. Beach Ball, 581
Stobbs, Joanna, and William Stobbs.
    One Sun, Two Eyes, and a Million
    Stars, 593
Tafuri, Nancy. All Year Long, 598
_____. Who's Counting?, 605

Country life
Anno, Mitsumasa. Anno's Counting
    Book, 25
Arnosky, Jim. Mud Time and More:
    Nathaniel Stories, 38
_____. Nathaniel, 39
Blanco, Josette. On the Farm, 66
Capdevila, Roser. At the Farm, 101
Dupasquier, Philippe. Our House on the
    Hill, 176
Ernst, Lisa Campbell. Up to Ten and
    Down Again, 212
Euvremer, Teryl. Sun's Up, 213
Florian, Douglas. Year in the Country,
    A, 224
Goodall, John S. Edwardian Christmas,
    An, 243
_____. Lavinia's Cottage: Imagined by
    Her Devoted Grandfather, 250
Keussen, Gudrun. This Is How We Live
    in the Country, 365
Muller, Jorg. Changing Countryside,
    The, 485
Rappus, Gerhard. When the Sun Was
    Shining, 537
Sacre, Marie-Jose. Dandelion, The, 562
Stobbs, Joanna, and William Stobbs.
    One Sun, Two Eyes, and a Million
    Stars, 593
Watson, Aldren A. Town Mouse
    Country Mouse: A Book of Story
    Pictures, 652

Lemke, Horst. Places and Faces, 401
Mitchelhill, Barbara. Home from
    School, 469

Europe — history/geography
Goodall, John S. Story of the Seashore,
    The, 268
_____. Victorians Abroad, 270
Muller, Jorg. Changing City, The, 484
_____. Changing Countryside, The, 485

Everyday life. *See also* **Cities/city life;**
Country life; Family life; Farms/farm life
Baker, Jeannie. Window, 45
Bonners, Susan. Just in Passing, 70
Capdevila, Roser. What We Do, 106
Florian, Douglas. City, The, 220
Gray, Nigel. Country Far Away, A, 272
Hom, Jesper, and Sven Gronlykke. For
    Kids Only, 334
Raynor, Dorka. My Friends Live in
    Many Places, 538
Reich, Hanns. Children of Many Lands,
    542
_____. Human Condition, The, 543
Reich, Hanns; text by Eugen Roth.
    Children and Their Fathers, 545
Roennfeldt, Robert. Day on the Avenue,
    A, 557
Schories, Pat. Mouse Around, 570
Shore, Stephen. Uncommon Places, 576

Exploration
Gilbert, Elliott. Cat Story, A, 236
Goodall, John S. Lavinia's Cottage:
    Imagined by Her Devoted
    Grandfather, 250
MacGregor, Marilyn. Baby Takes a
    Trip, 412
_____. On Top, 413
Schories, Pat. Mouse Around, 570
Sugano, Yoshikatsu. Kitten's Adventure,
    The, 596

Fables. *See* **Moral tales**

Faerie folk. *See also* **Little people**
Butterworth, Nick. Amanda's Butterfly,
    99
Collington, Peter. On Christmas Eve,
    134

Grimm, Jacob, and Wilhelm Grimm;
    retold by M. Eulalia Valeri; tr.
    by Leland Northam. Sleeping
    Beauty, 280
Hyman, Trina Schart. Enchanted Forest,
    The, 344
Mogensen, Jan. 46 Little Men, The, 477
Perkins, Diana. Have You Seen My
    Shoe?, 519
Perrault, Charles; retold by M. Eulalia
    Valeri; tr. by Leland Northam.
    Cinderella, 521

Fairs. *See* **Circuses/carnivals**

Fairy tales. *See* **Folk/fairy tales**

Fall. *See* **Autumn; Seasons**

Falling
Blanco, Josette. Sport, 68
Hughes, Shirley. Up and Up, 339
Krahn, Fernando. Little Love Story, 391
Mayer, Marianna. Alley Oop!, 430
Winter, Paula. Sir Andrew, 679
Young, Ed. Up a Tree, 684

Family life. *See also* **Fathers and children;**
Grandparents; Mothers and children;
Parents and children; Siblings
Adams, Pam. Angels, 1
Adoff, Arnold. Ma nda La, 3
Alexander, Martha. Out! Out! Out!, 8
Ardizzone, Edward. Wrong Side of the
    Bed, The, 35
Baker, Madeleine. I Got Lost, 46
_____. We Went to the Pond, 47
Capdevila, Roser. Our House, 103
_____. Weekend, The, 105
Carrick, Donald. Drip, Drop, 113
Carroll, Ruth, and Latrobe Carroll.
    Christmas Kitten, The, 120
Dupasquier, Philippe. I Can't Sleep, 175
_____. Our House on the Hill, 176
Endersby, Frank. Holidays, 195
_____. Man's Work, 200
_____. My Baby Sister, 201
_____. Nuisance, The, 202
_____. Pet Shop, The, 203
_____. Plumber, The, 204
_____. Waiting for Baby, 206
_____. Wallpaper, 207
_____. Wash Day, 208
_____. What about Me?, 209

Fantasy/reality

Farms/farm life. *See also* Animals — farm; *names of individual animals*

Schubert, Dieter. Where's My Monkey?, 571

Sis, Peter. Beach Ball, 581

Tafuri, Nancy. Have You Seen My Duckling?, 602

Willey, Lynne. Up in the Big Tree, 676

Machinery

Hoban, Tana. Dig, Drill, Dump, Fill, 305

Koren, Edward. Behind the Wheel, 378

Wood, Leslie. Dig Dig, 681

Magic

Alexander, Martha. Magic Box, The, 5

_____. Magic Hat, The, 6

_____. Magic Picture, The, 7

Collington, Peter. On Christmas Eve, 134

Grimm, Jacob, and Wilhelm Grimm; retold by M. Eulalia Valeri; tr. by Leland Northam. Sleeping Beauty, 280

Hughes, Shirley. Up and Up, 339

Lisker, Sonia O. Attic Witch, The, 406

Mayer, Mercer. Bubble Bubble, 433

Perrault, Charles; retold by M. Eulalia Valeri; tr. by Leland Northam. Cinderella, 520

Valeri, M. Eulalia, reteller; tr. by Leland Northam. Pied Piper of Hamelin, The, 632

Ward, Nick. Bag of Tricks, A, 647

_____. Surprise Present, The, 648

Wetherbee, Holden. Wonder ring, The, 659

Magpies

Mari, Iela. L'albero, 415

Schubert, Dieter. Where's My Monkey?, 571

Willey, Lynne. Up in the Big Tree, 676

Mail. *See* **Letters and invitations**

Making things

Arnosky, Jim. Mouse Numbers and Letters, 36

Briggs, Raymond. Snowman: Building the Snowman, The, 72

Craig, Helen. Mouse House ABC, The, 137

Emberley, Ed. Ed Emberley's ABC, 187

Felix, Monique. Further Adventures of the Little Mouse Trapped in a Book, The, 216

Krahn, Fernando. April Fools, 380

_____. Self-Made Snowman, The, 396

Meyer, Renate. Vicki, 463

Mitchelhill, Barbara. Going to School, 468

Remington, Barbara. Boat, 547

Roberts, Thom. Barn, The, 555

Sewell, Helen. Head for Happy, A, 574

Turk, Hanne. Friendship Max, 612

Mammoths

Martin, Rafe. Will's Mammoth, 428

Manners. *See* **Customs**

Maps

Burningham, John. Come Away from the Water, Shirley, 87

Florian, Douglas. Airplane Ride, 218

Mogensen, Jan. 46 Little Men, The, 477

Sewell, Helen. Head for Happy, A, 574

Wiesner, David. Free Fall, 662

Markets

Anno, Mitsumasa. Anno's Flea Market, 28

Capdevila, Roser. Shopping, 104

Marriages. *See* **Weddings**

Mathematics

Anno, Mitsumasa. Anno's Counting Book, 25

_____. Anno's Counting House, 26

Burningham, John. Count Up: Learning Sets, 88

_____. Five Down: Numbers as Signs, 89

_____. Just Cats: Learning Groups, 93

_____. Pigs Plus: Learning Addition, 94

_____. Read One: Numbers as Words, 95

_____. Ride Off: Learning Subtraction, 96

Chwast, Seymour, and Martin Stephen Moskof. Still Another Number Book, 129

McMillan, Bruce. One, Two, One Pair!, 456

Migration

Mimes. *See* **Pantomime**

Misbehavior. *See* **Behavior/misbehavior**

Mischief

Mishaps. *See also* **Accidents**

Morning

Mother Goose. *See* **Nursery rhymes**

Mothers and children

Mothers/baby

Moths. *See* **Butterflies/moths**

Mountains

Movies

Moving

Multi-ethnic

Nursery rhymes

Nursery schools

Object identification

Oceans. *See* **Sea**

Old age. *See* **Elderly; Grandparents**

Only child

Oxenbury, Helen. Beach Day, 500
_____. Good Night, Good Morning, 504
Rispin, Colin. Off on Holiday, 554

Opposites
Burningham, John. John Burningham's
Opposites, 92
Daughtry, Duanne. What's Inside?, 146
Duke, Kate. Guinea Pigs Far and Near,
173
Hoban, Tana. Exactly the Opposite, 307
_____. Push-Pull Empty-Full, 318
Kightley, Rosalinda. Opposites, 370
McMillan, Bruce. Becca Backward,
Becca Frontward: A Book of
Concept Pairs, 451
_____. Dry or Wet?, 453
Pragoff, Fiona. Opposites, 532
Sis, Peter. Beach Ball, 581
Spier, Peter. Fast-Slow High-Low, 586
Webber, Helen. What Is Sour? What Is
Sweet?, 655

Optical illusions
Anno, Mitsumasa. Anno's Alphabet:
An Adventure in Imagination, 22
_____. Topsy-Turvies: Pictures to
Stretch the Imagination, 34

Optimism
Richter, Mischa. Quack?, 549
Tanaka, Hideyuki. Happy Dog, The, 606

Organ grinder
Goodall, John S. Edwardian
Entertainments, 244
_____. Jacko, 248

Outdoor activities
Amery, Heather. Seaside Picture Book,
The, 11
Blades, Ann. Fall, 62
_____. Summer, 64
_____. Winter, 65
Blanco, Josette. Playtime, 67
Briggs, Raymond. Snowman: Building
the Snowman, The, 72
Bruna, Dick. Another Story to Tell, 80
Burningham, John. John Burningham's
1 2 3, 90
_____. John Burningham's Colors, 91
Capdevila, Roser. Weekend, The, 105
Davis, Annelies. This Is My Garden, 147

dePaola, Tomie. Flicks, 159
Duke, Kate. Guinea Pigs Far and Near,
173
Dupasquier, Philippe. Our House on the
Hill, 176
Florian, Douglas. Summer Day, A, 222
_____. Winter Day, A, 223
_____. Year in the Country, A, 224
Heuninck, Ronald. Rain or Shine, 292
Howe, Caroline Walton. Counting
Penguins, 337
Keats, Ezra Jack. Skates!, 361
Keussen, Gudrun. This Is How We Live
in the Country, 365
_____. This Is How We Live in the
Town, 366
Mayer, Mercer. Bubble Bubble, 433
McCully, Emily Arnold. First Snow, 446
Meyer, Renate. Hide-and-Seek, 462
_____. Vicki, 463
Oxenbury, Helen. Monkey See, Monkey
Do, 505
Roennfeldt, Robert. Day on the
Avenue, A, 557
Spier, Peter. Dreams, 585
_____. Peter Spier's Rain, 590
Tafuri, Nancy. Do Not Disturb, 599
Turk, Hanne. Raking Leaves with Max,
623
_____. Rope Skips Max, The, 625
Watson, Aldren A. Town Mouse
Country Mouse: A Book of
Story Pictures, 652
Weiss, Nicki. Dog Boy Cap Skate, 657
Wood, Leslie. Dig Dig, 681

Outings
Adams, Pam. Zoo, The, 2
Bradman, Tony. Sandal, The, 71
Burgin, Norma. Just Out for a Walk, 84
Capdevila, Roser. Weekend, The, 105
Collington, Peter. Little Pickle, 132
Ernst, Lisa Campbell. Up to Ten and
Down Again, 212
Florian, Douglas. Beach Day, A, 219
_____. Nature Walk, 221
_____. Summer Day, A, 222
Goodall, John S. Surprise Picnic, The,
269
Krahn, Fernando. Secret in the Dungeon,
The, 395
Lisker, Sonia O. Lost, 407
Mayer, Mercer. Frog on His Own, 435

Photograms

Photographs—black and white

Photographs—color

Mitchelhill, Barbara. Home from
School, 469
_____. Shoes, 471
_____. Supermarket, The, 473
Munro, Roxie. Christmastime in New
York City, 486
Oxenbury, Helen. Shopping Trip, 508
Schories, Pat. Mouse Around, 570
Simmons, Ellie. Wheels, 579
Spier, Peter. Peter Spier's Christmas,
589

Short stories
Arnosky, Jim. Mud Time and More:
Nathaniel Stories, 38
_____. Nathaniel, 39
Blanco, Josette. On the Farm, 66
_____. Playtime, 67
_____. Sport, 68
_____. Weather, The, 69
Burton, Marilee Robin. Elephant's Nest:
Four Wordless Stories, The, 98
Charlip, Remy, and Jerry Joyner.
Thirteen, 124
dePaola, Tomie. Flicks, 159
Emberley, Ed. Ed Emberley's ABC, 187
Fromm, Lilo. Muffel and Plums, 227
Giovannetti. Max, 237
Krahn, Fernando. Here Comes Alex
Pumpernickel!, 388
_____. Journeys of Sebastian, 390
_____. Sleep Tight, Alex Pumpernickel,
397
Mayer, Mercer. Two Moral Tales, 440
_____. Two More Moral Tales, 441
Pierce, Robert. Look and Laugh, 523
Schweninger, Ann. Dance for Three,
572
Steiner, Charlotte. I Am Andy:
You-Tell-a-Story Book, 591
Tanaka, Hideyuki. Happy Dog, The, 606
Van Soelen, Philip. Cricket in the Grass
and Other Stories, 636
Wijngaard, Juan. Bear, 664
_____. Cat, 665
_____. Dog, 666
_____. Duck, 667

Showing off
Aruego, Jose. Look What I Can Do, 40
Baum, Willi. Birds of a Feather, 59
Ringi, Kjell. Winner, The, 553

Shows. *See* **Drama; Theater**

Shrews
Goodall, John S. Shrewbettina Goes to
Work, 262
_____. Shrewbettina's Birthday, 263

Siblings. *See also* **Family life; New baby**
Adams, Pam. Angels, 1
Dubois, Claude K. He's MY Jumbo!, 170
_____. Looking for Ginny, 171
Endersby, Frank. My Baby Sister, 201
_____. Nuisance, The, 202
_____. What about Me?, 209
Grimm, Jacob, and Wilhelm Grimm;
retold by M. Eulalia Valeri; tr.
by Leland Northam. Hansel and
Gretel, 279
Heuninck, Ronald. Rain or Shine, 292
Ichikawa, Satomi. Let's Play, 346
McMillan, Bruce. Dry or Wet?, 453
Meyer, Renate. Hide-and-Seek, 462
Prater, John. Gift, The, 535
Riggio, Anita. Wake Up, William!, 551
Simpson, Kate. All Dressed Up, 580
Spier, Peter. Peter Spier's Rain, 590
Venus, Pamela. I Had Measles, 637
Ward, Nick. Surprise Present, The,
648

Sickness. *See* **Illness**

Signs/signboards
Crews, Donald. Truck, 139
Hoban, Tana. I Read Signs, 308
_____. I Read Symbols, 309
_____. I Walk and Read, 310
Rice, Brian, and Tony Evans. English
Sunrise, The, 548

Silhouettes
Gardner, Beau. Guess What?, 229
Hoban, Tana. A, B, See!, 300
_____. Shapes and Things, 322
Wetherbee, Holden. Wonder Ring, The,
659

Sisters. *See* **Siblings**

Sizes and shapes. *See* **Shapes and sizes**

Skating. *See* **Roller skating; Ice skating**

Snowmen

Soccer

Social history

Social studies

Sounds